P9-DHP-434

DISCARD

37-949 780.92

37-949 B(780.92) Q

Orga, Ates BEE L

Beethoven: his life and times

DATE DUE

[illegible] 4 '85			
JE 23 '86			
JY 10 '86			
AP 27 '87			
NO 15 '88			
JE 7 '94			
JA 11 '95			

CULVER PUBLIC LIBRARY
CULVER, INDIANA 46511
TELEPHONE 219-842-2941

Mon.-Fri. 12 noon-8 P.M.
Sat. 12 noon-4 P.M.

BEETHOVEN

his life and times

Ateş Orga

Paganiniana Publications, Inc.
211 West Sylvania Avenue, Neptune City, N.J. 07753

For Marion and Sidney Prior

CULVER PUBLIC LIBRARY

ISBN 0-87666-646-2

37-949 780.92

Beethoven: His Life and Times by Ates Orga was originally published in 1978 by Midas Books, 12 Dene Way, Speldhurst, Tunbridge Wells, Kent TN3 0NX England. Copyright ©1978 by Ates D'Arcy-Orga, reprinted by permission of the publisher.

Expanded Edition of *Beethoven: His Life and Times* ©1980 by Paganiniana Publications, Inc. A considerable amount of new material has been added to the original text, including but not limited to illustrations and their captions. Copyright is claimed for this new material.

All rights reserved. No part of this publication may be reproduced, stored in a retrieval system, or transmitted, in any form or by any means, electronic, mechanical, photocopying, recording or otherwise without the prior permission of Midas Books and Paganiniana Publications, Inc.

Published by PAGANINIANA PUBLICATIONS, INC.
211 West Sylvania Avenue
Neptune City, New Jersey 07753

Contents

1 Omega 7

2 Canonisation 11

3 Origins 21

4 The Early Years: 1770-92 27

5 Vienna: 1793-99 41

6 Revolution and Change 60

7 Landmarks: 1800-04 70

8 Hero and Heroine 88

9 Passions and Enigmas 96

10 'A pure romantic': 1806-08 106

11 Entr'acte: 1809-13 118

12 The Congress of Vienna 132

13 'The most celebrated of living composers' 141

14 Apotheosis 159

Acknowledgements

In finishing this book I have to first thank my wife Josephine for her immense patience and help, and for all the stimulating hours of discussion that she gave me. For a moment of crucial rescue, Ronald and Rosslyn Farren-Price are owed a debt of gratitude. Thanks must also go to my students for their enthusiastic tolerance and interest, as well as in retrospect to Reginald Smith Brindle, Mosco Carner, Hans Gál, Arthur Hutchings and Basil Lam who all so actively kindled and encouraged my early interest in Beethoven and his work.

My thanks are additionally due to the following for kindly granting permission to quote extracts:

William Kimber & Co., Ltd (George R. Marek, *Beethoven*)
Macmillan & Co., Ltd./St. Martin's Press (Emily Anderson, *The Letters of Beethoven*). Except where otherwise stated, translations of Beethoven's letters are taken from this edition
G. Schirmer Inc./Dover Publications Inc. (O.G. Sonneck, *Beethoven: Impressions by his Contemporaries*)

Some of the illustrations have come from my own collection or from original prints and engravings. Thanks, however, are due to the following for helpfully granting reproduction rights:

Beethoven-Archiv, Bonn
Beethoven-Haus, Bonn
British Museum, London
Columbia Records

E.M.I.
Gesellschaft der Musikfreunde,
Vienna Historisches
Museum, Vienna
Institute of Arts, Detroit
Kunsthistorisches Museum,
Vienna

Landesmuseum, Brunswick
National Gallery, London
Niederösterreichisches
Landesmuseum,
Vienna Österreiche
Nationalbibliothek, Vienna
R.C.A.
Royal College of Music, London
Staatsbibliothek, Berlin
Staats/Universitätsbibliothek,
Hamburg

Wadhurst, April 1978 *A.O.*

Bibliography

Anderson, Emily *The Letters of Beethoven*, 3 vols. (London, New York 1961)

Arnold, Denis & Fortune, Nigel *The Beethoven Companion* (London 1971)

Cooper, Martin *Beethoven: The Last Decade* (London 1970)

Gál, Hans *The Golden Age of Vienna* (London 1948)

Grove, Sir George *Beethoven-Schubert-Mendelssohn* (London 1951)

Hamburger, Michael *Beethoven: Letters, Journals and Conversations* (London 1951)

Kerst, Friedrich & Krehbiel, Edward *Beethoven: The man and the artist* (1905, New York 1964 reprint)

Kinsky-Halm *Das Werk Beethovens* (Munich 1955)

Landon, H.C. Robbins *Beethoven: a documentary study* (Zürich, London 1970)

— *Beethoven*, abridged version of above (Zürich, London 1974)

Marek, George R. *Beethoven* (New York 1969, London 1970)

McNaught, William 'Beethoven' *Grove's Dictionary of Music and Musicians,* Vol. I (London, New York 1954 ed.)

Orga, Ateş 'Beethoven for Voices', *Music & Musicians*, XVIII/viii (April 1970)

—'Genesis of the Ninth', *Music & Musicians,* XVIII/xi (July 1970)

Schindler, Anton F., edit. D. MacArdle, trans. C. S. Jolly *Beethoven as I knew him* (London 1966)

Schmidt-Görg, Joseph & Schmidt, Hans *Ludwig van Beethoven* (Hamburg 1969, London 1970)

Scott, Marion *Beethoven* (1934, London 1974 rev.)

Solomon, Maynard *Beethoven* (New York 1977, London 1978)

Sonneck, O.G. *Beethoven: Impressions by his Contemporararies* (1926 New York 1967 reprint)

Thayer, Alexander Wheelock, rev. and edit. Elliott Forbes *Life of Beethoven* (Princeton 1967)

Wegeler, Franz & Ries, Ferdinand *Biographische Notizen* (Coblenz 1838, 1845)

Willets, Pamela J. *Beethoven and England* (London 1970)

Beethoven. From a late 19th century engraving taken from a Victorian collection of the composer's piano music originally published by Augener of Great Marlborough Street, London.

Chapter 1

Omega

'When beggars die, there are no comets seen;
The heavens themselves blaze forth the death of princes'—Shakespeare, *Julius Caesar*.

Monday the 26th of March 1827 was a freezing day. From Silesia and the Sudeten peaks, a north wind blew across the Wienerwald. Everywhere the ground lay under a soft blanket of fresh, silent snow. The long winter had been 'raw, damp, cold and frosty': on that day it showed no sign of releasing its grip on the land.

By four o'clock the lights of Vienna, the street lamps, the candles of a myriad rooms, began to pierce the overcast gloom. The day had all but run its course. On the second floor of the Schwarzspanierhaus, the House of the Black Spaniard to the west of the old city walls, lay a man who had also all but run his course. In a large, sparsely furnished room of 'sad appearance', amid squalor and books and manuscript paper, and within sight of his prized mahogany Broadwood grand, Beethoven, the 'General of Musicians', lost hold of life. On a roughly made bed, unconscious, he was at that moment as broken and finished as his piano. The elements continued to rage. Flurries of snow drifted against the window. Then 'there was suddenly a loud clap of thunder accompanied by a bolt of lightning . . . Beethoven opened his eyes, raised his right hand, and, his fist clenched, looked upwards for several seconds . . . As he let his hand sink down onto the bed again, his eyes half closed . . . There was no more breathing, no more heartbeat! The great composer's spirit had fled from this world of deception into the kingdon of truth'. So remembered Anselm Hüttenbrenner. Another contemporary, Joseph Carl Rosenbaum, recorded Beethoven's end even more poignantly in the terseness of a *Diary* entry: 'Ludwig van Beethoven's death, in the evening, towards six o'clock, of dropsy in his fifty-sixth year.* He is no longer! His name lives in fame's illumination.'

* Actually his fifty *seventh* year.

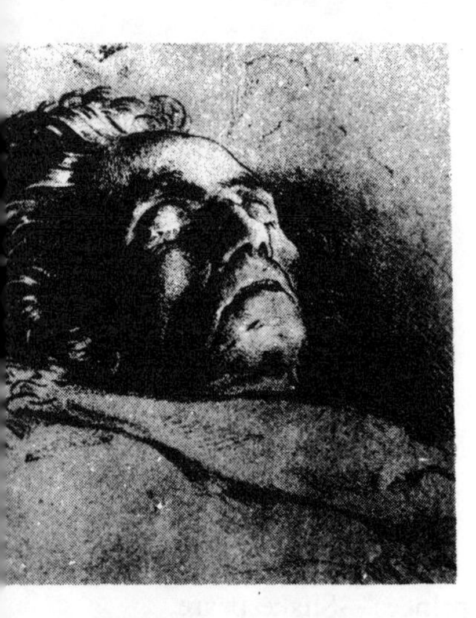

Beethoven on his deathbed. Lithograph by J. Danhauser

The funeral took place on the afternoon of 29 March 1827. By contrast with three days earlier, the weather was now 'lovely, warm': spring had kissed winter. A grief-stricken multitude turned up to pay their last homage. The *Allgemeine Theater Zeitung* (12 April) reported some 15,000. Others estimated a figure nearer 20,000. By all accounts the ceremony was one of the most spectacular seen in post-Napoleonic Vienna. According to a detailed account of the funeral in the archives of the Supreme Court, the courtyard of the house was 'filled to overflowing, and outside the crowd stormily demanded entrance. The military assistance from the Alser Barracks . . . was hardly able to ward off the crowd. Even the schools were closed. At 3 o'clock the coffin was closed, carried down and placed in the court. The pall, ordered by Anton Schindler from the 2nd Civil Regiment, was spread over the coffin, the cross was adorned with a "very beautiful" wreath, and the Evangelical book and the "very beautiful" civic Crown set up . . . the door was opened; the crowd was so jammed that only with the greatest difficulty was the director of ceremonies and his helpers able to organise the procession'. The pall bearers included Hummel and Gyrowetz, carrying candles draped in crêpe, while among the torchbearers the names of Castelli, Czerny, Grillparzer, Graf, Paccini, Schubert and Schuppanzigh, stand out from a distinguished company. In the centre of the procession came 'the "very lovely ceremonial carriage" pulled by four horses which had been ordered from the office of the *Kirchenmeister* of St Stephen's Cathedral'. The cortège wound its way past the Lichnowsky Palace. A choir sang the *Miserere* in an arrangement from one of Beethoven's *Equali* for trombones; a band offered the funeral march from the Op 26 Piano Sonata. The report continues:

The church was filled to capacity; the soldiers on duty did not want to admit anyone after the coffin had been carried in. The relatives and friends of the master succeeded only with difficulty to get inside the church. Those who had fainted from the pressure of the crowd were taken across to the hospital.

The inside of the church shone with candle-light. Zeller's receipt for the cost of lighting the three main altars showed that the town wax dealer had supplied $6\frac{1}{2}$ lbs. But Johann Wolfmayer had candles at all altars, wall brackets and chandeliers lit at his own expense. The nine priests from the Schottenstifte sang the *Libera* by Seyfried. Then the bier was carried by the bearers, led by the trombonists and priests and followed by the funeral guests. It was taken through the nave and to the door. The ceremony was over.

After the religious service the ceremonial carriage took the coffin. A part of the crowd was dispersed but thousands closed in on the procession going slowly along the hospital street. It crossed the Alserbach by the Namentur, passed by the almshouse and the brick-kiln, reached the Währing line, crossed it, reached the right bank of the Währing Brook and went along the brook to the village parish church. The minister, Johann Hayeck, and a second priest were waiting there. The procession stopped; the coffin was carried into the church and blessed by both of the priests, candles were burning on three altars. After the ceremony the parish singers sang the *Miserere* and the *Libera* . . . Now the bearers again took the bier. Many people were still following the procession, the village school-children were there, supervised by the school assistants; then came the local poor people. Before the coffin went the priests, the sacristan, and the acolyte with the censer. The funeral guests followed the coffin accompanied by the prayer leader. The Währing master of ceremonies arranged the procession. With the brook on the right and a slope falling gently on the left, the funeral procession approached the fields of the parish cemetery amid the sound of bells. Before the gates . . . the bearers put their load down. Before the coffin stepped the great tragedian, Heinrich Anschütz, and delivered the gripping obituary by Grillparzer. Thereupon a poem by Schlechta was passed out. And now the great man joined the other dead. The priests consecrated the tomb and blessed the body for the last time. By the last light of the spring day the coffin was lowered into the earth . . . . Tobias Haslinger had brought three laurel wreaths which Hummel placed on the grave. According to an old custom, those standing near threw earth on the grave and the torches were extinguished.

Grillparzer's oration, no less than the two hundred carriages which accompanied the coffin on its last journey, is confirmation enough, should we need it, that by 1827 Beethoven's fame was

The funeral cortège. Watercolour by F. Stöber. The Schwarzspanierhaus is in the background to the right of the church (Beethoven-Haus, Bonn)

already immense. Grillparzer immortalised him as 'the hero of verse in German speech and tongue . . . the last master of tuneful song, the organ of soulful concord, the heir of Handel's and Bach's, of Haydn's and Mozart's immortal fame'. He observed that Beethoven 'was an artist, and all that was his, was his through art alone'. And he ended:

> He was . . . a man as well. A man in every sense—in the highest. Because he withdrew from the world, they called him a man-hater, and because he held aloof from sentimentality, unfeeling. Ah, one who knows himself hard of heart, does not shrink! The finest points are those most easily blunted and bent or broken. An excess of sensitiveness avoids a show of feeling! He fled the world because, in the whole range of his loving nature, he found no weapon to oppose it. He withdrew from mankind after he had given them his all and received nothing in return. He dwelt alone, because he found no second Self. But in the end his heart beat warm for all men, in fatherly affection for his kindred, for the world his all and his heart's blood.
>
> Thus he was, thus he died, thus he will live to the end of time.
>
> You, however, who have followed after us hitherward, let not your hearts be troubled! You have not lost him, you have won him. No living man enters the halls of the immortals. Not until the body has perished, do their portals unclose. He whom you mourn stands from now onward among the great of all ages, inviolate forever. Return homeward therefore, in sorrow, yet resigned! And should you ever in times to come feel the overpowering might of his creations like an onrushing storm, when your mounting ecstasy overflows in the midst of a generation yet unborn, then remember this hour, and think, We were there, when they buried him, and when he died, we wept.

Franz Grillparzer (1791-1872) who had known Beethoven since 1805 and was a prominent Austrian national poet. Watercolour by M.M. Daffinger, 1827. (Historisches Museum, Vienna)

A modern view of Beethoven's grave in Waehringer Cemetery (now Schubert Park), in area shared with Franz Schubert

Tributes to Beethoven

Chapter 2

Canonisation

'History is the most partial of the sciences. When it becomes enamoured of a man, it loves him jealously; it will not even hear of others'—Romain Rolland

Future generations were to echo the sentiments and admiration of Grillparzer time and again. In 1837 in *The Musical Library*, an early Victorian anthology, William Ayrton, for instance, spoke for many when he wrote that Beethoven 'was indisputably the musical glory of the present century'. In the Hanover Square Rooms that same season, the Philharmonic Society of London included the Third and Fifth Piano Concertos in their programmes, as well as the Second Symphony, the *Eroica*, the Fifth and Seventh Symphonies, and, on 17 April, the Ninth Symphony, 'composed expressly for this society', in a complete performance with chorus conducted by Moscheles, a friend and associate of Beethoven at the time of the Congress of Vienna. A few years earlier, on 18 May 1832, His Majesty's Theatre had in the meantime staged the first complete performance in London of *Fidelio*: 'Let . . . all true lovers of music hear *Fidelio*', exclaimed one critic. Then there was Thomas Alsager of *The Times*, 'a complete fanatic in his Beethoven worship', who gave a number of private concerts at his house in Queen Square in which Beethoven's music featured prominently: on Christmas Eve 1832, the first English performance of the *Missa Solemnis* was given under Moscheles' direction. The following year Moscheles appeared as a pianist playing the late Op 109 and Op 111 sonatas ('I found some of my hearers listening with deep devotion', he recalled); some time later on 9 March 1845 he played no less gigantic a work than the B flat *Hammerklavier* Sonata, Op 106, the work that Berlioz had nine years earlier called 'the Sphinx's enigma of almost every pianist'. That same year, 1845, Alsager created the Beethoven Quartet Society which gave its first concert at 76 Harley Street on 21 April. The programme included Op 18, No 1, the third of the *Rasumowsky* Quartets, and Op 127. In that first season alone *all* Beethoven's quartets were played—an impressive testament of faith. By now others had taken up

Sir Charles Hallé (1819-95). 'What a contrast 1848 offers to 1895,' Hallé wrote in his *Autobiography*. '*Then* the question was: Can this or that sonata be understood by the audience? Nowadays the difficulty lies in finding one not too hackneyed'. From a photograph by Walery, 1890

Beethoven's cause, not least Joachim, who as a twelve-year-old had offered the Violin Concerto at an historical Philharmonic Society concert on 27 May 1844. The work had long been dismissed as 'a *fiddling* affair [that] might have been written by any third or fourth-rate composer' (*The Harmonicon*). But that night, with Mendelssohn—Queen Victoria's favourite—conducting, the Violin Concerto finally won that cherished place in the repertoire which it has held ever since.

Four years on, Charles Hallé, a sometime intimate in Paris of men like Chopin, Liszt, Berlioz and Thalberg, took up the challenge with his Covent Garden début when he offered a triumphally received performance of the Beethoven E flat Piano Concerto.

Later, as a conductor in Manchester, he championed Beethoven exhaustively. In the thirty-seven seasons between 1858 and 1895, for instance, he conducted all nine symphonies, the five piano concertos, the Violin Concerto, the Triple Concerto, the Choral Fantasia, and all the overtures, and also included a number of the piano sonatas in his programmes. Compared with the Philharmonic Society in London, this activity was notable. It was also at times better balanced: the Philharmonic may have given in this same period some 163 performances of the symphonies against Hallé's 123, but Hallé was prepared to give less emphasis to those two already universal favourites—Nos 5 and 6—in an effort to devote more relative attention to works such as the Seventh and the Ninth (eight performances of the latter against the Philharmonic's five). The concertos, too, received more attention: as in London the Fourth and Fifth for piano and the Violin Concerto enjoyed the most popularity, but with Hallé's public in the Free Trade Hall so, too, did such unlikely candidates as the Choral Fantasia (13 performances against the Philharmonic's five) and the Triple Concerto (11 against one), while the first three piano concertos also featured to a much greater degree in Hallé's plans. The Philharmonic, too, paid less attention to the piano sonatas: all they offered in fact was the *Waldstein* in 1876 with Anton Rubinstein; and the *Eroica* Variations and Fugue, Op 35, in 1884, with Hans von Bülow. By contrast Hallé presented the sonatas on no less than thirty-four occasions with the *Waldstein* alone receiving seven performances. For Hallé, of course, the canon of thirty-two sonatas was sacrosanct, and he had the distinction of being the first to play them all in public as a complete cycle: in 1861 at the old St. James's Hall in London. Hallé had to repeat the cycle in later seasons.

At a less exalted level, but no less significant in the wider dissemination of Beethoven's music, were the efforts in the 1840s and 50s of that great showman, Jullien, who in his early London

Jullien in 1843

promenade concerts featured everything from the Fifth arranged for four military bands and orchestra, and the *Pastoral* with the addition, in the 'Thunderstorm' movement, of dried peas in a tin box, to such 'obscure' items as the First Symphony and such 'serious' ventures as the weighty Beethoven Festival of 1846. The outcome of this activity, at once commercial yet boldly enterprising for the period, was that the *Musical World* could write in their issue of 2 December 1854 that Jullien had 'created a new taste for music among the middle classes, and they now listen to Beethoven and Mendelssohn because they really love and partly appreciate their works'.

Ever since the early 1790s when William Gardiner of Leicester 'claimed with justice to be the first to introduce the name and genius of Beethoven into England' (notably with the Op 3 String Trio) 'played over with surprise and delight in a room in the town in 1794, several years before the works of Beethoven were introduced to London', in the words of Mrs. T. Fielding Johnson's *Glimpses of Ancient Leicester*, 1806), England, it is obvious, had offered Beethoven a positive response. During his lifetime he often had cause to be gratified: in a letter to the publisher George Thomson of Edinburgh, 15 September 1814, he went so far as to remark on the 'very particular regard and affection I feel for the English nation'.

William Gardiner (1770-1853). Portrait attributed to W. Artaud

It was not only England, however, that revered Beethoven. If *The Times* in their obituary had tartly observed that 'a little more attention to him [in Vienna] would have been more to the purpose' than all the expressions of condolence symbolised by the carriages that had followed the coffin, there is no doubt that his admirers and supporters in the Habsburg capital were still legion—and not least among the nobility who more often than not had been able to implement their regard in practical terms.

In the years after Beethoven's death, musicians elsewhere often found themselves united in collective praise in spite of differing temperaments and philosophical outlooks. Mendelssohn and Schumann, not to mention later the young Brahms, had nothing but admiration for the 'Grand Mogul'. When Liszt played the *Hammerklavier* in the Salon Érard in Paris in 1836 he declared his allegiance overwhelmingly. In the *Gazette Musicale* for 12 June of that year, Berlioz chronicled the fact that he played it 'in a manner that, if the composer could have heard it in his grave, would have sent a thrill of joy and pride over him. Not a note was left out, not one added (I followed, score in hand), no inflection was effaced, no change of tempo permitted . . . Liszt, in thus making comprehensible a work not yet comprehended has proved that he is the pianist of the future'. Forty years later, at the time of the first Bayreuth Festival, Liszt was again to cast a spell over his listeners with this same sonata, or rather more specifically with its *Adagio* heart.

In a letter written earlier to Wilhelm von Lenz, author of *Beethoven et ses trois styles,* Liszt considered Beethoven's music to parallel 'the pillar of smoke and fire which led the Israelites through the desert, a pillar of smoke to lead us by day, and a pillar of fire to light the night' (1852). In France, not always a receptive environment, Bizet placed Beethoven 'above the greatest, the most famous . . . this Titan, this Prometheus of music' (1867). For Busoni, Beethoven was the personification of great humanity, of ideals that were 'high and pure', of 'liberty, equality, fraternity'. He was 'a product of 1793, and he was the first great democrat in music' (1920). For many others he remained the archetypal example of the 'great man' theory put forward by Georg Kisewetter in 1834 in his *History of the Modern Music of Western Europe.* He was a symbol of 'absolute genius', he was also the dominant symbol of an epoch. After more than a century he remains so. The 'Age of Beethoven' is a favourite phrase of the modern historian.

In spite of this, not *everyone* at first adulated Beethoven—as we know from some of Hallé's early experiences. In Paris in 1828, for example, his music was regularly frowned upon, as von Lenz confirms:

> Beethoven was not yet understood; of his thirty-two sonatas, three were played—the A flat major Sonata with variations (Op 26), the C sharp minor *quasi Fantasia* [*Moonlight*], and the Sonata in F minor, which a publisher's fancy—not Beethoven's—christened *Appassionata.* The last five sonatas passed for the monstrous abortions of a German idealist who did not know how to write for the piano.

In London *The Harmonicon* was often a source of statements designed to curtail the spread of enthusiastic acceptance. We read in their pages that if the *Eroica* 'is not by some means abridged it will soon fall into disuse' (April 1829), that the Seventh Symphony indulges in 'a great deal of disagreeable eccentricity', that it is 'a kind of enigma—we had almost said a hoax' (July 1825), and that the Ninth Symphony is long and wanting in 'intelligible design' (April 1825, following the first performance of it in England at a Philharmonic Society concert on 21 March under the direction of Sir George Smart). In America the response to the Ninth was as

Liszt plays the *Hammerklavier* to Wagner. Silhouette by Bithorn

Engraving of Beethoven

BOSTON DAILY TRAVELLER.

PUBLISHED BY TRAVELLER PUBLISHING CO., AT 307 WASHINGTON STREET, OPP. OLD SOUTH MEETING HOUSE.

MONDAY, MARCH 19, 1894.

SYMPHONY CONCERT.

An Excellent Programme Made Up of Familiar Numbers.

MR. PAUR'S COURAGE.

Beethoven's Music Treated with Loving Regard.

The Oberon Overture Very Well Given—The Drum Again a Nuisance.

The nineteenth concert of the Boston Symphony Orchestra took place in Music Hall Saturday evening. The following was the programme:

Symphony in G minor....................Mozart
Aria, "With Verdure Clad"..............Haydn
Adagio and Scherzo from Ninth symphony, Beethoven
Aria, "Voi che sapete," from "Marriage of of Figaro"..............................Mozart
Overture to "Oberon"....................Weber
Mrs. Lillian Blauvelt was the soloist.

As all the numbers performed are familiar, comment upon the compositions is unnecessary.

It only remains to speak of the performance, which as far as the orchestra is concerned, was admirable.

The delightful Mozart symphony was finely read by Conductor Paur; he giving himself some little latitude in the expression of the andante movement, but it was only the conception of a discreet musician and was not of an exaggerated form in the least, the effect of the music being enhanced thereby.

Mr. Paur always treats the music of Beethoven with loving regard for the great master's evident intentions, and so in these two movements we were vouchsafed a remarkably faithful rendering. These movements are the only ones worthy of perpetuation in this extraordinary composition of Beethoven's latest period, and it was gratifying to hear them unencumbered with the wearisome monotone of the first movement and the eccentricities of the finale. Mr. Paur is to be commended for his courage in so happily dismembering this uncouth specimen of the immortal master of symphonic composition.

The performance of the "Oberon" overture was an excellent one, but the rendering lacked that marvellous refinement that was such a positive characteristic of unrivalled interpretations of the Weber overtures by the master hand of Wilhelm Geircke. The admirable first horn player made much of the opening phrase for horn solo, but the diminuendo of the prolonged note was marred because of the falling from the pitch. The overture was played with remarkable precision and spirit.

The tympani as usual were out of tune. In the Scherzo of the Ninth Symphony the upper drum was nearly F sharp, which did not make a harmonious concord with the contrabasses playing F natural, to which pitch the drums are expected to be tuned. Besides, F sharp given by the drums as a minor third in the key of D minor is a little queer to a musical ear against the F natural of the rest of the instruments.

The sound of these drums when subjected to the herculean thumps of the player always reminds me of the sheet-iron thunder of a theatrical storm. Mr. Paur should see that this overpowering nuisance is abated. It is the last relic of musical barbarism that existed during the incumbency of Mr. Nikisch.

Boston Daily Traveller clipping of March 19, 1894, referring to a performance of Beethoven's Ninth Symphony

unflattering. The first performance, in New York on 21 March 1846, was a failure, and later the Boston *Daily Atlas* for 6 February 1853 felt that 'if the best critics and orchestras have failed to find the meaning of Beethoven's Ninth Symphony, we may well be pardoned if we confess our inability to find any . . . an incomprehensible union of strange harmonies'. Another American commentator reported in *The Orchestra*, London 20 June 1868, that the 'commonplace' theme of the Finale was 'very much like *Yankee Doodle* . . . the general impression it left on me is that of a concert made up of India war-whoops and angry wild cats'. No less a mind than Philip Hale's (in the Boston *Musical Record*, 1 June 1899) thought that to worship this symphony was 'mere fetishism'. He went on to talk about 'pages of stupid and hopelessly vulgar music' and then asked: 'Do you believe way down in the bottom of your heart that if this music had been written by Mr. John L. Tarbox now living in Sandown, N.H., any conductor here or in Europe could be persuaded to put it into rehearsal?'

Yet for others this self-same, apparently naïve, meaningless symphony spelt the future. When Wagner arranged it for piano in 1830, a mere six years after its first performance, he was just seventeen, and at the most impressionable stage of his life. Bruckner never got over the shock of hearing it for the first time: its elemental, cosmic dawn, its hammering scherzo, its idyllic slow movement—all were to haunt his greatest creative moments. Mahler, too, never quite got over it. When he appeared in New York in 1909 at the end of his life, he took audiences and critics by storm with a blazing and impassioned performance, and in the 1909-10 season conducted it again as part of an historical Beethoven cycle arranged by the New York Philharmonic Society. The Ninth was the inspiration of the Romantic age. Liszt transcribed it for piano,* Smetana spoke of it as 'no earthly music [but] a divine revelation', and the visionary Berlioz extolled its virtues in essays and lectures, defended its case as early as 1829, argued that modern music began with it, and then came to London in 1852 to conduct two legendary performances. Another French visionary, Debussy, found it to be 'a magnificent gesture of musical pride' (*Monsieur Croche, Antidilettante*). Quinet, in a moment of Gallic fervour, even saw it as 'the *Marseillaise* of humanity'.

By the 1840s Beethoven was, for some at any rate, all but canonised.† The great Romantics of the age set him on a pedestal. The first edition of Schindler's *Biographie von Ludwig van Beethoven* had been published in Münster in 1840, and an English version by Moscheles had appeared in London the following year. A Beethoven Festival was then held in Bonn in August 1845 and a

* Along with the other eight, 1837-64.

† To use Denis Arnold's phrase

statue was unveiled. Liszt played an active rôle in the organising of the event, wrote a new *Festival Cantata* based on the slow movement of Beethoven's *Archduke* Trio, and conducted a performance of the *Missa Solemnis*. At least one member of the audience found it 'incomprehensible': however, that old Beethovenian, William Gardiner, prophesied that 'the time will come (though I shall not live to see it) when the *Missa Solemnis* of Beethoven will be regarded as we now regard the greatest works of Handel'. Friedrich Wilhelm IV of Prussia came, Victoria and Albert came, a host of other distinguished guests came.

Berlioz, in the Second Epilogue to his *Les Soirées de l'Orchestre* (1852) summed it up regretfully: 'It is very fine in the end' he wrote 'to glorify in this fashion the demigods who are no more . . . Today all these intelligent and sensitive beings on whom [Beethoven's] genius had shed its radiance, turn to him as to a benefactor and a friend . . . But it is too late. This Beethoven in bronze is unaware of all this homage, and it is sad to think that the living Beethoven, whose memory is thus honoured, might not have obtained from his native town in the days of suffering and destitution which were so numerous during his troubled life, the ten-thousandth part of the sum lavished upon him after his death'. At the same time, nevertheless, he fully acknowledged and chronicled the significance of the occasion. On the unveiling of the statue, he wrote, 'applause, cheers, trumpet fanfares, drum rolls, volleys of gunfire, the pealing of bells, all the hullabaloo of admiration which is the voice of fame in civilised nations, blazed out . . . and hailed the figure of the great composer.' When the following year Wagner conducted a performance of the Ninth in Dresden, he as much realised the convictions of his youth and gave substance to his very personalised and emotional assessment of the work, as he built on the aftermath of this Bonn memorial. Its repercussions were to ultimately prove highly consequential.

Title page of the first edition of the Ninth Symphony (Beethoven-Archiv, Bonn)

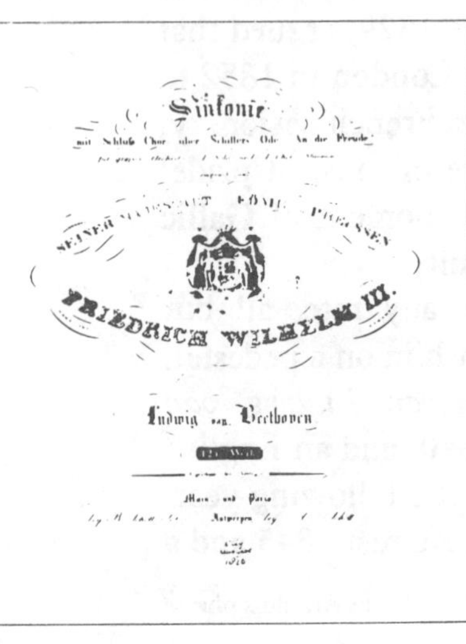

* * *

Immortality is to be remembered. With Beethoven, man has never stopped remembering. From the fictional asides of Schindler to the

Beethoven's room and his Broadwood Piano of 1817. Coloured lithograph from a sepia drawing by J.N. Noechle, *c.* April 1827

Berlioz conducting.
Caricature by Doré, 1850

digressions of Huxley, Mann and E. M. Forster, from the philosophical stands of Wagner and von Bülow to the psychological half-truths of Newman and Sullivan, from the profundity of Thayer and Nottebohm to the science of modern research, from hostility to admiration, from poetic celebration to the romanticism of Rolland, from reported fact to literary recreation—for nearly two centuries Beethoven has been a catalytic inspiration. That is the measure of his greatness, of his claim to posterity.

The Romantics saw to it that the landmarks of his survival in history would be monuments on a grand scale. Studies like Thayer's *Life of Beethoven* (1866-79), Nottebohm's examination of the surviving sketchbooks (1865-80) and Sir George Grove's book on the symphonies (1896), not to mention the outcome of the *Gesamtausgabe*, the complete edition of Beethoven's works published by Breitkopf & Härtel in 1864-88, helped to point the way to the future in no uncertain terms. Later came Donald Francis Tovey who in his *Essays in Musical Analysis* established criteria in examining the substance of Beethoven's art that have yet to be entirely surpassed, in spite of having been published as long ago as the 1930s. His 45-page study of the Ninth Symphony, quite apart from his 16 page *précis* analysis of the same work, stands perhaps as one of the most remarkable literary illuminations of all time. The legacy of such achievement has been rich and stimulating. It has also been an affirmation of the eagle-like hold which Beethoven still has over our lives and thoughts.

The Romantics forged no less conspicuous landmarks in the way Beethoven's music should be played and interpreted. The rise of distinctive performing traditions in the nineteenth century proved in fact to be of crucial importance in the survival and projection of Beethoven's art, and no more so than when they purported to have origins in the master's own ideas. A significant line, elements of which are still with us in a few celebrated cases, was begun, for instance, with Czerny. He had studied the piano with Beethoven, and then in turn taught, among others, the young Franz Liszt. Liszt's Weimar pupils subsequently formed a legendary group, many of whom survived well into the age of the gramophone. Among these, the Beethoven playing of the Scottish pianist, Frederic Lamond, was renowned, as was the conducting of Felix Weingartner who in 1907 published a book *On the performance of Beethoven's Symphonies* which was to have widespread influence and which is still provocative in spite of its continual advice to re-touch Beethoven's orchestration. It early on ran to several editions.

Felix Weingartner (1863-1942), the Austrian conductor and composer. He wrote six symphonies, and arranged Beethoven's *Hammerklavier* Sonata for orchestra. Photograph (Columbia Records)

Theoretically, Weingartner belonged to that broad Austro-German line of conducting which had its roots in Wagner (Liszt's

Hector Berlioz (1803-1869)

Carl Czerny (1791-1857)

Hans von Bulow (1830-1894)

Arthur Nikisch (1855-1922)

son-in-law) and which ran through Mahler and Strauss to Furtwängler, Bruno Walter and Klemperer. Yet whereas someone like, say, Mahler or Furtwängler, identified strongly with Wagner's liberal ideas, projecting their own philosophy into Beethoven's music, viewing each work as a self-expression of themselves—with results that were predictably contrary and variable—Weingartner, opposed to the Wagner-von Bülow concept, endeavoured to introduce greater objectivity into his performances. In this sense he shared something in common with Toscanini, a man who stood outside the Austro-German tradition, and for whom authenticity and an avoidance of over-programmatic characterisation were important factors. Toscanini dismissed the example of Furtwängler in abrupt terms: 'Tradition', he said 'is to be found only in one place—in the music!' In 1926 he viewed the *Eroica* with pristine objectivity: 'Some say this is Napoleon, some Hitler, some Mussolini. For me it is simply *allegro con brio*.' Such purity was to pave the way for a new style of Beethoven performance, a twentieth century one, closer perhaps to the spirit of the printed page than almost anything in the nineteenth century, yet at times still arguably less personal than the elaborately imagined realisations of all those Romantics who had been brought up so intensely in the first-hand shadow of Beethoven's might. Perhaps the solution lies somewhere between these extremes: if the reports of Beethoven's contemporaries are to be believed, and particularly those of Czerny and Schindler, Beethoven himself seems after all to have had as much concern for strictness and purity as for elements of a more fanciful and unpredictable nature. As Edwin Fischer (like Arrau a pupil of Martin Krause who had studied with Liszt) once commented:

NEW RECORDS

'His Master's Voice'
RECORDS

AUGUST 1914

12-inch Records 5s. 6d.; 10-inch 3s. 6d.

Orchestral

BERLIN PHILHARMONIC ORCHESTRA
(conducted by NIKISCH)

12-inch Records, 5s. 6d. each.

040790 Fifth Symphony—Finale, Part III. *Beethoven*
040791 Fifth Symphony—Finale, Part IV. *Beethoven*

THIS month's issue of records brings to a conclusion the set which together covers the whole of the wonderful Fifth Symphony. We have already had the three complete movements—the 1st Movement Part I., the 1st Movement Part II., and the Scherzo, as well as a portion of the Finale. The remaining portion of the Finale is dealt with in the present two records.

Again in these records do we remark the delicate and poetical precision of the maestro Nikisch in the soft passages that lead to the Presto. The definition of those celebrated pianissimos is superb alike in the

H.M.V.'s completion of the Nikisch recording of Beethoven's Fifth Symphony (040786-91). Catalogue announcement, August 1914 (E.M.I.)

> Two dangerous paths lie open before the interpreter. On one of them the performer's own passion makes use of Beethoven's music to express itself, while on the other the player simply obeys slavishly all the instructions given in the written music. One has to steer between this Scylla and Charybdis: neither expressing oneself without restraint, nor being petrified with too much reverence.

One other conductor who had a hand to play in the fashioning of a Beethoven tradition ought to be mentioned: Nikisch. As a young violinist he had played for Wagner in 1872 in a performance of the Ninth Symphony, and he later worked with Liszt, Brahms and Anton Rubinstein. Like Furtwängler, a disciple by example, he was moulded in the Liszt-Wagner style: he was, he claimed, 'a re-creator of the masterpieces according to my own ideas'. Harold Schonberg has said that 'Nikisch worked through intuition and emotion rather than planning or scholarship'. In spite of this he is remembered for being 'one of the finest of orchestral conductors in musical history', and the example he set his students lived on through several generations. In 1913 he further had the distinction of making the first *complete* gramophone recording of Beethoven's Fifth Symphony—with the Berlin Philharmonic, on eight acoustic 78 discs. By then von Bülow had already committed (in 1891 in fact) part of the *Eroica* on to some Edison cylinders: recorded sound, however much in its infancy, was here to stay, and Beethoven's music was to be a cornerstone from the outset.

If such landmarks of heritage and tradition are beyond erosion, so, also, of course, are the reminiscences of Beethoven's contemporaries, and the voluminous correspondence and conversation books which he kept. In his 1946 Presidential Address to the English Association, Arthur Bryant defined biography as 'the art of making the dry bones of a dead man live'. In Beethoven's case we are fortunate: nearly 2,000 letters remain extant, and out of some 400 original conversation books 136 have survived (the rest were destroyed by Schindler in an attempt to whitewash the character of his hero). The letters, reaching back forty years, make particularly unique reading, and especially the later ones. There is no denying of course that in literary terms they may lack the finesse and elegant phrasing of, say, Mendelssohn, the etiquette of Chopin, the philosophical musing of Liszt, or even the earthiness of things in Mozart . . . Yet, just because of their clumsiness, their deficiencies, their 'constipated' command of language (with acknowledgement to Winton Dean), they come alive in a way that is at once spontaneous. They are, one feels, sincere expressions, with no time for the elaborate pleasantries or conventions of the Napoleonic period to which they belong historically. The result very often is that Beethoven emerges not as an impersonal, unreal figure, but as a plain-speaking, hasty, argumentative, complaining, sarcastic and often rash man, yet with nevertheless that renowned sense of 'unbuttoned' humour, that shrewd, if unscrupulous, business mind which his business associates had good reason to fear, and that sense of fair play when faced with injustice which made him so loved by those close to him. The impact is so vivid that just occasionally it seems almost possible to turn the clock back, to become a part of Beethoven's time and place, ready to split a flagon of rough red wine, enjoy a meal at a favourite fish restaurant, while away the small hours in the half world of some Viennese coffee house, and witness the philosophy, mood and temper of the man and his era . . .

Arturo Toscanini conducting the NBC Symphony Orchestra. He made several recordings of the Beethoven symphonies and his integral cycle with the NBC Symphony, dating mainly from the early fifties, has long been a classic of the gramophone. Photograph (R.C.A.)

Chapter 3
Origins

'Tis virtue, and not birth that makes us noble:
Great actions speak great minds, and such should govern'
Beaumont and Fletcher, *The Prophetess*

Ludwig van Beethoven was born in Bonn on either the 15th or 16th of December 1770. He himself believed the former, but the latter date is traditionally accepted since it is known that he was baptised on the 17th: the custom of the day in Catholic Germany was to baptise a child within twenty-four hours of birth. Interestingly there was for some time an added confusion as to the exact *year* of Beethoven's birth. He himself was convinced that he was born in 1772: a letter written as late as 2 May 1810 (to his friend in youth and subsequent biographer, Franz Wegeler) contains the comment 'Unfortunately I lived for a while without knowing how old I was—I had a family book but it was lost, Heaven knows how'. This situation led early on to a number of errors and contradictions and to Thayer's conclusion that Beethoven's age was actually falsified by his father in an effort to make his son out as an infant prodigy whose abilities could compare with those of the child Mozart that had so captured the imagination of Europe in the 1760s. In his revision of Thayer's *Life of Beethoven,* Elliot Forbes (1967) questions the validity of this argument, adding that many family records of the period were, after all, 'imperfectly kept [as] is amply illustrated by the discrepancies of birth dates mentioned in contemporary writings'.

The second son of Johann van Beethoven and Maria Magdalena (*née* Keverich), Beethoven's lineage has been traced back directly to the fifteenth century when members of the 'van Beethoven' family worked as peasant farm labourers in the Spanish-dominated Flemish Brabant region of what is now Belgium.* The family tree is complex but it appears that descendants of these early Low Country Beethovens settled in various towns, gradually improving

* The prefix 'van' confirms Beethoven's plebeian Flemish ancestry. Though originally a sign of social standing, it in no way had the connotations of the German 'von', a sign of noble birth.

Beethoven's birthplace, the courtyard. Pencil drawing by R. Beissel, 1889

their status and working as tradesmen and artisans. One document of 1594 registered 'Arnoldus beethoven filius quondam Marci' as belonging to the Brabant town of Kampenhout. Another branch of the family made their home in Malines (now Mechelen) to the south of Antwerp. Here Beethoven's great-grandfather, Michael van Beethoven, worked as a master-baker and lace merchant, eventually becoming bankrupt and fleeing to Bonn in 1741. In so doing he followed in the footsteps of his two sons, Cornelius and Ludwig, who had already arrived in Bonn in around 1731 and 1733 respectively. Ludwig became a Court Musician shortly afterwards and assumed the post of *Kapellmeister* in 1761. His wife, Maria-Josepha Poll, probably came of Rhineland stock, although her family name is known in both Southern Germany and Austria. Their son, Johann—Beethoven's father—became a Court Musician in turn and at the time of Beethoven's birth was a tenor in the service of the then Elector and Archbishop of Cologne, Maximilian Friedrich. Johann's wife, Maria Magdalena, had origins in the Rhineland and Moselle regions, and on her mother's side could boast of councillors, mayors and merchants among her forebears. Before her marriage to Johann she had been the wife of a chamberlain to the Elector of Trēves. Their one son had died in infancy and Maria Magdalena was herself a widow after less than three years. She married Johann against the wishes of his father ('I would never have believed or expected of you that you should sink so low') in 1767. They had a first son, Ludwig Maria, who was baptised on 2 April 1769. He died, however, six days later and so Ludwig van Beethoven was actually the first of their children to survive. That he did at all was perhaps something of a miracle. Infant mortality was high in the eighteenth century, and Bonn, like so many places, was not the healthiest of cities. The Rhine would overflow in bad weather, spreading its effluent through those kind of 'narrow, nasty streets out of repair, wretchedly thin of inhabitants and [with] above half of the common sort asking alms' which Mary Montagu witnessed in one of her letters from Germany. The poorer sections of the city were unpaved and poisonous. People thought nothing of urinating in the street, ditches and ruts were choked with sewage, pigs and chickens roamed the streets, offal was thrown out of doors or windows and left to rot and putrefy. Rats and vermin were everywhere. A document of 1786 complains ineffectually about the 'intolerable stink' of the city.

Ludwig van Beethoven, the grandfather (1712-73). Beethoven had this painting sent from Bonn to Vienna in 1801, and after his death it passed on to his nephew, Karl. Portrait in oils by L. Radoux (Otto Reichert, Vienna)

Illuminating descriptions have come down to us about Beethoven's immediate family. The image of his grandfather, reputedly a fine bass singer, for instance, long remained implanted in his memory, even though the old man was dead by December

View of Bonn from the Rhine, *c.* 1792-94. Anonymous coloured etching

1773. Franz Wegeler reported in his *Notizen* that he 'was a man short of stature, muscular, with extremely animated eyes, and was greatly respected as an artist'. The Fischer family, friends of the Beethovens for at least two generations, and in whose house Beethoven himself was born, give us a picture of life in the household of the patriarchal Ludwig: 'everything was so beautiful and proper and well arranged, with valuables, all six rooms were provided with beautiful furniture, many paintings and cupboards, a cupboard of silver service, a cupboard with fine gilded porcelain and glass, an assortment of the most beautiful linen which would be drawn through a ring; everything from the smallest article sparkled like silver.'

Of Beethoven's father we know that he entered the Court Chapel as a boy soprano in 1752. He was then twelve, and also showed an ability on the violin and clavier. Later, as a Court Musician (he assumed a salaried post by a decree dated 24 April 1764) he gave lessons to the children of wealthy families in Bonn, teaching singing and keyboard playing. In his prime it seems clear that for all the 'dark side of his character', he was esteemed as a competent official at Court, as a fine musician, and as an excellent teacher. One contemporary described him as tall and handsome with powdered hair. Another (Gottfried Fischer) says that he was in fact 'of medium height', with a 'longish [somewhat scarred] face, broad forehead, round nose, broad shoulder, serious eyes . . . [and a] thin pigtail'.

As for Beethoven's own mother, we have a description of her as a 'handsome, slender person' with a 'rather tall, longish face, a nose somewhat bent [and] spare, earnest eyes'. She was a serious person, whose whole life and character seem to have been fatefully marked by the deaths of her father, her first husband, and, shortly after her marriage to Beethoven's father, her mother. According to the so-called Fischer manuscript, compiled by Gottfried Fischer with the help of his elder sister, Cäcilia, she 'was a clever woman; she could give converse and reply aptly, politely and modestly to high and low, and for this reason she was much liked and respected.' Long suffering, she died from consumption in 1787. She was forty: Beethoven, grief-stricken, was to lament her passing to the end of his days.

The Beethovens lived on the second floor of a house in the Rheingasse (No 934, now No 7) which belonged to the Fischer family. It was here, as we have noted, that Ludwig was born, and it was this same street that offered a home to his grandfather the *Kapellmeister*, to the horn-player Simrock, who later became a well-known publisher, to the Ries family, and to the Salomons, one of whom, Johann Peter, later brought Haydn to London.

Bonn at that time was a small and, to European minds, an otherwise relatively provincial Rhineland city of Roman origin, with a close-knit population of less than ten thousand. It was important, however, being the capital seat of Maximilian Friedrich the Archbishop and Elector of Cologne. As such it commanded a position second to none for out of all the petty and largely independent sovereignties (some 300 in all) which together made up the multi-layered structure of the German nation in the eighteenth century, it was specifically the Archbishopric of Cologne, together with those of Mainz and Trèves, which carried the most political and strategic weight. As upholders of the last bastions of the ancient, thousand-year-old Holy Roman Empire, with the right to elect the 'Holy Roman Emperor' (at that time Joseph II of the Habsburg-Lorraine dynasty, the son of Maria Theresa of Austria), and with positions and titles confirmed by the Pope, the ecclesiastical princes of these three particular courts possessed power and influence. As 'Electors of the Empire and rulers of the fairest regions of the Rhine' (to use Thayer's words), they additionally took their place in the imperial Diet, the *Reichstag* or German legislative assembly, and acted as a counterforce against royal absolutism. The Holy Roman Empire itself came to an end in 1806 but the legacy of the Electoral courts lasted well into the nineteenth century. As for Bonn, which had been the centre of the Cologne Archbishopric from 1263 to 1794, time was to rob it of none of the splendour and pomp that had created it at the outset. It is still a majestic, imperial place.

The Fischer House in Bonn. Engraving by C.C. Rordorff

An English visitor, Henry Swinburne, discovered Bonn in 1780. In a letter to his brother (29 November) he wrote:

Bonn is a pretty town, neatly built, and its streets tolerably well paved, all in black lava. It is situated in a flat near the river. The Elector of Cologne's palace faces the South entry. It has no beauty of architecture and is all plain white without any pretensions.

We went to court and were invited to dine with the Elector (Königsegg). He is 73 years old, a little, hale, black man, very merry and affable. His table is none of the best; no dessert wines handed about, nor any foreign wines at all. He is easy and agreeable, having lived all his life in ladies' company, which he is said to have liked better than his breviary. The captains of his guard and a few other people of the court form the company, amongst whom were his two great-nieces, Madame de Hatzfeld and Madame de Taxis. The palace is of immense size, the ball-room particularly large and low . . . The Elector goes about to all the assemblies and plays at tric-trac. He asked me to be of his party, but I was not acquainted with their way of playing. There is every evening an assembly or play at court.

The pace of aristocratic life in the town makes interesting reading. Joseph Clemens, for instance, one of the Bavarian Electors of Cologne, 'held the opinion, universal in the courts of those days, that he might with a clear conscience enjoy life after the manner of secular princes. In pleasing the ladies, he was utterly regardless of expense and for their amusement gave magnificent balls, splendid masquerades, musical and dramatic entertainments, and hunting parties' (Karl Eduard Vehse, *Geschichte der deutschen Höfe seit der Reformation*, Hamburg 1857). To this end Clemens found it necessary in 1698 to employ some 22 musicians with a total salary of nearly 9,000 florins. His successor (and nephew), Clemens August, took office in 1724, later becoming Grand Master of the Teutonic Order. In his book *Der Spanische Erbfolgekrieg und Kurfürst Joseph Clemens von Cöln* (Jena 1851), Leonhard Ennen wrote that 'monstrous were the sums squandered by [Clemens August] in the purchase of splendid ornaments, magnificent equipages, furniture, costly for its variety, and of rare works of art; upon dazzling court festivities, sleighing-parties, masquerades, operas, dramas and ballets; upon charlatans, swindlers, female vocalists, actors and dancers. His theatre and opera alone cost him 50,000 thalers annually and the magnificence of his masked balls twice a week in winter, is proof that no small sums were lavished upon them'. Clemens August died from exertion on the dance floor in February 1761.

Maximilian Friedrich of Königsegg-Rothenfels Archbishop and Elector of Cologne (1708-84). Oil painting by J. E. Marteleux (Städtische Kunstsammlung, Bonn)

He was succeeded by Maximilian Friedrich who was elevated to the Electorship of Cologne on 6 April 1761. Through his prime minister, Kaspar Anton von Belderbusch, an admirer of Friedrich II of Prussia, the lavish expenditure of his predecessor was curtailed. Ennen says that Belderbusch 'put a stop to building, dismissed a number of the actors, restricted the number of concerts and court balls, dispensed with the costly hunts, reduced the salaries of court officials, officers and domestics, lessened the *état* for the kitchen, cellar and table of the prince, turned the property left by Clemens August into money and comforted the latter's creditors with the hope of better times'. For all this, musical activity at Court does not seem to have suffered to any great degree. A document, dated 16 July 1761, appointed Beethoven's grandfather as the new *Kapellmeister*, and orchestral and operatic activities were encouraged to continue. In the court calendar for 1774, some fourteen instrumentalists are listed (all string players, save for two bassoonists), together with an organist and a small mixed choir of nine singers. In addition there was the Band of the Life Guards, a minute company of trumpeters and Court kettledrummer.

When Beethoven's grandfather died, Andreas Lucchesi was appointed *Kapellmeister* (26 May 1774). Later that year the nineteen-year-old Franz Anton Ries, sometime child prodigy, an outstanding violinist and a stalwart friend of the Beethoven family, was placed on a salary and a few months subsequently, on 23 March 1775, Nikolaus Simrock joined the Bonn musicians as 'Court Hornist on the Electoral Toxal, in the cabinet and at table'. Christian Gottlieb Neefe (1748-98), a North German musician Burney regretted not having met when he visited Leipzig in 1772, joined the Court as organist in 1781.

Outside the court in the wealthier areas of the city, there was also much activity, as is clear from a letter of 2 March 1783 sent by Neefe to Cramer's *Magazin der Musik*. From this we learn that Berlderbusch kept an unusual wind quintet, made up of two horns, a bassoon and, exceptionally for the period, two clarinets. The Countess von Hatzfeld, niece of the Elector, 'plays the fortepiano brilliantly' and was in addition a fine singer. Another, Johann Gottfried von Mastiaux, was 'a devoted admirer of Haydn, with whom he corresponds . . . in his large collection of music there are already [amazingly] 80 symphonies, 30 quartets and 40 trios by that master. His rare and valuable instruments are so numerous that he could almost equip a complete orchestra'. Yet another, Count Alstädter, possessed a good string quartet. Neefe felt that 'a stranger fond of music need never leave Bonn without nourishment': even so he found it necessary to conclude that 'a large public concert institution under the patronage of His Electoral Grace is still desirable. It would be one more ornament of the capital, and a promoter of the good cause of music'.

Chapter 4

The Early Years: 1770-92

'Keep your eyes on him; some day he will give the world something to talk about'—Mozart

It was in such an environment, at once civilised and cultured, squalid and servile, that Beethoven was brought up. His early childhood is best described in the Fischer manuscript. The Fischers, it will be remembered, had plenty of opportunity to observe the young boy and his family (the eldest Fischer child, Cäcilia, was born in 1762, the youngest, Gottfried, in 1780). From this source we learn something of how the Beethovens would celebrate an occasion:

> Every year, on Saint Magdalen's day, the name and birthday of Madame van Beethoven would be celebrated festively. The music stands would be brought out of the *Tucksaal*. The chairs would then be placed right and left in the rooms facing the street and a canopy set up in the room where the portrait of Grandfather Ludwig van Beethoven hung, and handsomely decorated with flowers, laurel branches and foliage. Early in the evening Madame van Beethoven would be requested to retire betimes, and by ten o'clock everyone would be assembled and ready in the most complete silence. The tuning up would now begin and Madame van Beethoven would be awakened. She would then dress and be led in and seated on a beautifully decorated chair under the canopy. At that very moment magnificent music would strike up, resounding throughout the whole neighbourhood so that everyone who was preparing to go to bed became gay and cheerful. When the music ended a meal would be served up and the company ate and drank until those who had become light-headed and wished to dance would take off their shoes and dance in their stockinged feet in order not to make a commotion in the house. In this fashion the celebration would come to an end.

Later documents confirm, however, that in spite of such scenes of merriment the family lived in fact under conditions of extreme poverty.

Beethoven's ability as a musician manifested itself around 1775, the year in which his grandmother, Maria-Josepha, died. Whether, nevertheless, he showed signs of any extraordinary talent at so early an age remains in doubt. Two years later in 1777, and, according to one schoolfellow, 'distinguished by uncleanliness and negligence', he began lessons at the so-called Tirocinium, a Latin primary school. These lasted until probably 1780 or the summer of 1781: he did not subsequently go to the Gymnasium for higher education, and had no formal lessons in general subjects after this time, devoting his entire effort to music. To all intents and purposes, therefore, it can be said that by the age of ten, Beethoven had learnt what he could: thereafter he lived off his wits and his insatiable natural curiosity. The Fischers remembered this period. It was thought apparently that Beethoven

did not learn very much at school; that is why his father so early seated him at the clavier and kept him at it so severely. Cäcilia Fischer related that when his father led him to the clavier he had to stand on a small bench to play. *Oberbürgermeister* Windeck also saw this . . . Ludwig van Beethoven also received daily instruction on the violin. Once he happened to be playing without notes when his father came in and said 'What is all that silly nonsense you are scraping away so badly? You know that I cannot stand it. Scrape from notes otherwise all your scraping will not be of any use to you.' When Johann van Beethoven received an unexpected visitor and Ludwig happened to come into the room, he would generally walk around the clavier and press down the keys with his right hand. Then his father would say 'What are you splashing there again; go away or I'll box your ears.' His father finally paid attention to him when he heard him play the violin; he was again playing out of his head without notes. His father said 'Don't you ever stop doing that in spite of what I have told you.' The boy went on playing and said to his father, 'But isn't that beautiful?' His father replied, 'That is another matter. You are not ready to play things out of your head. Work hard at the clavier and on the violin. Play the notes correctly; that is more important. When you have become good enough, then you can and will have to work out of your head hard enough.' Ludwig van Beethoven later also received daily lessons on the viola.

Beethoven's parents had a further five children: Caspar Anton Carl (baptised 8 April 1774); Nikolaus Johann (baptised 2 October 1776); Anna Maria Franziska (first daughter, baptised 23 February 1779, died 27 February); August Franz George (fifth son, baptised 17 January 1781, died 16 August 1783) and Maria Margaretha Josepha (second daughter and seventh and last child, baptised 5 May 1786, died 25 November 1787). The Fischer manuscript tells how on fine summer days the surviving children

would be taken out by the serving maids to the Rhine or to the Palace garden, where they played in the sand with other children. At the proper time they would have to find their own way home. When the weather was

Maximilian Franz, the last Archbishop and Elector of Cologne (1756-1801). Copy in oils after an original portrait in the Brühl Palace (Beethoven-Haus, Bonn)

The handbill marking Beethoven's first appearance in public, 26 March 1778. From a photograph (Beethoven-Haus, Bonn)

AVERTISSEMENT

Heut dato den 26ten Martii 1778. wird auf dem musikalischen Akademiesaal in der Sternengass der Churkölnische Hoftenorist BEETHOVEN die Ehre haben zwey seiner Scholaren zu produciren; nämlich: Mdlle. Averdonc Hofaltistin, und sein Söhngen von 6 Jahren. Erstere wird mit verschiedenen schönen Arien, letzterer mit verschiedenen Clavier-Concerten und Trios die Ehre haben aufzuwarten, wo er allen hohen Herrschaften ein völliges Vergnügen zu leisten sich schmeichlet, um je mehr da beyde zum grösten Vergnügen des ganzen Hofes sich hören zu lassen die Gnade gehabt haben.

Der Anfang ist Abends um 5. Uhr.

Die nicht abbonnirte Herren und Damen zahlen einen Gulden.

Die Billets sind auf ersagtem musikalischen Akademiesaal, auch bey Hrn. Claren auf der Bach im Mühlenstein zu haben.

not favourable, the children played in the Fischer's courtyard with the Fischer and other children from the neighbourhood.

In an all too short childhood that had its harsh moments, Beethoven the musician was finally thought ready by his father to make his first public appearance in Cologne on 26 March 1778. Though billed as Johann's 'little son of six years', he was in fact seven years and three months: not, certainly, as young as Mozart was when he first demonstrated his genius (perhaps to Johann's regret), but still astonishingly youthful. What he played, or how he was received, is not on record.

It was in 1778 that the young Beethoven began studying with the ageing Court Organist, Heinrich van den Eeden—in all probability he took lessons in musical theory as well as learning the clavier. Between 1779 and 1781—the exact period is vague—further study was undertaken with Tobias Friedrich Peiffer, a tenor and a skilled keyboard player and oboist; with Franz George Rovantini, a relative (violin and viola); with Willibald Koch, a Franciscan monk (organ?); with Zenser, organist of the Münsterkirche in Bonn; and perhaps also with one Father Hanzmann, an organist in the Minorite cloisters. He was described by a Dr. Müller of the time as being 'a shy, and taciturn boy, the necessary consequence of the life apart which he led, observing more and pondering more than he spoke, and disposed to abandon himself entirely to the feelings awakened by music and (later) by poetry and to the picture created by fancy'. In spite of passages in the Fischer manuscript and in one or two other reliable sources, Thayer emphasised this lone manner and aloofness further when he remarked that not one of Beethoven's childhood friends ever spoke of him as a 'playfellow'.

The Fischers have the last word on Beethoven as a boy growing up—and one in which Johann himself, for a change, is seen depicted in a better light than usual:

When Johann van Beethoven visited the Fischer family on a Sunday evening, he talked about a number of things. Then he also said: 'My son Ludwig, he is now my only comfort in life. He is improving in his music to such an extent that he is admired by everyone. My Ludwig, my Ludwig, I foresee that in time he will be a great man in the world. Those of you who are gathered here and see it come about, remember these words of mine.'

Ludwig van Beethoven, when he was somewhat older, was often dirty and unkempt, so much so that Cäcilia [Fischer] said to him: 'How dirty you look. You really should be tidier.' To which he answered: 'What difference does it make. When I become a gentleman, no one will notice.'

Once Ludwig van Beethoven was sitting at the window of his bedroom overlooking the courtyard. He held his head in both his hands and looked

Christian Gottlob Neefe (1748-98)

very pensive: Cäcilia Fischer, coming across the courtyard, called up to him: 'What are you looking at, Ludwig?' But she received no answer. Later she asked him: 'What does that mean? No answer is also an answer.' He said: 'Oh no, it's not that. Forgive me; I was so taken up with profound and beautiful thoughts that I could not bear to be disturbed.'

In 1781 (towards the end of which year Beethoven and his mother visited Rotterdam), Beethoven graduated to lessons in thorough-bass, composition and keyboard with Neefe, the newly appointed Court Organist. At first he complained about the older man's 'too sharp criticism of his first attempts at composition' (Wegeler), but later thanked him 'for the counsel you have so often given me in the progress of my God-Given art. Should I ever become a great man, you will have contributed to it . . .'. In 1782 we find Beethoven, aged eleven, deputising as organist for Neefe (a complex and involved task for one so young) and the following year, by which time Götz of Mannheim had published the young boy's Variations for fortepiano on a March by Dressler—his first work to appear in print—we come across a printed notice about Beethoven, in Cramer's *Magazin der Musik* for 2 March: 'Ludwig van Beethoven, son of the above-mentioned Tenor, is an eleven-year-old boy [actually twelve] and of very promising talent. He plays on the piano in a very finished manner and powerfully, reads at sight and, to put it briefly, he plays the greater part of the *Well Tempered Clavier* of Sebastian Bach which Herr Neefe gave him. Those who are familiar with this collection of Preludes and Fugues in every tonality (which one could practically term the *non plus ultra*) will know what this means. Herr Neefe, insofar as his other duties permitted, has given him instruction in thorough-bass. Now he is teaching him composition . . . This young genius deserves a subsidy in order to enable him to travel. He will undoubtedly become a second Mozart, if he progresses as well as he has begun.'

Beethoven at the age of thirteen, *c.* 1784. Anonymous half-length portrait, formerly in the possession of Dr. Klamann-Parlo, a Silesian art collector (Historisches Museum, Vienna)

On Neefe's recommendation, Beethoven was that same year created (without salary however) 'cembalist in the orchestra' and accompanist, a responsible post. Then on 14 October 1783, Bossler of Speier announced the publication of Beethoven's most substantial opus yet, the three so-called *Electoral* Sonatas for piano, dedicated, perhaps not entirely dutifully, to 'my gracious Sovereign', Maximilian Friedrich.

The old Elector died on 15 April 1784, and was succeeded by Maximilian Franz, younger brother of the Emperor Joseph, Maria Theresa's favourite son, and a man destined to be the last Elector of Cologne. Swinburne summed him up as 'a good-natured, neither here-nor-there kind of youth': others gave him little credit for intelligence or ability. At twenty-eight he was nevertheless no

Beginning of the E major fugue from Bach's *Well Tempered Clavier*

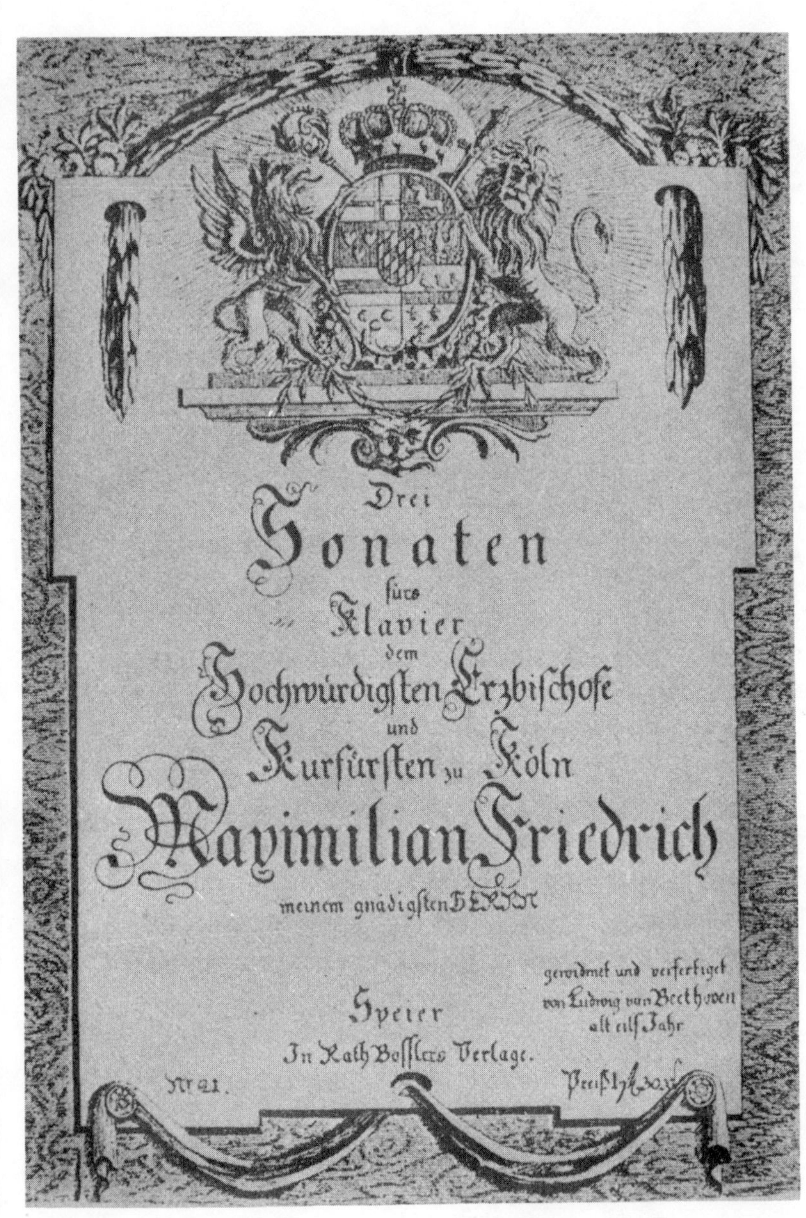
Drei
Sonaten
fürs
Klavier
dem
Hochwürdigsten Erzbischofe
und
Kurfürsten zu Köln
Maximilian Friedrich
meinem gnädigsten Herrn
gewidmet und verfertiget
von Ludwig van Beethoven
alt eilf Jahr
Speier
In Rath Bosslers Verlage.
Nr 21.

Title page for three sonatas dedicated to Maximilian Friedrich

Stephan von Breuning (1774-1827)

The Breuning house. Watercolour by M. Frickel (Stadtarchiv, Bonn)

apron-string child, and, on arriving in Bonn, he ordered a full account to be prepared of court activities. In a subsequent official report dated 25 June of that year, we learn that 'Johann Beethoven has a definitely decaying voice [but that] he has been long in service, is very poor, of respectable conduct, and married'. Lower down we read that 'Ludwig Beethoven . . . receives no stipend but, in the absence of *Kapellmeister* Lucchesi, has taken over the organ. He has good ability, is still young and his conduct is quiet and upright'. Two days later, in a list of annual salaries, we find Beethoven suddenly with a salary of 150 florins as against a *reduced* salary of 200 florins for Neefe: it seems clear a delicate issue had arisen in which Beethoven now found himself as second organist, but in a position of conflict between gratitude to Neefe and the furtherance of his own future. In the months that followed, new musicians entered the service of the Elector, and others were promoted; the most notable of these was possibly Joseph Reicha who in June 1785 became Concert Director.

It was at about this time that Beethoven established a close friendship with the Wegeler and von Breuning families. In his *Aus dem Schwarzspanierhaus* (Vienna 1874), Gerhard von Breuning, born in 1813 and the son of Stephan von Breuning, imagined what it must have been like:

Children attract playmates, school children bring home friends after school. So must have grown the little family circle in the house of my grandmother through the years from the outside; the cultivated influence of this virtuous woman extended not only to her children but also to other young people . . . A poor student of amiable and industrious character soon became daily a member of this household. This was Franz Gerhard Wegeler, the son of an Alsatian burgher, who sensed early a craving for knowledge, for expanding the limitations of his poor origin in order to develop himself in the career for which he was to be known by those around him.

After he had already become attached to this house, he made the acquaintance in 1782 of the son of a musician of the Electoral Court Chapel who, although still more a boy than a young man, already was burning with enthusiasm for the muse of music, just as the other was for science and art, and already he was playing the piano admirably.

Eleonore and Lenz needed a piano teacher and Wegeler's young friend needed to give lessons for the support of himself and his parents. Thus is was that the young Ludwig van Beethoven became introduced into the hospitable home of my grandmother.

The importance of the von Breuning family on Beethoven is emphatically illustrated in the *Notizen* of Wegeler:

Ludwig received his first acquaintance with German literature, especially poetry, as well as his first training in social behaviour in the midst of the von Breuning family in Bonn . . . In this house reigned an unconstrained tone of culture in spite of youthful wilfulness. Christoph von Breuning made early essays in poetry, as was the case (and not without success) with Stephan von Breuning much later. The friends of the family were distinguished by indulgence in social entertainments which combined the useful and the agreeable. When we add that the family possessed considerable wealth, especially before the war [with the French], it will be easy to understand that the first joyous emotions of Beethoven found vent here. Soon he was treated as one of the children in the family, spending in the house not only the greater part of his days, but also many nights. Here he felt that he was free, here he moved about without constraint, everything conspired to make him cheerful and develop his mind.

As Gerhard von Breuning suggests, Beethoven by this time (1785-86) had followed in his father's footsteps by giving music lessons to supplement his income and to support his ailing mother and his increasingly drunk father. Impressionable and idealistic, there is good reason to suppose that he was even then infatuated with some of his pupils: his feelings for Eleonore von Breuning, for instance, may have been quite deep (she later married Wegeler in 1802).

Franz Anton Ries (1755-1846). Portrait in oils by J.G. Schallenberg

It was during these years that Beethoven took further violin lessons — from Franz Anton Ries, Music Director of the Electoral Chapel and a faithful friend. He also composed a set of three piano quartets and continued to play an active rôle in the musical life of both the Chapel and the Court. On occasion he seems, too, to have indulged in good-humoured fun which amused some but offended

Beethoven in court dress. Silhouette attributed to Neesen, 1786

others. One well-known anecdote tells, for example, of how he succeeded one day in distracting a singer who had to deliver a long passage in Latin against a reciting note. Beethoven 'asked the singer, who sat with unusual firmness in the tonal saddle, if he would permit him to throw him out, and utilised the somewhat too readily granted permission to introduce so wide an excursion in the accompaniment while persistently striking the reciting note with his little finger that the singer got so bewildered that he could not find the closing cadence. Father Ries, the first violinist . . . tells with details how *Kapellmeister* Lucchesi, who was present was astonished by Beethoven's playing. In his first excess of rage Heller entered a complaint against Beethoven with the Elector, who commanded a simpler accompaniment, although the spirited and occasionally waggish young prince was amused at the occurrence' (Wegeler, March 1785).

In Cramer's *Magazin der Musik* for 8 April 1787, Neefe tells us something further about the musical life of Bonn under Maximilian Franz:

> Our residence city is becoming more and more attractive for music-lovers through the gracious patronage of our beloved Elector. He has a large collection of the most beautiful music and is expending much every day to augment it. It is to him, too, that we owe the privilege of hearing often good virtuosi on various instruments. Good singers come seldom. The love of music is increasing greatly among the inhabitants. The pianoforte is especially liked; there are here several *Hammerklavier* by Stein of Augsburg, and other correspondingly good instruments.

Beethoven, the 'young genius', had in the meanwhile momentarily left Bonn and had actually arrived in Vienna, the Habsburg capital, the day before this issue of Cramer's journal appeared. It seems that he had left his birthplace around 20 March, reaching Munich on 1 April, when the *Münchener Zeitung* listed one 'Herr Peethofen [sic], Musikus von Bonn bei Köln'. Beethoven stayed in Vienna for less than two weeks. The highlight of the visit was a meeting with Mozart, then working on *Don Giovanni*. Otto Jahn, in his biography of Mozart (1851) says that Beethoven, then sixteen,

> was taken to Mozart and at that musician's request played something for him which he, taking it for granted that it was a show-piece, prepared for the occasion, praised in a rather cool manner. Beethoven, observing this, begged Mozart to give him a theme for improvisation. He always played admirably when excited and now he was inspired, too, by the presence of the master whom he reverenced greatly; he played in such a style that Mozart, whose attention and interest grew more and more, finally went

silently to some friends who were sitting in an adjoining room, and said vivaciously, 'Keep your eyes on him; some day he will give the world something to talk about.'

He had a few superficial lessons and, if Czerny, one of his later pupils, is right, must have also heard Mozart play the clavier: 'he had a fine but choppy way of playing, no *legato*.'

The tragedy of the year was the death of Beethoven's mother on 17 July. In a letter to Dr. Joseph Wilhelm von Schaden in Augsburg, dated 15 September 1787, and the earliest surviving correspondence of Beethoven, the trauma of that moment is sadly communicated:

Wolfgang Amadeus Mozart (1756-91). Silverpoint drawing by D. Stock, 1789 (City Music Library, Leipzig)

> I found my mother still alive, but in the most wretched condition. She was suffering from consumption and in the end she died about seven weeks ago after enduring great pain and agony. She was such a good, kind mother to me and indeed my best friend. Oh! who was happier than I, when I could still utter the sweet name of mother and it was heard and answered; and to whom can I say it now? To the dumb likenesses of her which my imagination fashions for me? Since my return to Bonn I have as yet enjoyed very few happy hours. For the whole time I have been plagued with asthma; and I am inclined to fear that this malady may even turn to consumption. Furthermore I have been suffering from melancholia which in my case is almost as great a torture as my illness.

Years later, Beethoven could still say that he had not forgotten the way his mother died.

Even more pitiful though was the state of Beethoven's father. Deeply in debt, broken in spirit, mentally and physically worn, and sodden with drink, he sent this request to the Elector just a week or so before his wife's death: 'Court Musician makes obedient representation that he has got into a very unfortunate state because of the long-continued sickness of his wife and has already been compelled to sell a portion of his effects and pawn others and that he no longer knows what to do for his sick wife and many children. He prays for the benefaction of an advance of 100 thlr on his salary.' No reply was forthcoming and the only person to help financially was Franz Anton Ries. The social standing of the family had sunk to its lowest point, far below that enjoyed by old Ludwig van Beethoven, the *Kapellmeister*, and from which the future was scarcely discernible.

At the beginning of 1788 Count Waldstein arrived at the Electoral Court. Though nearly nine years older than Beethoven, a strong spiritual bond sprang up between the two men and was encouraged to flourish within the all-important von Breuning household. Wegeler (*Notizen*) chronicled its significance:

The first, and in every respect the most important, of the Maecenases of Beethoven was Count Waldstein, Knight of the Teutonic Order, and (what is of greater moment here) the favourite and constant companion of the young Elector, afterwards Commander of the Order at Virnsberg and Chancellor to the Emperor of Austria. He was not only a connoisseur but also a practitioner of music. He it was who gave all manner of support to our Beethoven, whose gifts he was the first to recognize worthily. Through him the young genius developed the talent to improvise variations on a given theme. From him he received much pecuniary assistance bestowed in such a way as to spare his sensibilities, it being generally looked upon as a small gratuity from the Elector. . . .

Beethoven, now seventeen, continued to widen his intellectual horizons. Neefe's interest in German literature and the association with the von Breunings and with Waldstein encouraged him in particular to not only discover other literary influences (including such classical models as Homer and Plutarch), but also to explore science, philosophy and politics in general. He may have left school at ten, and lacked higher education, but this did not prevent him from attending philosophy lectures at the newly founded University in Bonn; he is actually listed as a candidate in 1789, together with his friend the flautist Anton Reicha. Additionally he used often to take his meals at the Zehrgarten, a haunt of the professors, artists and literary men of Bonn.

Such intellectual pursuit was nurtured within a cultural climate in Bonn that had in no way lessened with Maximilian Franz's accession. The performances of plays by Lessing and Schiller and (in translation) by Garrick, Voltaire, Beaumarchais, Molière, Sheridan and Shakespeare—highlights in the era of the old Elector—were followed in the 1785 Carnival season, for instance, by a string of operas which included Gluck's *Alceste* and *Orpheus*, Salieri's *Armida* and various Paisiello and French offerings. In 1788 a National Theatre in Bonn was planned. Fine actors were engaged and among the theatre musicians (thirty-one strong) the names of Neefe (pianist and opera stage manager), Joseph Reicha

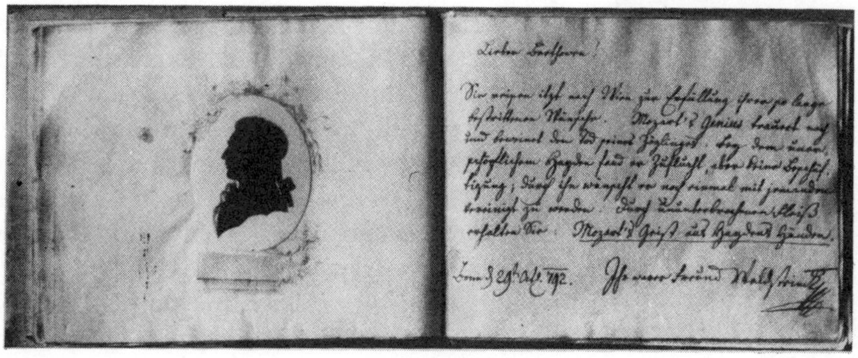

Count Ferdinand Waldstein (1762-1823): a silhouette and the famous words he wrote in Beethoven's farewell autograph album from Bonn, 1792. Later in life he fell on hard times and died in poverty (Fischer & Kock)

(director), Franz Ries and Andreas Romberg (violins), Bernhard Romberg (cello), Simrock (horn), and Anton Reicha (flute) stand out. Beethoven played the viola (the Elector's instrument), as well as still retaining his organist's appointment. The accent was on youth and the first season was from 3 January to 23 May 1789. Operas by Benda, Grêtry and Salieri catch the attention as well as a performance of Mozart's *Seraglio*. The second season ran from 13 October 1789 to 23 February 1790 (the news of Joseph II's death closed the theatre the following day). The repertoire included Mozart's *Don Giovanni* and *Le Nozze di Figaro*. Further seasons followed during which Beethoven must have gained incalculable experience as an orchestral player working in close harmony with a select band of good musicians.

By 1789, Beethoven's in many ways exceptional association with the nobility and with families of good social standing, and his desire to better himself was beginning to be noticed in several quarters, and towards the end of that year (in a decree dated 20 November), he found himself made effectively the head of the family, entitled to draw half of his father's salary in addition to his own. Johann by now was infirm and alcoholic and had to be repeatedly rescued by Beethoven from the hands of the police: the Court, not surprisingly, found it necessary to dismiss him from service.

The highlight of 1790 came in December with a visit from Haydn who, with Salomon, was on his way to London. Dies in his *Biographische Nachrichten von Joseph Haydn* (Vienna 1810) described the event:

Franz Joseph Haydn (1732-1809). Portrait in oils by Thomas Hardy, 1791 (Royal College of Music, London)

In the capital, Bonn, he was suprised in more ways than one. He reached the city on Saturday 25 December and set apart the next day for rest. On Sunday, Salomon accompanied Haydn to the court chapel to listen to mass. Scarcely had the two entered the church and found suitable seats when high mass began. The first chords announced a product of Haydn's muse. Our Haydn looked upon it as an accidental occurrence which had happened only to flatter him; nevertheless it was decidedly agreeable to him to listen to his own composition. Towards the close of the mass a person approached and asked him to repair to the oratory, where he was expected. Haydn obeyed and was not a little surprised when he found that the Elector, Maximilian, had had him summoned, took him at once by the hand and presented him to the virtuosi with the words: 'Here I make you acquainted with the Haydn whom you all revere so highly.' The Elector gave both parties time to become acquainted with each other, and, to give Haydn a convincing proof of his respect, invited him to dinner. This unexpected invitation put Haydn into an embarrassing position, for he and Salomon had ordered a modest little dinner in their lodgings, and it was too late to make a change. Haydn was therefore fain to take refuge in excuses which the Elector accepted as genuine and sufficient. Haydn took his leave and returned to his lodgings, where he was made aware in a special manner of the good will of the Elector, at whose secret command the little dinner had been metamorphosed into a banquet for twelve persons to which the most capable musicians had been invited.

Whether Beethoven was among these 'most capable musicians' remains in doubt: he had yet to attain the status of colleagues like Neefe or Reicha. What is certain, however, is the kind of scene that Haydn must have witnessed in the court chapel. The Fischer manuscript gives one vivid account of a typical Bonn Christmas mass:

At Christmas time when the Elector, as Bishop, celebrated Mass in the Court chapel, from 11 to 12 midnight, the musicians and the Court Choir ladies in the Court *Tucksaal* had to give proof of their best strength and ability. All the Court nobility and servants attended in gala dress. The Electoral bodyguard lined each side in parade uniform, the entire regiment from the Koblenzer gate to the Palace chapel in full dress. After the first Gospel, half-way through the Mass and also after the last Gospel, they would fire three volleys followed by the cannon on the city ramparts. At this season it was often very cold. After the celebration, when Johann Beethoven and his family, with other friends had arrived home, following an old custom, they broiled fresh sausages and drank hot wine, punch and coffee. In this way, Christmas Eve would be celebrated and come to an end . . . Court musicians would be in gala dress: sea-green tail coat, short green knee-breeches with buckles, white or black silk hose, shoes with black bows, a white flowered silk waistcoat with flap pockets, the waistcoat bordered with pure gold cord, hair dressed in curls and pigtail, a cocked hat under . . . left arm and a sword, carried also on the left, with a silver sword belt.

Apart from playing in the orchestra and fulfilling his other Court obligations, Beethoven managed increasingly to find time for composition. In 1790, for instance, he wrote two cantatas, one on the death of Joseph II, the other on the accession of Leopold II. He also finished a set of twenty-four variations on a theme by Righini (*Kapellmeister* at the electoral court in Mainz), dedicating them to the Countess von Hatzfeld. Then on Carnival Sunday, 6 March 1791, came a performance of a *Ritterballet*, designed to illuminate a masked pantomime depicting 'the predilection of the ancient Germans for war, the chase, love and drinking' but given without the composer's name. Other work included songs and piano and chamber music. Sketchbooks (even then Beethoven had them) offer unfulfilled plans for a violin concerto and an oboe concerto. That he early on had ambitions for larger-scale compositions is suggested time and again in these sketches: a Symphony in C minor, for example, was contemplated sometime around 1788-89.

As for publications, the *Righini* Variations were announced by Götz in the *Wiener Zeitung* in August 1791. The Abbé Sterkel, one of the greatest keyboard players of the age, saw the music and on meeting Beethoven a month or so later expressed the doubt that the young composer could actually play them. Wegeler says that in response to this challenge Beethoven, in a typical gesture of pride and defiance, 'played not only these variations so far as he could remember them (Sterkel could not find them), but went on with a number of others no less difficult, all to the great surprise of the listeners, perfectly, and in the ingratiating manner that had struck him in Sterkel's playing'.

Shortly after, Beethoven travelled along his favourite Rhine as a member of the Court orchestra on the way to Mergentheim where, as capital of the Teutonic Order of which Maximilian Franz was Grand Master, there was a protracted meeting of knights and commanders. Carl Ludwig Junker published an account of the visit in Bossler's *Musikal. Correspondenz* for 23 November 1791. It is a verbose narrative but the life and colour of the observation and gossip is worth recalling:

> . . . Here I was also an eye-witness to the esteem and respect in which this chapel stands with the Elector. Just as the rehearsal was to begin Ries was sent for by the Prince, and upon his return brought a bag of gold. 'Gentlemen', said he, 'this being the Elector's name-day he sends you a present of a thousand thalers'. And again, I was eye-witness of this orchestra's surpassing excellence. Herr Winneberger, *Kapellmeister* at Wallenstein, laid before it a symphony of his own composition, which was by no means easy of execution, especially for the wind-instruments, which had several solos *concertante*. It went finely, however, at the first trial, to the great surprise of the composer. An hour after the dinner-music the concert began. It was opened with a symphony of Mozart; then followed a recitative and air sung by Simonetti; next, a violoncello concerto played by

The Market Place in Bonn, with the Town Hall in the background. Beethoven's favourite eating-place and intellectual haunt, the Zehrgarten, is on the right. Engraving by C. Dupuis after F.J. Roussaux

Herr [Bernhard] Romberger [*sic*]; fourth, a symphony by Pleyel; fifth an air by Righini, sung by Simonetti; sixth a double concerto for violin and violoncello played by the two Rombergs; and the closing piece was the symphony of Winneberger, which had very many brilliant passages. The opinion already expressed as to the performance of this orchestra was confirmed. It was not possible to attain a higher degree of exactness. Such perfection in the *pianos, fortes, rinforzandos*—such a swelling and gradual increase of tone and then such an almost imperceptible dying away, from the most powerful to the lighest accents—all this was formerly to be heard only in Mannheim. It would be difficult to find another orchestra in which the violins and basses are throughout in such excellent hands . . . The members of the chapel, almost without exception, are in their best years, glowing with health, men of culture and fine personal appearance. They form truly a fine sight, when one adds the splendid uniform in which the Elector has clothed them—red, and richly trimmed with gold.

I heard also one of the greatest of pianists—the dear, good Bethofen . . . True, he did not perform in public . . . but, what was infinitely preferable to me, I heard him extemporise in private; yes, I was even invited to propose a theme for him to vary. The greatness of this amiable, light-hearted man, as a virtuoso, may in my opinion be safely estimated from his almost inexhaustible wealth of ideas, the altogether characteristic style of expression in his playing, and the great execution which he displays. I know, therefore, no one thing which he lacks, that conduces to the greatness of an artist. I have heard Vogler upon the pianoforte . . . have often heard him, heard him by the hour together, and never failed to wonder at his astonishing execution; but Bethofen, in addition to the execution, has greater clearness and weight of idea, and more expression—in short he is more for the heart—equally great, therefore, as an *adagio* or *allegro* player. Even the members of this remarkable orchestra are, without exception, his admirers, and all ears when he plays. Yet he is exceedingly modest and free from all pretension.

The following summer Leopold II died and Franz II was crowned Holy Roman Emperor in Frankfurt-am-Main. Then in July, Haydn, returning from London on his way to join his patron, Anton Esterházy, in Frankfurt, passed once again through Bonn. It seems that on this occasion he may have met Beethoven and may even have seen some of his music (the *Cantata on the Death of Leopold II* is usually singled out). The exact details of the event, however, are blurred and chronologically confused in early reports: suffice to say that as a result of the support and encouragement of men like Waldstein, Beethoven was shortly afterwards granted leave of absence to be sent to Vienna 'at the expense' of the Elector in order to actually study with Haydn and to 'perfect himself . . . more fully in the art of composition' (Neefe).

October marked the start of the fifth theatre season, the last in which Beethoven would play in the electoral orchestra. The old order, however, was not quite the same, the atmosphere was tenser and less abandoned or joyous. In the end, following a period in which the acceleration of war with France had seen the downfall of Mainz and the left bank of the Rhine, in which the streets of Bonn became overrun with refugees and funerals, and in which the wealthy had been prompted to pack their valuables in time for a hurried exit, Beethoven left for Haydn and Vienna. The date was 2 November 1792. He was not to see Bonn again.

He arrived in the capital towards the middle of the month, having journeyed by the post road through Coblenz, Frankfurt, Nuremburg and Linz. He travelled economically, keeping a careful account of his expenses, at one point driving 'like the Devil' through the Hessian army, at another narrowly missing an encounter with an advancing corps of the French. He took with him an autograph album full of messages from his friends in Bonn, but with nothing from his fellow musicians or his debilitated father (who was to die weeks later on 18 December). In it Waldstein wrote:

Dear Beethoven!

You are now going to Vienna in fulfilment of a wish that has for so long been thwarted. The *genius* of Mozart still mourns and weeps the death of its pupil. It has found a refuge in the inexhaustible Haydn, but no occupation; through him it desires once more to find a union with someone. Through your unceasing diligence, receive *Mozart's spirit from the Hands of Haydn*. Bonn, the 29th Oct. 1792

Your true friend Waldstein

Eleonore von Breuning quoted some lines from Herder:

Friendship, with that which is good,
Grows like the evening shadow
Till the setting sun of life.

Beethoven kept the album for the rest of his life. It was Bonn's farewell to him. Vienna was now to become the stage on which his hopes and disappointments, his successes and failures, his loves and hates, his life and death were to be played out.

Chapter 5

Vienna: 1793-99

'Beethoven will in time fill the position of one of Europe's greatest composers' — Haydn

At the end of the eighteenth century Vienna lay sprawled along the Danube, a series of districts, villages and suburbs clustered around a central walled and gated citadel, a defence originally built on higher ground to withstand the Ottomans. Little more than a mile at its widest point, this citadel housed the complex that made up the Imperial Palace (the Hofburg), as well as the Lobkowitz Palace, the influential Burgtheater, the Kinsky Palace, the old Town Hall, the Kärntnertortheater, the Kohlmarkt — a busy street in which the music publishers Artaria had their premises — the Herrengasse (the street of gentlemen) and the Neuermarkt, a *piazza* sometimes used for winter sleighrides. The whole was dominated by the towering Gothic spire of St Stephen's Cathedral, an imposing landmark that could be seen for miles. The top of this citadel wall provided the citizens of Vienna with a panoramic walk, while outside at the base lay the Glacis, an open space that had once been a moat. To the north west, on the other side of the river lay the Augarten, to the east the Prater. To the south of the citadel there were some spectacular palaces, built in vast open tracts of land, sur-

Vienna seen from the Josephstadt. Coloured engraving by C. Schütz, 1785

Vienna, the Paradeplatz — a popular walking spot. Coloured engraving by L. Beyer, 1805

rounded by trees and sculpted gardens, and permeated everywhere by the scent and sounds of the Wienerwald, the Vienna woods. Not least among these was the Belvedere, a glorious baroque building designed for Prince Eugen of Savoy, an Italian brought up in Versailles. Then a few miles to the west on the way to Linz there was the Schönbrunn, the summer residence of the Imperial family, completed by Maria Theresa.

The magic and character of the city was well captured by Mary Montagu when she visited it in the early years of the eighteenth century. In a letter to her sister, the Countess of Mar (8 September 1716), she wrote:

This town, which has the honour of being the emperor's residence, did not at all answer my ideas of it, being much less than I expected to find it; the streets are very close, and so narrow, one cannot observe the fine fronts of the palaces, though many of them very well deserve observation, being truly magnificent, all built of fine white stone, and excessive high, the town being so much too little for the number of the people that desire to live in it, the builders seem to have projected to repair that misfortune, by clapping one town on the top of another, most of the houses being of five, and some of them of six storeys. You may easily imagine, that the streets being so narrow, the upper rooms are extremely dark; and, what is an inconvenience much more intolerable, in my opinion, there is no house that has so few as five or six families in it. The apartments of the greatest ladies, and even of the ministers of state, are divided but by a partition from that of a tailor or a shoemaker; and I know nobody that has above two floors in any house, one for their own use, and one higher for their servants. Those that have houses of their own, let out the rest of them to whoever will take them; thus the great stairs (which are all of stone) are as common and as dirty as the street. 'Tis true, when you have once travelled through them, nothing can be more surprisingly magnificent than the apartments. They are commonly a suite of eight or ten large rooms, all inlaid, the doors and windows richly carved and gilt, and the furniture such as is seldom seen in the palaces of sovereign princes in other countries — the hangings the finest tapestry of Brussels, prodigious large looking-glasses in silver frames, fine japan tables, beds, chairs, canopies, and window curtains of the richest Genoa damask or velvet, almost covered with gold lace or embroidery. The whole made gay by pictures, and vast jars of japan china, and almost in every room large lustres of rock crystal.

I have already had the honour of being invited to dinner by several of the first people of quality; and I must do them the justice to say, the good taste and magnificence of their tables very well answers to that of their furniture. I have been more than once entertained with fifty dishes of meat, all served in silver, and well dressed; the dessert proportionable, served in the finest china. But the variety and richness of their wines is what appears the most surprising. The constant way is, to lay a list of their names upon the plates of the guests, along with the napkins; and I have counted several times to the number of eighteen different sorts, all exquisite in their kinds.

Palatial Vienna was indeed on a scale conceived by few. In the Hofburg alone, during the Congress of 1814, for instance, forty banqueting tables were laid each night, the guest suites were scenes of lavish elegance and decoration, the royal stables boasted fourteen hundred horses and several hundred carriages. For the rest, masked balls, the opera, firework displays, and hunting parties were some of the daily pleasures provided by the music-loving Franz II. No one, it seems, could have enough of anything, and nothing was an obstacle when it came to the pursuit of pleasure and entertainment. It was at one and the same time a life of richness and decadence, of idle pleasure and frivolity which had relatively little time, it seems, for anything else. Even the common populace who, like their Bonn counterparts, lived in a state of diseased squalor, tried to emulate the life-style of their overlords.

Given such conditions, the upheavals of the age all but swept past the Viennese until it finally consumed them almost unawares. The Parisian consequences of 1789, the rise of the Corsican Bonaparte, the break-up of old orders — all somehow remained the concern of another world, another time. Not until the invasion of the Empire itself and the French occupation of Vienna did the Viennese wake up to the reality of the situation and to the fact that their leisurely, self-indulgent, uncomplicated way of life was already part of a history that was rapidly receding into the past. By then, however, it was too late: 1806 came and the Holy Roman Empire was no more.

In his bicentenary study of Beethoven, George Marek summed up the Vienna of the 1790s and early 1800s as 'a city of palaces and parks; of ill-lit sour-smelling little rooms and sunlit suburban houses; of representational buildings designed by a great baroque architect and quite a few buildings designed by hobbling imitators; of churches which better induced pageantry than worship; of quiet, restful places near the river, and muddy side streets where prostitutes prowled; of a university which became one of Europe's leading institutions of learning and which, even then, in spite of censorship and chicanery, managed to expose its students to Leibnitz, Kant, Home and Voltaire'. It was to such a city, ruled by an emperor who loved his gardens more than his armies, dominated by a sense of history reaching back to Marcus Aurelius, a sometime bulwark against the barbarians, and a melting pot of German, Slav, Latin and Magyar thought, that the young, impressionable Beethoven came.

Some biographers have painted a romantic picture of his arrival. Yet in spite of Neefe having seen him as 'the foremost pianoforte player' of the day, and regardless of the fact that his friends in Bonn held him to be a composer of aspiration, the truth was that at that moment in time, Beethoven was a relative unknown, who had exchanged the closed, introverted, provincial community of Bonn for a city that was not only worldly, competitive and the undisputed centre of both European musical life to the east of Lorraine and the Austro-German tradition, but also the capital of an empire that stretched across half Europe. With its population of around 200,000 it was twenty times the size of the Bonn Beethoven knew, and offered as many new obstacles to overcome. As a 'small, thin, dark-complexioned, pock-marked, dark-eyed, bewigged young musician of 22 years [who] had quietly journeyed to the capital to pursue the study of his art with a small, thin, dark-complexioned, pockmarked, black-eyed and bewigged veteran composer' (Thayer), Beethoven was just like any other unheralded apprentice in search of a future. Given the environment, the choice open to him was clear: he could either be a success or a failure, a master or a nonentity. As far as Vienna was concerned, no one but himself really cared one way or the other.

Beethoven's first lodgings in the city were in an attic room. His memorandum book shows him keeping a careful account of his expenditure. It also shows, however, that he intended to cultivate a style and manner suited to the society he was about to enter. He may have looked like 'a Moor', with protruding teeth and lips, a broad, flattened nose and rounded, full forehead, but that did not prevent a desire to take lessons with a dancing master, nor did it stop him buying new clothes: 'Black silk stocking, 1 ducat; 1 pair of winter silk stocking, 1 florin 40 kreutzers; boots, 6 florins; shoes, 1 florin 30 kreutzers'. Later we find that his rent was 14 florins, that

Painting of Beethoven

Engraving of Beethoven

a meal with wine could cost 16½ florins. Within weeks he had moved to a ground floor room in Prince Karl Lichnowsky's house on the Alserstrasse. Such a move, however, indicated neither affluence nor influence. As Mary Montagu had noticed, many Viennese palaces rented their garrets and ground floors cheaply: only second floors had the official distinction of being royal residences. To all intents and purposes therefore Beethoven continued to live as an impecunious music student, saving some money, living off his talent, and trying to make the most of the letters of introduction he had brought with him from Bonn. He needed to: with his father so recently dead, he was now the head of the family, and his Bonn allowance was meagre. That he lived in proximity to a Prince who happened to be musical was in those early days of no consequence. He was still unproven.

Lessons with Haydn began early on. There is a reference to him in Beethoven's memorandum book under 12 December 1792, and in October 1793 we see master and pupil sharing cups of chocolate and coffee. Although Beethoven outwardly kept on good terms with the venerated old man, then in his early sixties, he was inwardly dissatisfied with what he had learnt — or rather not learnt. In his *Notizen* of 1838, Ferdinand Ries confirms this: 'Haydn had wished that Beethoven might put the word "pupil of Haydn" on the title of his first works. Beethoven was unwilling to do so because, as he said, though he had had some instruction from Haydn he had never learnt anything from him'. As a result Beethoven, possibly within weeks of starting lessons with Haydn, turned to one Johann Schenk for guidance in counterpoint and theory, in which area, in spite of his training with Neefe, he was surprisingly deficient. Many years later, Schenk actually spoke of unfamiliarity 'with the preliminary rules of counterpoint', a remarkable statement if it is to be believed. The lessons were kept secret from Haydn.

Haydn went to London in January 1794. Shortly before leaving Vienna, on 23 November 1793, he wrote to the Elector of Cologne reporting on Beethoven's progress:

I am taking the liberty of sending to your Reverence in all humility a few pieces of music, a quintet, an eight-voice *Parthie*, an oboe concerto, a set of variations for the piano and a fugue composed by my dear pupil Beethoven who was so graciously entrusted to me. They will, I flatter myself, be graciously accepted by your Reverence as evidence of his diligence beyond the scope of his own studies. On the basis of these pieces, expert and amateur alike cannot but admit that Beethoven will in time become one of the greatest musical artists in Europe, and I shall be proud to call myself his teacher. I only wish that he might remain with me for some time yet.

While I am on the subject of Beethoven, may your Reverence permit me to say a few words concerning his financial affairs. For the past year he was allotted 100 ducats. That this sum was insufficient even for mere living expenses your Reverence will, I am sure, be well aware. Your Reverence, however, may have had good reason for sending him out into the great world with so small a sum. On this assumption, and in order to prevent him from falling into the hands of usurers, I have on the one hand vouched for him and on the other advanced him cash, so that he owes me 500 fl., of which not a kreutzer has been spent unnecessarily. I now request that this sum be paid him. And since to work on borrowed money increases the interest, and what is more is very burdensome for an artist like Beethoven, I thought that if your Reverence would allot him 1000 fl. for the coming year, your Reverence would be showing him the highest favour and at the same time would free him of all anxiety. For the teachers which are absolutely indispensable to him and the expenses which are unavoidable if he is to be admitted to some of the houses here, take so much that the barest minimum that he needs comes close to 1000 fl. As to the extravagance that is to be feared in a young man going out into the great world. I think I can reassure your Reverence. For in hundreds of situations I have always found that he is prepared, of his own accord, to sacrifice everything for his art. This is particularly admirable in view of the many tempting opportunities and should give your Reverence the assurance that your gracious kindness to Beethoven will not fall into the hands of usurers.

Joseph Haydn

The Nationalbibliothek in the Josephplatz, Vienna. Baron Gottfried van Swieten (1733-1803) had rooms in this building. Coloured engraving by C. Schütz. 1780

The Elector's reply, exactly a month later, put Beethoven into an embarrassing position:

The music of young Beethoven which you sent me I received with your letter. Since, however, this music, with the exception of the fugue, was composed and performed here in Bonn before he departed on his second journey to Vienna, I cannot regard it as progress made in Vienna.

As far as the allotment which he has had for his subsistence in Vienna is concerned, it does indeed amount to only 500 fl. But in addition to this 500 fl. his salary here of 400 fl, has been continuously paid to him, he received 900 fl. for the year. I cannot, therefore, very well see why he is as much in arrears in his finances as you say.

I am wondering therefore whether he had not better come back here in order to resume his work. For I very much doubt that he has made any important progress in composition and in the development of his musical taste during his present stay, and I fear that, as in the case of his first journey to Vienna, he will bring back nothing but debts.

Haydn can hardly have been pleased: he left for London without, as had been expected, taking Beethoven with him. Three months later, in March 1794, Beethoven's allowance from Bonn ceased, though he still officially remained on the Elector's staff.

How concerned he was, however, remains questionable. Other things of more immediate relevance were on his mind. The memorandum book shows that by now he was taking lessons from Ignaz Schuppanzigh, about five years his junior, but even then a noted musician and first violinist in Karl Lichnowsky's string quartet. He was also taking lessons in counterpoint with Albrechtsberger, 'the most famous teacher of that science', as well as studying vocal writing, prosody, and the setting of Italian and dramatic composition with none other than the Imperial *Kapellmeister*, Salieri, a man willing 'to give gratuitous instruction to musicians of small means'. The lessons with Salieri continued sporadically up to at least 1802.

There was plenty else, too, to make up for the censure of Bonn. Within a very short time of arriving in Vienna, Beethoven's reputation as a pianist, for instance, was beginning to spread — as one fashionable player of the time, the Abbé Joseph Gelinek, had cause to know: 'I am asked to measure myself with a young pianist who is just arrived; I'll work him over'. A few days later, rather less confidently: 'Ah, he is no man; he's a devil. He will play me and all of us to death. And how he improvises!' Beethoven's tricks were soon being copied by everyone. A letter to Eleanore von Breuning in Bonn, enclosing a set of variations for violin and piano on a popular theme from Mozart's *Le Nozze di Figaro,* reports in a postscript (June 1794):

Prince Karl Lichnowsky (1756-1814) pupil and patron of Mozart, friend and patron of Beethoven. It was at one of the Prince's Friday morning concerts that Beethoven first played the Op. 2 Sonatas dedicated to Haydn and published in March 1796. Anonymous portrait in oils

> The v[ariations] will be rather difficult to play, and particularly the trills in the coda. But this must not intimidate and discourage you. For the composition is so arranged that you need only play the trill and can leave out the other notes, since these appear in the violin part as well. I should never have written down this kind of piece, had I not already noticed fairly often how some people in Vienna after hearing me extemporize of an evening would note down on the following day several peculiarities of my style and palm them off with pride as their own.

The *Figaro* Variations had by then been published by Artaria who announced them in the *Wiener Zeitung* for 31 July 1793 — a mere eight months or so after Beethoven had come to Vienna. By now he had managed to cultivate not only a number of influential musicians but also, more importantly, members of the nobility. As in Bonn such association with the highest in the land was less exceptional than it might have been elsewhere. There were many artistic circles in which a common love of music blotted out all kinds of class distinctions. J. F. Reichardt was one reliable contemporary source who illuminated the kind of life that existed in Vienna at the turn of the century, with its cultural groups and its *Assembleen* or evening meetings which began at ten o'clock and which were devoted to poetry readings, music making and drama. One inevitable and important consequence of this was the gradual emergence of the musician as an independent artist rather than a bonded servant, as a dominant rather than a lesser intellectual force. With this change of emphasis came a new kind of patronage as well, one in which material commitment or service on the part of the musician was no longer necessarily expected. To support and nurture the strangely inexplicable aspirations of the creative or the re-creative mind was often to become compensation enough for those wealthy enough to indulge.

Once accepted within this receptive, often adulatory environment, Beethoven flourished. An early admirer was the Baron Gottfried van Swieten, Director of the Imperial Library. He was a champion of Handel and Bach, and it was he who, more than anyone else, instilled in Beethoven a lasting regard for these masters' oratorios and choral works, which he had in manuscript and several of which he used to have privately performed in his rooms. Beethoven, in his turn, used to play Bach fugues 'as an evening blessing' for the old Baron.

Another new friend was his landlord, Prince Karl Lichnowsky. Wegeler tells us in his *Notizen* how when he (Wegeler) arrived in Vienna in October 1794, a fugitive from the French occupation of Bonn (the Cologne Electorate had by then fallen, to be annexed by the French in 1797), he was surprised to find his old childhood friend no longer 'on the ground floor' where 'it was not necessary to pay the housekeeper more than seven florins', but instead living as a guest of the Prince, with rooms in his quarters. Wegeler says that 'the Prince was a great lover and connoisseur of music. He played the pianoforte, and by studying Beethoven's pieces and playing them more or less well, sought to convince him that there was no need of changing anything in his style of composition'. Another contemporary, Frau von Bernhard, recalled the atmosphere, the contrast, between Lichnowsky and Beethoven, in especially vivid terms:

When he [Beethoven] came to us, he used to stick his head in the door and make sure that there was no one there whom he disliked. He was small and plain-looking, with an ugly, red, pock-marked face. His hair was quite dark and hung almost shaggily around his face. His clothes were very commonplace, not differing greatly from the fashion of those days, particularly in our circles. Moreover, he spoke in a strong dialect, and in a rather common manner. In general his whole being did not give the impression of any particular cultivation; in fact, he was unmannerly in both gesture and demeanour. He was very haughty; I myself have seen the mother of Princess Lichnowsky, Countess Thun, going down on her knees to him as

Title page of the original edition of the Op 1 Piano Trios

he lolled on the sofa, and begging him to play something. But Beethoven did not. Countess Thun was, however, a very eccentric woman.

I was frequently invited to the Lichnowsky's in order to play there. He was a friendly and distinguished gentleman, and she [his wife] a very beautiful woman. Yet they did not seem happy together; she always had such a melancholy expression on her face, and I hear that he spent a great deal of money, far beyond his means. Her sister who was even more beautiful, had a husband [Count Rasumowsky] who was a patron of Beethoven. She was almost always present when music was performed. I still remember clearly both Haydn and Salieri sitting on a sofa on one side of the small music-room, both carefully dressed in the old-fashioned way, with perruque, shoes and silk hose, whereas even here Beethoven would come dressed in the informal fashion of the other side of the Rhine, almost ill-dressed.

It was at a *soirée* at Karl Lichnowsky's that Beethoven's Op 1 Piano Trios were first tried out sometime toward the end of 1793 or the beginning of 1794. Ferdinand Ries chronicled the scene as recalled for him by Beethoven himself:

Most of the artists and music-lovers were invited, especially Haydn, for whose opinion all were eager. The Trios were played, and at once commanded extraordinary attention. Haydn also said many pretty things about them, but advised Beethoven not to publish the third, in C minor. This astonished Beethoven, inasmuch as he considered the third the best of the Trios, as it is still the one which gives the greatest pleasure and makes the greatest effect. Consequently, Haydn's remark left a bad impression on Beethoven and led him to think that Haydn was envious, jealous and ill-disposed toward him.

The Op 1 Trios represented a substantial achievement. They were subsequently published by Artaria in the summer of 1795, with a subscription list of 123 names that included not only the Lichnowsky family (the Trios were dedicated to Karl) but also the Erdödys, Prince Nicholas Esterházy, Prince Lobkowitz, the Russian Ambassador Count Rasumowsky, the Schwarzenburgs and Baron van Swieten — as Robbins Landon has said the list already contained 'the cream of the Austro-Hungarian nobility', all of them to play a part in Beethoven's life. 241 copies were sold and Beethoven made a handsome profit for himself. As one of Beethoven's first patrons, Lichnowsky was a considerable force, helping him out financially after his Bonn salary ceased, and generally giving him the envouragement and security he needed — yet, as far as we can tell, with no special obligation on Beethoven's part.

By the time these Trios were published, Beethoven's red-headed brother Caspar Anton Carl had arrived in Vienna from Bonn (in June 1794) and had set himself up as a music teacher (he later held a post in the office of taxes). Other old ties were renewed too as more and more of Beethoven's Bonn friends fled the French occupation. By far the most important event of the period, however, was Beethoven's public début in Vienna as a pianist and composer. In those days concerts were on a casual, less formal scale. Public or semi-private functions used to be given in ballrooms, in the spacious, colonnaded, music rooms of the great palaces and houses of the city, or in one or other of the several theatres that existed. The Augarten, 'the Tuileries of Vienna', was another well-known place, a public garden, rather like those in eighteenth century London, between the Danube and the Danube canal. Opened by Joseph II on 30 April 1775, a concert room was built and summer morning concerts began in 1782. They lasted well into the 1820s. The fame of the place was known throughout the Empire. Mozart appeared here in triumph with his concertos and symphonies, and all the great musicians of Beethoven's time came as well, regardless of the fact that concerts often began as early as seven o'clock in the morning. Benefit concerts or *Akadamien* on behalf of charities or the artists themselves were the norm for the period, as were the numerous masked balls that used to be held in the winter. Then, of

The Augarten concert rooms. Coloured engraving by L. Poratzky

Heute Sonntag den 29. März 1795.
wird
die hiesige Tonkünstlergesellschaft
im k. k. Nazional-Hof-Theater
zum Vortheil ihrer Wittwen und Waisen
Eine große musikalische Akademie
in zwey Abtheilungen zu geben, die Ehre haben

Erste Abtheilung.
1) Eine große neue Symphonie vom Hrn. Kapellmeister Cardellieri.
2) Ein neues Konzert auf dem Piano-Forte, gespielt von dem Meister Herrn Ludwig von Beethoven, und von seiner Erfindung.

Zweyte Abtheilung.
Der erste Theil des in wälscher Sprache abgefaßten Oratoriums
betittelt:
Gioas, König in Judäen,
von der Erfindung des obbenannten Hrn. Cardellieri.
Dabey werden die Hauptstimmen absingen:

Gioas,	Hr. Viganoni.	()	Giojada,	Hr. Saal.
Sebia,	Mlle. Sessi.	()	Mathan,	Hr. Vogel.
Athalia,	Delle. Mareschalchi.	()	Ismael,	Hr. Spangler.

NB. Da die Recitative zu lange sind, so traf man in einigen Stellen eine Abänderung.

Diese Akademie, mit Instrumenten und Singstimmen gerechnet, wird von mehr denn 150 Personen aufgeführt.

Die Eintrittspreise sind wie gewöhnlich im Nazionaltheater.

Diejenigen, welche sonst einen geringeren Eintrittspreis zahlen, erhalten das Billet für 30 kr.

Jene von der hohen Noblesse, welche ihre bey den sonst gewöhnlichen Schauspielen abbonirten Logen nicht beybehalten wollen, werden geziemend ersucht, es der Kassa beyzeiten melden zu lassen.

Die Büchel von dem Oratorium sind ebenfalls bey der Kasse für 7 kr. zu haben.

Der Anfang ist um 7 Uhr.

Oggi Domenica il 29. Marzo 1795.
nel Teatro Nazionale
la Società della Musica
avrà l'onore di dare
a benefizio delle Vedove, ed Orfani di essa
UNA GRANDE
ACCADEMIA DI MUSICA,
in due parti, nella quale si eseguirà

Per prima parte:
1) Una grande nuova Sinfonia del Sigre. Maestro Cardellieri.
2) Il Sigre. Maestro Ludovico de Beethoven, suonerà sul Piano Forte un Concerto nuovo di sua composizione.

Per seconda parte:
Sarà eseguito in lingua italiana il primo Atto d' un Oratorio
intitolato:
GIOAS, RE DI GIUDA,
composto dal sudetto Sigre. Maestro Cardellieri.
Le parti principali saranno cantate dalli Signori professori:

Gioas,	Sigre. Viganoni.	()	Giojada,	Sigre. Saal.
Sebia.	Sigra. Sessi.	()	Matan,	Sigre. Vogel.
Atalia,	Sigra. Marescalchi.	()	Ismaele,	Sigre. Spangler.

L'Academia fra cantanti e suonatori sarà eseguita da più di 150 Persone.

Li prezzi per l'ingresso sono come il solito al Teatro Nazionale.

Li Signori, che sono soliti pagar meno per l'entrata, riceveranno il viglietto a 30 car.

Per li Palchi abbonati quelli Signori, che non sono intenzionati di ritenerli, sono rispettosamente pregati di darne avviso a tempo alla Cassa.

I Libretti dell' Oratorio si trovano alla Cassa per 7 car.

Il principio dell' Accademia sarà alle ore 7 in punto.

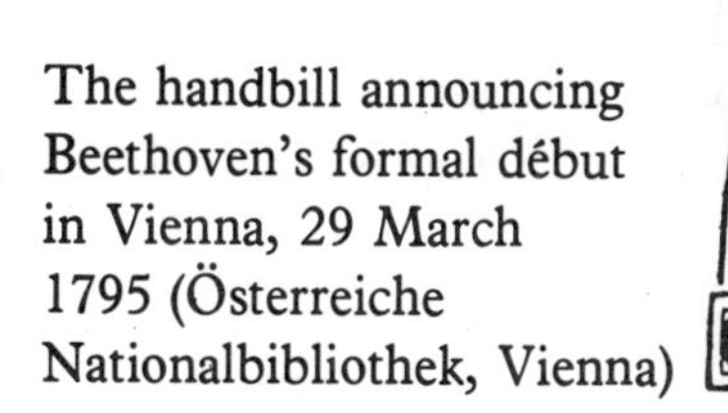

The handbill announcing Beethoven's formal début in Vienna, 29 March 1795 (Österreiche Nationalbibliothek, Vienna)

course, there was the opera and ballet. Public concerts such as we know today were relatively infrequent, though the breakdown of the old patronage system and the effects of the Napoleonic wars hastened their development. Nevertheless in Beethoven's time they were still rare: it may be worth recalling to this end that the Concerts of Ancient Music in London did not begin until as late as 1776, the Leipzig Gewandhaus concerts not until 1781, the Philharmonic Society of London and the Gesellschaft der Musikfreunde of Vienna not until 1813. The public *solo* recital was an even later phenomenon, which did not become manifest until the 1840s. The Sunday morning Musikverein subscription concerts of the Vienna Philharmonic did not in their turn begin until 1860.

Beethoven's formal Viennese début took place at a 'Grand Musical Academy' held on 29 March 1795 for the benefit of orphans and widows of the Society for Musicians at the Burgtheater, one of the most prestigious platforms in all Vienna. 'More than one hundred and fifty participants' took part, and Beethoven played the original version of his new Piano Concerto in B flat, finished just hours before the first rehearsal. No doubt even then he possessed those qualities of playing that Czerny got to know a decade later:

Beethoven's manner: characteristic and passionate strength, alternating with all the charms of a smooth *cantabile*, is its outstanding feature.

The expressive means are often intensified to an extreme degree, especially as regards a humorous inclination. The piquant dominating manner is rarely employed. But for that reason total effects, partly by means of a full sounding *legato*, partly by a judicious use of the forte-pedal, etc., are more often applied.

Beethoven . . . drew entirely new and daring passages from the Forte-piano by the use of the pedal, by an exceptionally characteristic way of playing, particularly distinguished by a strict *legato* of the chords, and thus created a new type of singing tone and many hitherto unimagined effects. His playing did not possess that clean and brilliant elegance of certain other pianists. On the other hand, it was spirited, grandiose and, especially in *adagio*, very full of feeling and romantic.

Though unwell at the time he won his audience: the *Wiener Zeitung* reported that 'the famous Herr Ludwig van Beethoven reaped the wholehearted approval of the public'.

The following day there was a second benefit for the same cause. This time Beethoven improvised. Long experienced in the art, he no doubt more than justified his widely held reputation. Czerny, writing in the *London Musical Miscellany* (2 August 1852), remembered the power of his master:

His improvisation was most brilliant and striking. In whatever company he might chance to be, he knew how to produce such an effect upon every hearer that frequently not an eye remained dry, while many would break

Vienna, the Kohlmarkt. Artaria's building is in the right foreground. Coloured engraving by L. Beyer

out into loud sobs; for there was something wonderful in his expression in addition to the beauty and orginality of his ideas and his spirited style of rendering them. After ending an improvisation of this kind he would burst into loud laughter and banter his hearers on the emotion he had caused in them. 'You are fools!' he would say. Sometimes he would feel himself insulted by these indications of sympathy. 'Who can live among such spoiled children?' he would cry, and on that account (as he told me) he declined to accept an invitation which the King of Prussia gave him after one of the extemporary performances above described.

Ferdinand Ries never heard anyone to equal Beethoven as an improviser.

Following this success came another one on the last day of the month. Mozart's widow had arranged a performance of *La Clemenza di Tito* at the Burgtheater. In the course of it Beethoven offered the D minor Concerto of Mozart, one of his favourites, and one for which later he wrote out his own cadenzas.

Beethoven justifiably enjoyed the rest of the year. In May he signed a contract with Artaria, already the publishers of Haydn and Mozart, and had the satisfaction of seeing the Op 1 Trios announced in the *Wiener Zeitung*. Then around the 18th or so of the month at Emanuel Schikaneder's Friehaustheater, next to an open-air market and the scene of the first performance of *The Magic Flute*, a ballet, *Le Nozze Disturbate*, caught his attention: a set of variations on one of its tunes followed. Then in June he went to the Court Opera with a lady friend. Paisiello's *La Molinara* was on offer this time and another set of variations appeared.

As winter approached so Beethoven's activity increased. Though still pursuing his studies, he was more and more in demand as both composer and pianist. A singular honour came in November with the commission of two sets of dances from his 'master hand' for the annual masked ball of the Gesellschaft der bildenen Künstler. The ball took place annually at the Redoutensaal on the 22nd, St. Cecilia's Day, and the roll-call of composers who had provided dance music for it was notable, beginning with Haydn and including Kozeluh, the Royal Imperial Composer, as well as Dittersdorf. The 1795 ball also included music by the Imperial *Kapellmeister*, Süssmayr: Beethoven had indeed been favoured.

Three weeks or so later Beethoven appeared again at the Redoutensaal, this time on 8 December in a concert with Haydn. The programme included three of Haydn's *Salomon* symphonies written in London, and Beethoven played his B flat Concerto again. That the two men were on good terms once more seems evident: shortly afterwards, on 8 January 1796, they collaborated in another concert.

A masked ball in the great Redoutensaal of the Hofburg. Engraving by J. Schütz, *c.* 1800 (Hans Swarowsky)
'The halls are open from 9 p.m. to 6 a.m. . . . Entrance fee is two florins. Refreshments of all kinds are available. One can sup in private rooms which surround the grand halls. Two orchestras play minuets and waltzes, but few dance . . .' — from a guidebook of 1803

1796 began with a reuniting of all three Beethoven brothers — Nikolaus Johann, a 'complete dandy' according to Czerny, had arrived from Bonn on 26 December and within weeks was working as an apothecary. Later he set up in business on his own. Following the successes of 1795, Beethoven himself seemed all set for his future. He was no longer studying with Albrechtsberger, and his relationship with Salieri was on a casual basis. Lessons in violin playing, however, had been resumed, this time with Wenzel Krumpholz, one of the many Bohemians then living in Vienna, and a first violinist at the Court Opera. Beethoven grew very fond of him. According to Ries, Beethoven's violin playing was more enthusiastic than accurate: 'really dreadful . . . he did not hear when he began a passage with wrong fingering.'

Socially, Beethoven's position was good. He had left Lichnowsky's house and had rooms in the Kreuzgasse. He kept a servant and a horse, and seemed to have possessed a wardrobe that was fashionable if not always used. He gave lessons to the nobility — not always, however, with the greatest enthusiasm if little musical talent was in evidence. His friends included not only musicians but artists, writers and actors as well. Among the latter was Johann Heinrich Friedrich Müller, a particularly famous thespian of the day who lived next to the Kärntnertortheater, Vienna's other principal theatre besides the Burg. It was in Müller's house in 1796 that Beethoven met the Baron Kübeck von Kübau, an Austrian government official who recalled in his *Diary* how Beethoven, 'the hero of music, was a small man with unkempt, bristling hair with no powder which was unusual. He had a face deformed by pockmarks, small shining eyes, and a continuous movement of every limb in his body'. The following year, on 10 March, it was this same von Kübau who wrote that 'Whoever sees Beethoven for the first time and knows nothing about him would surely take him for a malicious, ill-natured and quarrelsome drunkard who has no feeling for music . . . on the other hand, he who sees him for the first time surrounded by his fame and his glory, will surely see musical talent in every feature of an ugly face . . .'

So far as Beethoven's letters of the year are concerned, there is a gap between 19 February when he wrote to his brother Johann, and 19 November when he wrote to Johann Andreas Streicher thanking him for having sent one of his new fortepianos. Streicher was a noted maker and his Viennese *salon* was a centre of musical life. In spite of this gap we know however that Beethoven undertook an important and successful tour of Prague, Dresden, Leipzig and Berlin between February and July. In the letter to his brother, for instance, we see him already in Prague, where he had gone with Karl Lichnowsky; 'I am well, very well. My art is winning me friends and renown, and what more do I want? And this time I shall make a good deal of money.' The visit to Dresden in April was similarly rewarding. One contemporary wrote to Maximilian Franz: 'Beethoven has delayed here almost eight days, everyone who heard him play was enchanted'. He had the further distinction of playing for the Elector of Saxony. Ferdinand Ries has left us an idea of Beethoven's stay in Berlin, the Prussian capital: 'He played several times at court (that of King Friedrich Wilhelm II), when he played the two grand sonatas with *obbligato* violoncello, Op 5, written for Duport, first violoncellist of the King, and himself. On his departure he received a gold snuffbox, filled with *Louis d'ors*. Beethoven declared with pride that it was not an ordinary snuffbox, but such a one as it might have been customary to give to an ambassador.' Beethoven also attended the Singakademie, and gave displays of improvisation. A sojourn in Vienna was then followed in the late autumn by another trip to Pressburg and Pesth. In the meantime on 21 November, in Leipzig, the Bohemian soprano Josefa Dušek, who had had such a rôle to play in Mozart's life, sang 'An Italian scene', specially composed for her by Beethoven — either *Ah perfido!* or *Primo amore* — no doubt embodying some of the fruits of the lessons with Salieri. The most significant publication of the year was that of the Op 2 Sonatas, dedicated to Haydn, and announced by Artaria in the *Wiener Zeitung* for 9 March.

More publications followed in 1797: the Cello Sonatas, Op 5, were issued in February, together with Beethoven's setting of Matthisson's *Adelaide.* Later in the year, in October, came the 'Grande Sonate pour le Clavecin ou Piano-Forte', Op 7, dedicated to the Countess Babette von Keglevics, and as notable for its classicism as its more revolutionary, progressive tenor. Beethoven gave the Countess piano lessons: according to her nephew, Beethoven 'had the curious habit — one of many — as he lived opposite her, of going across in his dressing gown, slippers and nightcap to give her lessons'. Of less substance was a popular set of Variations on a Russian dance from Paul Wranitzky's ballet, *Das Waldmädchen*, staged at the Kärntnertortheater on 23 September 1796. These variations were dedicated to the Countess Anna Margarete von Browne, one of the original subscribers of the Op 1 Piano Trios. In return for the dedication, her husband, according to Ries, gave Beethoven

> . . . a handsome riding-horse . . . as a gift. He rode the animal a few times, soon after forgot all about it and, worse than that, its food also. His servant, who soon noticed this, began to hire out the horse for his own benefit, and, in order not to attract the attention of Beethoven to the fact, for a long time withheld from him all bills for fodder. At length, however, to Beethoven's great amazement he handed in a very large one, which recalled to him at once his horse and his neglectfulness.

Two concerts of 1797 stand out: on Thursday 6 April, Schuppanzigh included Beethoven's Quintet for piano and wind, Op 16, modelled after Mozart and dedicated to another of Beethoven's early Viennese benefactors, Prince Josef von Schwarzenberg. An aria was also sung by Magdalena Willmann, whom Beethoven had known in Bonn and to whom he is supposed to have proposed marriage only to be turned down because, apparently, of his ugliness and his 'half crazy' manner. At the other end of the year, in November, came a repeat performance of the charming dances he had written in 1795, a singular honour.

1798 was a year again notable for highlights. On 29 March Beethoven and Schuppanzigh took part in a benefit concert for Josefa Dušek, offering almost certainly one of the Op 12 Violin Sonatas that Beethoven was still working on (they were not published until the end of the year, when Artaria issued them with a dedication to Salieri). In an age when music of this kind for two players was intended more for private salons than for public halls, such a performance must have been as unusual as it was rare. Following their subsequent publication, the influential *Allgemeine Musikalische Zeitung* of Leipzig carried a review (5 June 1799) which, however, was less than complimentary:

> The reviewer, who had no previous knowledge of this composer's piano music must confess, after working with great effort through these entirely personal Sonatas, overladen with uncommon difficulties, that his feeling on playing them really fluently and strenuously was that of a man who

desired to wander with a congenial friend through a pleasant wood, but was constantly impeded by tangled undergrowth, eventually emerging weary and exhausted, without pleasure. It is undeniable that Herr van Beethoven goes his own way; but what a bizarre and painful way it is! Full of scholarship and again scholarship, but no nature, no real singing is in here! If one considers this music carefully, one finds only a mass of material without good method; obstinacy in which one feels little interest, a striving after unusual modulation, a contempt of normal relationships, a heaping up of difficulty upon difficulty, which make one lose all patience and pleasure.

Antonio Salieri (1750-1825), admirer of Gluck, rival of Mozart, teacher of Beethoven, Schubert and Liszt. Anonymous oil painting (Gesellschaft der Musikfreunde, Vienna)

The exercise was a waste of time: Beethoven knew what he was doing.

A few days after this concert, Salieri gave two Widows and Orphans concerts at the Court Theater (1 and 2 April). The Emperor and the royal family attended in person, and on the 2nd, Beethoven once again played his Op 16 Quintet, as well as 'distinguishing himself at the piano . . . in improvising'.

Shortly afterwards Beethoven was introduced to Jean Baptiste Bernadotte, a young French general of just thirty-four who had been recently appointed to Vienna by Napoleon on the resumption of diplomatic relations with Austria following the peace of Campo Formio. According to Schindler it was Bernadotte who suggested that Beethoven write a 'Heroic' Symphony: 'the first idea for the [Third] Symphony is said to have gone out from General Bernadotte, then French Ambassador in Vienna, who esteemed Beethoven very highly. This I heard from several of Beethoven's friends. I was also told so by Count Moritz Lichnowsky (brother of Prince Lichnowsky), who was often in the society of Bernadotte with Beethoven'. Schindler confirmed, too, that as late as 1823 'Beethoven had a lively recollection that Bernadotte had really first inspired him with the idea of the *Eroica* Symphony'.

It was in 1798 that Beethoven encountered his first serious challenge as a pianist and composer in the shape of Joseph Wölffl, a Salzburg musician three years his junior who had studied with Mozart's father, Leopold, and with Haydn's younger brother, Michael. Many years later Ignaz von Seyfried, one of the conductors at the Freihaus, recalled the rivalry between the two men that was then the talking point of Vienna:

At the head of Beethoven's admirers stood the amiable Prince Lichnowsky; among the most zealous patrons of Wölffl was the broadly cultured Baron Raymond von Wetzlar, whose delightful villa (on the Grünberg near the Emperor's recreation-castle) offered to all artists, native and foreign, an asylum in the summer months, as pleasing as it was desirable, with true British loyalty. There the interesting combats of the two athletes not infrequently offered an indescribable artistic treat to the numerous and thoroughly select gathering. Each brought forward the latest product of his mind. Now one and anon the other gave free rein to his glowing fancy; sometimes they would seat themselves at two pianofortes and improvise alternately on themes which they gave each other, and thus created many a four-hand Capriccio which if it could have been put upon paper at the moment would surely have bidden defiance to time. It would have been difficult, perhaps impossible, to award the palm of victory to either one of the gladiators in respect of technical skill. Nature had been a particularly kind mother to Wölffl in bestowing upon him a gigantic hand which could span a tenth as easily as other hands compass an octave, and permitted him to play passages of double notes in these intervals with the rapidity of lightning. In his improvisations even then Beethoven did not deny his tendency toward the mysterious and gloomy. When once he began to revel in the infinite world of tones, he was transported also above all earthly things; his spirit had burst all restricting bonds, shaken off the yoke of servitude, and soared triumphantly and jubilantly into the luminous spaces of the higher aether. Now his playing tore along like a wildly foaming cataract, and the conjurer constrained his instrument to an utterance so forceful that the stoutest structure was scarcely able to withstand it; and anon he sank down, exhausted, exhaling gentle plaints, dissolving in melancholy. Again the spirit would soar aloft, triumphing over transitory terrestrial sufferings, turn its glance upwards in reverent sounds and find rest and comfort on the innocent bosom of holy nature. But who shall sound the depths of the sea? It was the mystical Sanscrit language whose hieroglyphs can be read only by the initiated. Wölffl, on the contrary, trained in the school of Mozart, was always equable; never superficial but always clear and thus more accessible to the multitude. He used art only as a means to an end, never to exhibit his acquirements. He always enlisted the interest of his hearers and inevitably compelled them to follow the progression of his well-ordered ideas.

But for this [the attitude of their patrons] the *protégés* cared very little. They respected each other because they knew best how to appreciate each other, and as straightforward honest Germans followed the principle that the roadway of art is broad enough for many, and that it is not necessary to lose one's self in envy in pushing forward for the goal of fame!

Later that year Beethoven returned once more to Prague, always a highly critical and informed city when it came to music. Tomásek heard him play both the newly finished C major Piano Concerto and the recently revised one in B flat, as well as movements from the Op 2, No 2 Sonata in A major. He also improvised. In his *Autobiography* published in 1845 after a lifetime of hearing the greatest of pianists play, Tomásek could still describe Beethoven as 'that giant among players'. The value of these reminiscences, however, lies not so much in their repetitious outpourings of adoration and adulation, as in their moments of constructive critical observation:

I listened to Beethoven's artistic work with more composure. I admired his powerful and brilliant playing, but his frequent daring deviations from one

Joseph Wolffl (1772-1812)

Scene of Prague

Johann Wenzel Tomasek
(Tomaschek) (1774-1850)

Domenico Dragonetti (1763-1846)

motive to another, whereby the organic connection, the gradual development of idea was broken up, did not escape me. Evils of this nature frequently weaken his greatest compositions, those which sprang from a too exuberant conception. It is not seldom that the unbiased listener is rudely awakened from his transport. The singular and original seemed to be his chief aim in composition, as is confirmed by the answer which he made to a lady who asked him if he often attended Mozart's operas. 'I do not know them', he replied [an exaggeration, he knew several], 'and do not care to hear the music of others lest I forfeit some of my originality'.

1799, the last year of the old century, saw Beethoven meeting the great Venetian double-bass virtuoso Domenico Dragonetti, then on his way to London. Dragonetti taught Beethoven things about the double-bass that few were capable of, and he astonished him by playing on the bass the second of the Op 5 cello sonatas — an astonishing achievement. Their paths were to cross again in the coming years. Another great artist of the day whom Beethoven met and admired without reservation at this time was the eminently refined pianist, Johann Baptist Cramer, then based in London. Largely self-taught, Cramer had nevertheless enjoyed two years with Clementi, and he was a noted classicist in his admiration for Bach, Handel, Scarlatti and Mozart. When Haydn had been in London, he singled out Cramer for special attention. According to Ries, Beethoven 'had praise for but one as being distinguished — John Cramer. All others were but little to him'. As for Cramer himself, he felt that 'no man in these days has heard extempore playing, unless he has heard Beethoven'.

Of all the works composed or planned or published in this period, one stands out for both its fame and its substance: the Piano Sonata in C minor, Op 13, called by Beethoven himself the *Pathétique* and published by Hoffmeister of Vienna in December 1799 with a dedication to Prince Karl Lichnowsky. The *Allgemeine Musikalische Zeitung* (19 February 1800) praised it in high terms. Modelled in its formal outline on ideas first tried out in one of the early *Electoral* Sonatas of 1783, it more than any other of Beethoven's works up to this time seemed to herald the dawn of the new century. From its dramatic opening *grave* chords, through its searchingly expressive, emotional *Adagio* to the nervous intensity and defiance of the final *Allegro*, the *Pathétique* was a burial of the past, a celebration of the future.

The years of apprenticeship were over, Beethoven had finally arrived.

Title page of the first edition of the *Pathétique* Sonata (Gesellschaft der Musikfreunde, Vienna)

Chapter 6
Revolution and Change

'No man lives *in vacuo*, and a biographer cannot hope to understand his subject if he cannot breathe the air of the age in which he lived' — Arthur Bryant

When Ferrucio Busoni saw Beethoven as not only a symbol of 'liberty, equality, fraternity' but also as 'a product of 1793 . . . the first great democrat in music', he expressed a view — that of the artist as the outcome, the reflection of his age — which was a prevalent assumption among many Romantic thinkers. Hegel in his Berlin *Lectures on the Philosophy of History* was one, for instance, who early on commented on the rise of the quintessential philosophy of the Romantic age which believed that 'art and literature, like laws and institutions [are] an expression of society and therefore inextricably linked with other elements of social development'. Gustav Schilling in 1841 went so far as to trace extensive parallels and analogies between music and politics — the changes of one being the changes of the other — and, like Busoni, expressed the belief of an epoch in viewing Beethoven as the spirit incarnate of freedom.

Such notions were to survive into our own time. In his *Music in Western Civilisation* (1941), Paul Henry Láng, for example, talks about Goethe and Schiller and the post *Sturm und Drang* period:

> They derived their peculiar energy from the forces of their times — an era whose strongest incentives for a new life were in the spirit of opposition against existing ideas and institutions. Men found themselves in social circumstances that led the nation from economic slavery to a free modern order, from princely autocracy to a participation of the middle classes in the government, from the domination of the nobility and the courts to an assertion of the rights of the citizenry. In the ensuing campaign wide possibilities of progress opened up, with new aims on the horizon. More than anyone else, Ludwig van Beethoven lived in this movement and was carried by it.

Later Láng goes on to describe Beethoven as 'the poet of the ideal'. For him, Beethoven 'proved convincingly that true idealism is heroism', he was 'the herald of the nineteenth century', 'the musical prophet of will power'. In *Man and His Music* (1962), Wilfrid Mellers similarly says that we cannot start to understand Beethoven 'unless we recognize that for him music was not merely a pattern of sounds nor even merely an aural means of self-expression; it was also a moral and ethical power'. A few sentences later he even asserts that 'there *is* a connection between Beethoven's music and the French Revolution'. In another document, this time that highly perceptive monograph *The Golden Age of Vienna* (1948), we find Hans Gál resorting to much the same kind of correlation:

> Beethoven's personal relations with his master, Haydn, were not always cordial but rather formal and sometimes even strained. A considerable difference of age had not prevented the most sincere friendship between Haydn and Mozart. Between Haydn and Beethoven [however] there were not only nearly forty years, but the greatest crisis in modern history. For Haydn, brought up under the conditions of the *ancien régime*, the French Revolution was just a horror. Mozart, whose *Figaro* had been his own choice — a revolutionary subject, though carefully expurgated — and who may have had some sympathy for the French people's struggle for liberty, died when it had only begun. But for Beethoven's generation it was a matter of passionate interest, and though he did not approve of its outrages, the ideals of the French Revolution were his own all his life.

Significantly, the age which originally encouraged this kind of thinking also bred it from early on as a conditioning inspirational force that was to mould ideas and attitudes, forge statements and philosophies, and consciously determine the creative direction of

An Afternoon at Liszt's: Liszt, possessed by inspiration, plays a Graf piano, a volume of Beethoven sonatas in front of him. Kriehuber listens on the left, Wilhelm Ernst, the violinist, contemplates from the right, Standing are Berlioz and Czerny. Lithograph by J. Kriehuber, 1846

the artist throughout Europe. In consequence fanciful comparisons were soon to become factual corroborations: so much so that composers like Weber or Schumann, Berlioz or Wagner, became epitomes of an age and place, barometers of a specific intellectual climate, voices of a definable political and social change. In Beethoven, a child of historical transition, we are faced with the dawn of this thought: as a man of politics, an idealist, a champion of liberty, a philosopher, a believer in universal divinity, his every gesture is as much a manifestation of the Romantic age to come as a farewell to the classical past of his predecessors. From his correspondence, and from his contemporaries, we know that he subscribed to many of the tenets of his times: confined though he was to Vienna and its surrounds, he was a man of the world, he followed newspapers avidly, he read widely. In the *Pathétique*, the *Eroica*, *Fidelio*, the *Missa Solemnis*, and the Ninth Symphony, he expressed beliefs of an independence and character that would have been inconceivable if it had not been for an awareness of and an identity with the revolutionary, freedom-seeking, new age in which he lived. To separate Beethoven from his period, to try to understand him without knowing the background of his historical time, is to realise but a one-dimensional view of the man and the artist. The Romantics rightly saw him within the frontiers of their own aesthetic creed, a luminary above all others: to see him as anything else would be to misattribute the intensity of his personality and expression, the essence of his Rousseau-like flowering.

Beethoven gained maturity during, as Gál says, the 'greatest crisis in modern history'. That fact is important. The political map of Europe during Beethoven's lifetime shows seas of relative calm at the beginning and end of his life. But then at the most impressionable stage of his creative evolution, 1789, came the fall of the Bastille. In Edmund Burke's words, the age of chivalry had gone: 'That of sophisters, economists, and calculators has succeeded, and the glory of Europe is extinguished for ever'. Austria itself was already at war with the Ottomans, old enemies, and for the next twenty-five or so years the whole of Europe was to be racked by battles, revolutions and short-lived truces. It was against such strife and bloody breakdown that Beethoven set out.

The storming of the Bastille, 1789

The landmarks of these years stand out like beacons. Those French apostles of the Enlightenment — Voltaire, Condorcet, Diderot, Rousseau — had inflamed a nation to bring the bourgeois and capitalist class to a dominating position and to bring feudalism to an end, to bring the house of Bourbon, the house of Louis XVI and his Queen, Marie Antoinette, to the guillotine in 1793. By then France had already declared war on Habsburg Austria, the so-called Reign of Terror was taking its horrific course, and the armies of

Napoleon asleep and awake at St. Cloud in 1812. From sketches by Girodet

Catherine the Great of Russia had invaded Poland. In 1799, with the French Revolutionary Wars still shaking Europe, the thirty-year-old Corsican Bonaparte became First Consul of the Republic. Five years later, in 1804, he declared himself Emperor. Then in 1805 came not only Trafalgar but the Austrian capitulation at Ulm, Napoleon's defeat of the Austrians and Russians at Austerlitz, and the French occupation of Vienna. Four years later they reoccupied the city. Haydn, defiant to the end, died within the sound of their cannon, and Metternich, the future arbiter of Europe, was appointed Chief Minister of Austria (a post he was to hold until 1848).

1812 marked the fateful year of the French alliance with Prussia, of the invasion of Russia, of Smolensk and Borodino, of Napoleon's entry into Moscow, and of the ultimate and ironic defeat of his *Grande armée* and his entire strategy at the hands of the Russian winter. The following year Austria declared war on the French, and Wellington defeated them at Vittoria. In 1814 Napoleon abdicated and at the end of that year the Congress of Vienna met to reunite and reorganise a divided Europe: in the process the final vestiges of its ancient structure were laid to rest, nationalism was born. A last ditch stand by Napoleon at Waterloo in 1815 only met with defeat and banishment to St. Helena. Subversive, revolutionary tendencies continued to smoulder on the horizon (the Wartburg Festival of 1817, the subsequent Carlsbad decrees of 1819, the 1820 Congress of Troppau), but for the most part Europe was once again at peace.

The advent of the steam railway

At an economic and social level the tide of change was just as apparent and relentless. In 1787, for instance, the Quakers in Britain had formed the Association for the Abolition of Slavery: twenty years later it was finally abolished, while at the same time in Prussia, Stein suppressed both serfdom and noble privilege; the destruction of the medieval guilds came in 1810. In 1812 the Jews found themselves emancipated in Russia. The right of the worker was similarly assuming importance: a general strike in Hamburg in 1791 was one manifestation; another was the recognition in 1825 of the legality of trade unions in Britain.

The rise of industry, modern armament, and the utilisation of gas and electricity were also significant factors of the age. The late 1780s and early 1790s, for example, saw the use of gas for illumination. Then in 1809 Sömmering in Munich invented electric telegraphy. The electromotor came in 1823, and the first German gasworks were opened in Hanover in 1826. That same year Ampère published his *Electrodynamics*; Ohm's Law concerning electric currents was formulated shortly afterwards in 1827. On a different front Senefelder's invention of lithography in 1796 proved to be a decisive step, while at another extreme we find the emergence of Congreve's artillery rocket in 1805, and the opening of the Krupp works at Essen in 1810. As a portent of alternative means of travel, Stephenson's first effective steam locomotive appeared in 1814, with the Stockton-Darlington railway coming eleven years later. By then, the first steamship had crossed the Atlantic (1818): the advent of steam was enthusiastically applauded by Beethoven.

The immense upheavals of the period, and the way classical, sedate Europe was positively torn up by its roots to be flung into the turbulence of the modern era, are nowhere better chronicled than in those epoch-making statements and narratives of the great philosophers and writers who joined Beethoven on that troubled bridge of no return which led to the nineteenth century. In their work we repeatedly came across pronouncements, sentiments, aspirations, and ideals that are entirely Beethovenian in spirit.

The monuments of those stressful fifty years became posterity's inheritance: Kant's *Critique of Pure Reason* appeared in 1781, his *Critique of Practical Reason* in 1788, his *Critique of Judgement* in 1790 and his *Religion within the Boundaries of Reason* three years later; a favourite phrase in one of Beethoven's 1820 conversation books, 'the moral law within us and the starry heavens above us', is actually a misquotation from the conclusion of the *Critique of Practical Reason*. Then between 1784-91 Herder published his *Ideas toward a philosophy of a History of Mankind*; Reid's *Essays on the Intellectual Powers of Man* appeared in 1785.

Five years later Edmund Burke's *Reflections on the Revolution in France* came out. Its aphoristic asides still sum up the Omega and Alpha of two civilisations, two orders of world, with a thrust that needs no elucidation: 'A state without the means of some change is without the means of its conservation'; 'Make the Revolution a parent of settlement, and not a nursery of future revolutions'; 'People will not look forward to posterity, who never looked backward to theit ancestors'; 'Government is a contrivance of human wisdom to provide for human *wants*. Men have a right that these wants should be provided for by this wisdom'; 'It is gone, that sensibility of principle, that chastity of honour, which felt a stain like a wound'; 'In the groves of *their* academy, at the end of every vista, you see nothing but the gallows'; 'Kings will be tyrants from policy, when subjects are rebels from principle'; 'Nobility is a graceful ornament to the civil order. It is the Corinthian capital of polished society'.

In 1791-92 Thomas Paine published his *Rights of Man*, with its Beethovenian sentiment, 'My country is the world, and my religion is to do good'. The philosophy of the age was to be reflected yet further in Fichte's idealistic *Two Pamphlets concerning the French Revolution* (1793), Schiller's *Letters concerning the aesthetic education of mankind* (1794), and Chateaubriand's *Essai sur les révolutions anciennes et modernes* (1797) — all of them documents revealing a mood of change and extensive thought and re-evaluation.

The first decades of the new century saw Hegel (whose attack on Kant had appeared in 1799) achieve prominence with his *Phenomenology of Spirit* (1807), his *Encyclopaedia of Philosophy* (1817), and his *Philosophy of Right* (1821). By then Schopenhauer had produced *The World as Will and Idea* (1819). With the growth of nationalism came a spate of nationalist philosophies as well: not least Fichte's *Sermons Addressed to the German Nation* (1807), Arndt's *Spirit of the Age* (1806-17), a study in four volumes promoting German nationalism and written by a man noted for his patriotic sentiments, and Lachmann's critical edition of the *Nibelungenlied* (1826). Another notable ethnic publication was the Grimm collection of *Fairy Tales* (1812).

In the literary world the appearance of Goethe's *Egmont* in 1788 was followed the next year with *Faust: A Fragment*. *Wilhelm Meister* appeared in 1795, and Part I of *Faust* proper in 1808. A. W. and F. Schlegel's *Athaneum* ('a Romantic journal') had in the meantime begun publication in 1798, while Jean Paul's novel *Titan* (the inspiration over eighty years later of Mahler's First Symphony), saw the light of day in 1800-03. The rest of Europe in the meantime witnessed the gradual emergence in the first decade of the nineteenth century of people like Scott, Jane Austen, Byron, Wordsworth, Shelley, Keats, Victor Hugo, Lamartine, Manzoni, Heine and Pushkin — all of them forces of elemental power.

Beethoven's own tastes, formed in his Bonn period and nurtured, however chaotically, throughout his life, ranged through most of the notable writings of his time and his interest seems to have embraced anything from philosophy and the classics to the latest inventions and scientific discoveries. He kept a careful note of books, prices, and second-hand bookshops in Vienna: the period 1816 to 1819 alone shows a listing of some 148 titles taken from daily newspapers. In his last home, at the House of the Black

Salisbury Cathedral from the Bishop's Garden: 'my light — my dews — my breezes — my bloom and my freshness'. Painting by John Constable (1776-1837. National Gallery, London)

Spaniard, Gerhard von Breuning reported that 'next to the door, between two windows, stood a set of drawers. On this was a black bookcase with four shelves, resting against the wall behind. It was filled with books and papers . . .' It seems that he read often: Franz Grillparzer recalled once finding him (in 1820) 'in a filthy nightshirt, lying on an unmade bed with a book in his hand'. His conversation books and his letters show further evidence of his passion for the written word: he judged a man on his ability to 'acquire new ideas through reading'.

Exactly what he read and when is less certain. We know, however, that he was familiar with Walter Scott (though he thought he was 'just writing for money'), and with Shakespeare in the Eschenburg translation (which he felt to be better than Schlegel's). His copies of the plays in particular contain many pencilled passages: 'Love is blind, and lovers cannot see', Jessica's words in *The Merchant of Venice*, is one heavily underlined example. Among the classics of antiquity he owned Plutarch's *Lives*, Cicero's *Letters*, Aristotle's *Politics*, and the *Republic* of Plato, as well as, according to Schindler, various writings by Euripides, Tacitus, Ovid, Lucian and Xenophon. He was a devoted admirer, too, of Homer and possessed the *Iliad* and the *Odyssey*, preferring the latter, which is again full of pencilled passages. He also knew Persian classical literature.

Among the Austro-Germans, he worshipped Schiller and Goethe, though he was by no means indifferent to people like Herder or Lessing, and he never quite lost his early admiration for Klopstock and Gellert. In his all-too few days reading philosophy at Bonn University, he had further come across some of the poetry of Eulogius Schneider which may have aroused feelings that were not to become tangible until some years later. In the words of Hans Konrad Fischer and Erich Koch, Schneider's 'poetry was pervaded with the French Revolution's wind of freedom and the poetic *Sturm und Drang* that coloured the enlightened Rhineland intellects of academic circles in Bonn'. Goethe, 'the great Goethe', was the one nevertheless, to most capture Beethoven's imagination. He possessed all his published works, and in a letter to the poet dated 8 February 1823 he speaks of 'the admiration, the love and the esteem which already in my youth I cherished for the one and only immortal Goethe'. A notebook at the time confirms that he regarded *Faust* (on which theme he often contemplated basing an opera) as 'the greatest achievement in art'.

As for his personal philosophy, Beethoven could be as revealing as the poets and writers and thinkers whom he read and quoted (or misquoted) so liberally. Schindler said that 'the Revolution had taken root in his bosom; it spread through him and will end with

The Nightmare. Painting by Henry Fuseli (1741-1825. Institute of Arts, Detroit)

him'. As early as 1797 we find him quoting from Schiller's *Don Carlos*: 'Truth is within the reach of the wise man. Beauty can be discerned by a sensitive heart. They belong to one another'. A year later — the period of the *Pathétique* Sonata — he writes: '*Power* is the moral principle of those who excel others, and it is also mine'. As an enemy of repression, he says 'Force is the one thing which is capable of every abuse against those greater things it cannot be'; as a republican thinker, he remarks in one of the late conversation books that 'It is our responsibility to exclude all kings from government'.

As a spiritual philosopher he had relatively little time for orthodox Catholicism or for the masonic persuasion of his friends (freemasonry in Austria, discouraged with the accession of Franz II in 1792, was actively suppressed by an Imperial edict of 1795), but it seems that he responded strongly to that all-embracing universality and infinity of oriental mysticism which was then beginning to attract the attention of the Western world. He admired these words from the Hindusthani:

> God is immaterial; since he is invisible he can have no form, but from what we observe in his works we may conclude that he is eternal, omnipotent, omniscient and omnipresent — The mighty one is he who is free from all desire; he alone; there is no greater than he.

On another occasion he read an essay by Schiller. Some lines of ancient Egyptian — 'I am that which is. I am all, what is, what was, what will be; no mortal man has ever lifted my veil. He is only and solely of himself, and to this only one all things owe their existence' — attracted his attention, and he framed them under glass to keep on his writing desk.

Concerning Beethoven's religious attitude in general, Schindler had this to reveal:

> Beethoven was brought up in the Roman Catholic religion. His entire life is proof that he was truly religious at heart. One of his marked characteristics was that he never discussed religious subjects or the dogmas of the various Christian churches. We can, however, say almost certainly that *his religious views were not so much based on church doctrine as on a sort of deism* [our italics]. Though he never elaborated a specific theory, he acknowledged God revealed in the world as well as the world in God. This view was formed in him as he observed all of nature, and under the tutelage of the much-cited book, Christian Sturm's *Betrachtungen der Werke Gottes in der Natur*, as well as through lessons derived from the philosophical systems of the wise men of Greece. No one who had seen how he absorbed the appropriate content of any writing into his inner life could deny what I have just said.

Herder, once wrote:

> Music rouses a series of intimate feelings, true but not clear, not even perceptual, only most obscure. You, young man, were in its dark auditorium; it lamented, sighed, stormed, exulted; you felt all that, you vibrated with every string. But about what did it — and you with it — lament, sigh, exult, storm? Not a shadow of anything perceptible. Everything stirred only in the darkest abyss of your soul, like a living wind that agitates the depths of the ocean.

Napoleon the Revolutionary

Such attitudes of mind in time prepared the way for that concept of Romanticism put forward by Friedrich Blume:

> The high-strung Romantic concept of music was rooted in a sort of confession of faith: in the circle of the arts music takes the lead. Superior to all the other arts through its 'immateriality', pure spirit, expression of the 'inmost self' (Hegel), or image of the will (Schopenhauer), it can, as no other utterance of the human mind, guide the soul towards the Infinite. In music the contradiction between finite and infinite is cancelled out and man finds salvation in his purer self.

Beethoven, the young Romantic revolutionary brought up within classical orders, anticipated these moods of change and impulse, these ideals of manner and philosophy, as surely as he breathed 'the air of the age in which he lived': his music, as the fruit of that anticipation, gave reality to his dreams, his visions, his quest.

Chapter 7

Landmarks: 1800-04

'He has felt, he has loved, he has suffered' — Vincent d'Indy

With 1800 and the dawn of the new century came not only the completion of such works as the six important Op 18 String Quartets but also Beethoven's first Viennese concert for his own benefit, given at 'the Royal Imperial Court Theatre beside the Burg' on Wednesday 2 April at 6.30 in the evening. 'Tickets for boxes and stalls are to be had of Herr van Beethoven at his lodgings in the Tiefen Graben, No. 241, third storey, and of the box-keeper'. The programme included a symphony by Mozart, two extracts from Haydn's recently completed *Creation*, a display of improvisation, an unspecified piano concerto by Beethoven himself, and the premiere of his First Symphony and the Septet Op 20, 'most humbly and obediently dedicated to Her Majesty the Empress'. The Leipzig *Allgemeine Musikalische Zeitung* reported in October:

On one occasion Herr Beethoven took over the theatre and this was truly the most interesting concert in a long time. He played a new concerto of his own composition, much of which was written with a great deal of taste and feeling. After this he improvised in a masterly fashion, and at the end one of his symphonies was performed in which there is considerable art, novelty and a wealth of ideas. The only flaw was that the wind-instruments were used too much, so that there was more *harmonie* than orchestral music as a whole. Perhaps we might do well to note the following about this concert. The orchestra of the Italian opera made a very poor showing. First, quarrels about who was to conduct. Beethoven thought quite rightly that he could entrust the conducting not to Herr Conti but to Herr Wranitzky. The gentlemen refused to play under him. The faults of this orchestra . . . then became all the more evident since B's compositions are difficult to execute. When they were accompanying, the players did not bother to pay any attention to the soloist. As a result there was no delicacy at all in the accompaniments and no response to the musical feeling of the solo player. In the second part of the symphony they became so lax that despite all efforts on the part of the conductor no fire whatsoever could be got out of them, particularly from the wind-instruments.

Heute Mittwoch den 2ten April 1800.
wird
im kaiserl. königl. National-Hof-Theater nächst der Burg
Herr Ludwig van Beethoven
die Ehre haben
eine große musikalische Akademie
zu seinem Vortheile zu geben.
Die darinn vorkommenden Stücke sind folgende:

1) Eine große Symphonie von weiland Herrn Kapellmeister Mozart.
2) [illegible] aus des [illegible] Herrn Kapellmeister Haydens Schöpfung, gesungen von Mlle. Saal.
3) Ein großes Konzert auf dem Piano-Forte, gespielt und komponirt von Hrn Ludwig van Beethoven.
4) Ein Sr. Majestät der Kaiserinn allerunterthänigst zugeeignetes, und von Hrn. Ludwig van Beethoven komponirtes Septett, auf 4 Saiten und 3 Blas-Instrumenten, gespielt von denen Herren Schuppanzigh, Schreiber, Schindlecker, Bär, Nikel, Matauschek, und [illegible]
5) Ein Duett aus Haydns Schöpfung, gesungen von Herrn und Mlle. Saal.
6) Wird Herr Ludwig van Beethoven auf dem Piano-Forte fantasiren.
7) Eine neue große Symphonie mit vollständigen Orchester, komponirt von Herrn Ludwig van Beethoven.

[illegible] sind sowohl bei Herrn van Beethoven, in dessen Wohnung im tiefen Graben Nro. 241. im 3ten Stock als auch [illegible] zu haben.

Die Eintrittspreise sind wie gewöhnlich.

Der Anfang ist um halb 7 Uhr.

The announcement of Beethoven's first benefit concert in Vienna, 2 April 1800

Following its publication in December 1801, the Symphony, inscribed to the Baron Gottfried van Swieten, soon grew in popularity, but it was outshone nevertheless by the Septet: Czerny said that Beethoven 'could not endure [the latter] and grew angry because of the universal applause with which it was received'.

Over two weeks later, on 18 April, Beethoven gave another concert, this time with the horn virtuoso Johann Wenzel Stich who was known by the name of Punto. The day before, Beethoven, according to Ferdinand Ries, began work on a Horn Sonata (Op 17) and actually managed to have it finished in time for the concert — though the piano part, as was his custom, was left only in sketch. Between the end of April and the beginning of July, Beethoven spend some time in Budapest as well as visiting regularly the country estate of the Brunsvik family at Martonvásár: he was more than attracted to the two Brunsvik sisters, Josephine and Therese. Whilst in Budapest, he gave another concert with Stich: a contemporary report remarks 'who is this Bethover [*sic*]? The history of German music is not acquainted with such a name. Punto, of course, is very well known . . .'. Another source, on the other hand, speaks of 'a famous *Musikus* named Beethoven [who] drew the attention of all present to himself from his artistic performance'.

Two other events of the year might be mentioned: Count Lichnowsky's continued patronage through an annuity of 600 gulden (about £60) to last until Beethoven could find some kind of permanent position; and Beethoven's agreement to teach the young

Carl Czerny, a native of Vienna. In 1842 Czerny vividly remembered his first encounter with the great man:

Prince Franz Joseph von Lobkowitz (1772-1816). A Bohemian nobleman, he had his own private orchestra, and was the dedicatee of such major works as the Op 18 Quartets, the *Eroica*, the Fifth and Sixth Symphonies, and the *An die ferne Geliebte* song cycle. Stippled engraving by C. H. Pfeiffer after F. A. Oelenhainz

I was about ten years old when I was taken to Beethoven through the kind offices of Krumpholz. It was the winter of 1799-1800. How I was overjoyed and terrified on the day when I was to meet the esteemed master! Even today every moment of it is still fresh in my memory. On a winter's day, my father, Krumpholz and I walked from the Leopoldstadt, where we still lived, into the city, to the so-called Tiefer Graben, climbed up as if in a tower, to the fifth or sixth floor, where a rather grubby-looking servant announced us to Beethoven and then showed us in. A very barren-looking room, papers and clothes strewn all over the place, a few boxes, bare walls, hardly a single chair save for a rickety one by the fortepiano — a Walter, at that time the best make. In this room were gathered six to eight persons, including both the brothers Wranitzky, Süssmayr, Schuppanzigh and one of Beethoven's brothers.

Beethoven himself was dressed in a jacket of some shaggy dark grey cloth and trousers of the same material, so that he immediately reminded me of Campe's *Robinson Crusoe*, which I had just then read. The coal-black hair cut *à la Titus* stood up around his head. His black beard, unshaven for several days, darkened the lower part of his already dark-complexioned face. Also I noticed at a glance, as children are wont to do, that his ears were stuffed with cotton-wool which seemed to have been dipped in some yellow fluid . . . I had to play something immediately, and since I was too shy to begin with one of his own compositions, I played Mozart's great C major Concerto [K.503] which begins with chords. Beethoven was immediately attentive; he came close to my chair and played with his left hand the orchestra part in those sections where I had only accompanying passages. His hands were very hairy and his fingers, especially at the tips, very broad. He expressed himself as being satisfied, so I made bold and played the *Pathétique* Sonata which had then just appeared, and finally the *Adelaide* which my father sang with his very good tenor voice. When I had finished, Beethoven turned to my father and said, 'The boy has talent. I will teach him myself and accept him as my pupil. Send him to me a few times a week. Before anything else, obtain for him Emanuel Bach's handbook on the proper way to play the clavier, so that he can already bring it with him the next time he comes.'

In the first lessons, Beethoven gave me scales in every key, showed me the only proper position of the hands and of the fingers and particularly the use of the thumb then unknown to the majority of players, rules whose complete scope I mastered only at a much later time.

The following year, 1801, saw the completion of several substantial sonatas (including the C sharp minor Sonata quasi una Fantasia, Op 27, No 2, the so-called *Moonlight*), the *Prometheus* ballet, and the String Quintet, Op 29, as well as the publication, in parts, of the First Symphony, the C major and B flat Piano Concertos (in that

Manuscript for beginning of last movement of the "Moonlight" Sonata

Gli Uomini di Prometeo

BALLO

per il Clavicembalo o Piano-Forte

Composto, e dedicato

á Sua Altezza la Signora Principessa

LICHNOWSKY nata CONTESSA THUNN

da

Luiggi van Beethoven

Opera 24

In Vienna presso Artaria e Comp.

872.

Title page of piano score for *Prometheus,* with Beethoven's notes regarding corrections to be made

order), the Op 16 Quintet, and the Op 18 Quartets dedicated to Prince Lobkowitz.

A series of public concerts at the beginning of the year, given to raise funds for soldiers wounded at the battle of Hohenlinden (where the Austrians had been decisively beaten by the French), included one on 30 January in which Beethoven and Stich played the Horn Sonata again. Haydn conducted two of his own symphonies as well. A more important event took place on 28 March with the first performance in the Burgtheater of the ballet *Prometheus*, Beethoven's first stage-work proper if we discount the early Bonn *Ritterballet*. Ballet was then on the ascendant in the Viennese court, not least due to the efforts of the ballet master, Salvatore Viganò (1769-1821).

Heinrich von Collin confirmed Viganò's importance in one of his reminiscences published posthumously in Vienna in 1814:

In the reign of Leopold II the ballet, which had become a well-attended entertainment in Vienna through the efforts of Noverre was restored to the stage. Popular interest was intensified in a great degree when, besides the ballet-master Muzarelli, a second ballet-master, Mr. Salvatore Vigano, whose wife disclosed to the eyes of the spectators a hitherto unsuspected art, also gave entertainments. The most important affairs of state are scarcely able to create a greater war of feeling than was brought about at the time by the rivalry of the two ballet-masters. Theatre-lovers without exception divided themselves into two parties who looked upon each other with hatred and contempt because of a difference of conviction . . . The new ballet-master owed his extraordinary triumph over his older rival to his restoration of his art back from the exaggerated, inexpressive artificialities of the old Italian ballet to the simple forms of nature. Of course, there was something startling in seeing a form of drama with which hitherto there had been associated only leaps, contortions, constrained positions, and complicated dances which left behind them no feeling of unity, suddenly succeeded by dramatic action, depth of feeling and plastic beauty of representation as they were so magnificently developed in the earlier ballets of Mr. Salvatore Viganò, opening, as they did, a new realm of beauty. And though it may be true that it was especially the natural, joyous, unconstrained dancing of Madame Viganò and her play of features, as expressive as it was fascinating, which provoked the applause of the many, it is nevertheless true that the very subject-matter of the ballets, which differentiate themselves very favourably from his later conceits, and his then wholly classical, skilful and manly dancing, were well calculated to inspire admiration and respect for the master and his creations.

Beethoven in his thirtieth year: 'the masculine sculptor who dominates his matter and bends it to his hand; the master-builder, with Nature for his yard' (Romain Rolland). A man 'like Lucifer, a son of the morning, glorying in his power' (Marion Scott). Engraving by J. Neidl from a drawing by G.E. Stainhauser von Treubert, 1800

The Vienna *Zeitung für die elegante Welt* (19 May 1801) was not wholly pleased, however, with the Viganò-Beethoven collaboration.

The music . . . did not completely come up to expectations, notwithstanding some uncommon virtues. Whether Herr van Beethoven can achieve

Maria Casentini, the prima ballerina of the Vienna Court Opera, for whose benefit *Prometheus* was first staged in 1801. After a stippled engraving. The original scenario depicted Prometheus, the hero of this allegorical ballet, as 'a lofty soul who drove ignorance from the people of his time, and gave them manners, customs and morals. As a result of this concept two statues which have brought to life are introduced into the ballet and these, through the power of harmony, are made sensitive to the passions of human life'

what audiences such as those here demand with so uniform — not to say monotonous — a subject, I leave undecided. There can scarcely be any doubt, however, that his writing here is too learned for a ballet, and pays too little regard to the dancing.

In spite of this *Prometheus* enjoyed a measure of immediate success: 16 performances in 1801, 13 in 1802, and the Artaria publication in June 1801 of Beethoven's own piano arrangement of the complete score.

Towards the end of 1801, in addition to Czerny and others, Beethoven took on another young pupil: Ferdinand Ries, seventeen in November, fresh from Munich, and the son of the Franz Ries who had so staunchly stood by the Beethoven family through the worst of their Bonn years. According to Ferdinand's *Notizen*, Beethoven taught him the piano:

When Beethoven gave me a lesson I must say that contrary to his nature he was particularly patient. I was compelled to attribute this and his friendly disposition, which was seldom interrupted, chiefly to his great affection and love for my father. Thus, sometimes, he would permit me to repeat a thing ten times or even oftener. In the Variations dedicated to the Princess Odescalchi (Op 34), I was obliged to repeat the last *Adagio* variation almost seventeen times; yet he was still dissatisfied with the expression of the little cadenza, although I thought I played it as well as he. On this day I had a lesson which lasted nearly two hours. If I made a mistake in passages or missed notes and leaps which he frequently wanted emphasized he seldom said anything; but if I was faulty in expression, in *crescendos*, etc., or in the character of the music, he grew angry because, as he said, the former was accidental, while the latter disclosed lack of knowledge, feeling, or attentiveness. The former slips very frequently happened to him even when he was playing in public.

Beethoven's letters of 1801 are among the first really significant documents to have survived from his pen. On about 15 January, for instance, he wrote to his Leipzig publisher, Franz Anton Hoffmeister, commenting on some of the adverse criticism that he had been receiving in the *Allgemeine Musikalische Zeitung*, whose recent pages had included such tirades as 'The composer with his unusual harmonic knowledge and love for serious composition, would provide us many things which would leave many hand-organ things far in the rear, even those composed by famous men, if he would but try to write more naturally' (on the Op 11 Trio), and 'Hr. van Beethoven may be able to improvise but he does not know how to write variations'. Another letter written on 22 April, this time to Breitkopf and Härtel, the publishers of the *Allgemeine Musikalische Zeitung*, refers even more specifically to the manner of their critics:

Advise your reviewers to be more circumspect and intelligent, particularly in regard to the productions of younger composers. For many a one, who perhaps might go far, may take fright. As for myself, far be it from me to think that I have achieved a perfection which suffers no adverse criticism. But your reviewer's outcry against me was at first very mortifying. Yet when I began to compare myself with other composers, I could hardly bring myself to pay any attention to it but remained quite calm and said to myself: 'They don't know anything about music'. And indeed what made it easier to keep calm was that I noticed how certain people were being praised to the skies who in Vienna had very little standing among the best local composers — practically none at all, whatever other excellent qualities they might possess — However, *pax vobiscum* — peace between you and me —

The letters of 1801, however, are demonstrably less notable for their business dealings, for their admiration of Bach, 'that first

Franz Gerhard Wegeler (1765-1848). Silhouette by Neesen

father of harmony', or for their humorous asides to the Hungarian, Nikolaus Zmeskall von Domanovecz, a close friend from Beethoven's early Vienna days, than for their sudden and dramatic revelation of hitherto unsuspected depths of spiritual and physical despair. Nothing in Beethoven's previous letters suggests the outpourings of 1801 that first became evident in a letter to Wegeler in Bonn, dated 29 June:

But that jealous demon, my wretched health, has put a nasty spoke in my wheel; and it amounts to this, that for the last three years my hearing has become weaker and weaker. The trouble is supposed to have been caused by the condition of my abdomen which, as you know, was wretched even before I left Bonn, but has become worse in Vienna where I have been constantly afflicted with diarrhoea and have been suffering in consequence from an extraordinary debility. Frank [Director of the General Hospital] tried to *tone up* my constitution with strengthening medicines and my hearing with almond oil, but much good did it do me! His treatment had no effect, my deafness became even worse and my abdomen continued to be in the same state as before. Such was my condition until the autumn of last year; and sometimes I gave way to despair. Then a medical asinus advised me to take cold baths to improve my condition. A more sensible doctor, however, prescribed the usual tepid baths in the Danube. The result was miraculous; and my inside improved. But my deafness persisted or, I should say, became even worse. During this last winter I was truly wretched, for I had really dreadful attacks of colic and again relapsed completely into my former condition. And thus I remained until about four weeks ago when I went to see *Vering*. For I began to think that my condition demanded the attention of a surgeon as well; and in any case I had confidence in him. Well, he succeeded in checking almost completely this violent diarrhoea. He prescribed tepid baths in the Danube, to which I had always to add a bottle of strengthening ingredients. He ordered no medicines until about four days ago when he prescribed pills for my stomach and an infusion for my ear. As a result I have been feeling, I may say, stronger and better; but my ears continue to hum and buzz day and night. I must confess that I lead a miserable life. For almost two years I have ceased to attend any social functions, just because I find it impossible to say to people: I am deaf. If I had any other profession I might be able to cope with my infirmity; but in my profession it is a terrible handicap. And if my enemies, of whom I have a fair number, were to hear about it, what would they say? — In order to give you some idea of this strange deafness, let me tell you that in the theatre I have to place myself quite close to the orchestra in order to understand what the actor is saying, and that at a distance I cannot hear the high notes of instruments or voices. As for the spoken voice it is surprising that some people have never noticed my deafness; but since I have always been liable to fits of absent-mindedness, they attribute my hardness of hearing to that. Sometimes, too, I can scarcely hear a person who speaks softly; I can hear sounds, it is true, but cannot make out the words. But if anyone shouts, I can't bear it. Heaven alone knows what is to become of me. *Vering tells me that my hearing will certainly improve, although my deafness may not be completely cured* — Already I have often cursed my Creator and my existence. *Plutarch* has shown me *that path of resignation*. If it is at all possible, I will bid defiance to my fate, though I feel that as long as I live there will be moments when I shall be God's most unhappy creature — I beg you not to say anything about my condition to any one, not even to *Lorchen* [Eleonore van Breuning]; I am only telling you this as a secret; but I should like you to correspond with *Vering* about it. If my trouble persists I will visit you next spring. You will rent a house for me in some beautiful part of the country and then for six months I will lead the life of a peasant. Perhaps that will make a difference. Resignation, what a wretched resource! Yet it is all that is left to me —

A letter written a few days later to Karl Amenda, a violinist and tutor to the children of Prince Lobkowitz, again draws attention to the same symptoms of deafness and speaks of 'sad resignation', while another one to Wegeler (16 November) reports further on Beethoven's suddenly grievous condition:

For the last few months Vering has made me apply to both arms *vesicatories* which, as you doubtless know, consist of a certain kind of bark. Well, it is an extremely unpleasant treatment, inasmuch as for a few days (until the bark has drawn sufficiently) I am always deprived of the free use of my arms, not to mention the pain I have to suffer. True enough, I cannot deny it, the humming and buzzing is slightly less than it used to be, particularly in my left ear, where my deafness really began. But so far my hearing is certainly not a bit better; and I am inclined to think, although I do not dare to say so definitely, that it is a little weaker — The condition of my abdomen is improving, and especially when I have taken tepid baths for a few days I feel pretty well for eight or even ten days afterwards. I very rarely take a tonic for my stomach and, if so, only one dose. But following your advice I am now beginning to apply *herbs to my belly* — Vering won't hear of my taking shower baths. On the whole I am not at all satisfied with him. He takes far too little interest in and trouble with a complaint of this kind. I should never see him unless I went to his house, which is very inconvenient for me — What is your opinion of Schmidt? It is true that I am not inclined to change doctors, but I think that V[ering] is too much of a practitioner to derive many new ideas from reading — In that respect S[chmidt], I consider, is a totally different fellow and, what is more, he might perhaps not be quite so casual —

The stress of this period reached its climax in the middle of 1802. As was the custom of the day the Viennese usually spent the hot summer months away in the country, and few years were to pass when Beethoven did not similarly pack his bags and head for the open spaces. In April 1802 on the advice of Schmidt, his new doctor, he accordingly took rooms in a house in the village of Heiligenstadt, famous for its sulphur springs. A view across fields to the Danube and the Carpathian mountains provided Beethoven with a solace to which he was to return again in later life: Thayer speaks of 'fresh air, sun, green fields, delightful walks, bathing, easy access to his physician, and yet a degree of solitude which is now not easy to conceive as having been attainable so near the capital'. In his *Notizen*, Ferdinand Ries confirmed Beethoven's enthusiasm for these quietly contemplative pastoral summer surroundings, no less than he recorded the first definite signs of deafness:

He lived much in the country, whither I went often to take a lesson from him. At times, at 8 o'clock in the morning after breakfast he would say: 'Let us first take a short walk.' We went, and frequently did not return till 3 or 4 o'clock, after having made a meal in some village. On one of these wanderings Beethoven gave me the first striking proof of his loss of hearing, concerning which Stephan von Breuning had already spoken to me. I called his attention to a shepherd who was piping very agreeably in the woods on a flute made of a twig of elder. For half an hour Beethoven could hear nothing, and though I assured him that it was the same with me (which was not the case), he became extremely quiet and morose. When occasionally he seemed to be merry, it was generally to the extreme of boisterousness; but this happened seldom.

By the end of the stay at Heiligenstadt, in early October, depression and despair finally overcame Beethoven's morale, and he wrote a remarkable document, a testament addressed to his brothers Carl and Johann (the latter remaining unnamed throughout, however), in which the extent of his spiritual downfall becomes all too painfully evident:

HEILIGENSTADT, 6 October 1802

FOR MY BROTHERS CARL AND [JOHANN] BEETHOVEN

O my fellow men who consider me, or describe me as, unfriendly, peevish or even misanthropic, how greatly do you wrong me. For you do not know the secret reason why I appear to you to be so. Ever since my childhood my heart and soul have been imbued with the tender feeling of goodwill; and I have always been ready to perform even great actions. But just think, for the last six years [i.e. since 1796] I have been afflicted with an incurable complaint which has been made worse by incompetent doctors. From year to year my hopes of being cured have gradually been shattered and finally I have been forced to accept the prospect of a *permanent infirmity* (the curing of which may perhaps take years or may even prove to be impossible). Though endowed with a passionate and lively temperament and even fond of the distractions offered by society I was soon obliged to seclude myself and live in solitude. If at times I decided just to ignore my infirmity, alas! how cruelly was I then driven back by the intensified sad experience of my poor hearing. Yet I could not bring myself to say to people: 'Speak up, shout, for I am deaf'. Alas! how could I possibly refer to the impairing *of a sense* which in me should be more perfectly developed than in other people, a sense which at one time I possessed in the greatest perfection, even to a degree of perfection such as assuredly few in my profession possess or have ever possessed — Oh, I cannot do it; so forgive me, if you ever see me withdrawing from your company which I used to enjoy. Moreover my misfortune pains me doubly, inasmuch as it leads to my being misjudged. For me there can be no relaxation in human society, no refined conversations, no mutual confidences. I must live quite alone and may creep into society only as often as sheer necessity demands; I must live like an outcast. If I appear in company I am overcome by a burning anxiety, a fear that I am running the risk of letting people notice my condition. — And that has been my experience during the last six months which I have spent in the country. My sensible doctor by suggesting that I should spare my hearing as much as possible has more or less encouraged my present natural inclination, though indeed when carried away now and then by my instinctive desire for human society, I have let myself be tempted to seek it. But how humiliated I have felt if somebody standing beside me heard the sound of a flute in the distance and *I heard nothing*, or if somebody heard *a shepherd sing* and again I heard nothing — Such experiences almost made me despair, and I was on the point of putting an end to my life — The only thing that held me back was *my art*. For indeed it seemed to me impossible to leave this world before I had produced all the works that I felt the urge to compose; and thus I have dragged on this miserable existence — a truly miserable existence, seeing that I have such a sensitive body that any fairly sudden change can plunge me from the best spirits into the worst of

Heiligenstadt, a place famous for its churches and medicinal baths. Coloured engraving by L. Janscha

humours — *Patience* — that is the virtue, I am told, which I must now choose for my guide; and I now possess it — I hope that I shall persist in my resolve to endure to the end, until it pleases the inexorable Parcae to cut the thread; perhaps my condition will improve, perhaps not; at any rate I am now resigned — At the early age of 28 I was obliged to become a philosopher, though this was not easy; for indeed this is more difficult for an artist than for anyone else — Almighty God, who look down into my innermost soul, you see into my heart and you know that it is filled with love for humanity and a desire to do good. Oh my fellow men, when some day you read this statement, remember that you have done me wrong; and let some unfortunate man derive comfort from the thought that he has found another equally unfortunate who, notwithstanding all the obstacles imposed by nature, yet did everything in his power to be raised to the rank of noble artists and human beings. — And you my brothers Carl and [Johann], when I am dead, request on my behalf Professor Schmidt, if he is still living, to describe my disease, and attach this written document to his record, so that after my death at any rate the world and I may be reconciled as far as possible — At the same time I herewith nominate you both heirs to my small property (if I may so describe it) — Divide it honestly, live in harmony and help one another. You know that you have long ago been forgiven for the harm you did me. I again thank you, my brother Carl, in particular, for the affection you have shown me of late years. My wish is that you should have a better and more carefree existence than I have had. Urge your children to be *virtuous*, for virtue alone can make a man happy. Money cannot do this. I speak from experience. It was virtue that sustained me in my misery. It was thanks to virtue and also to my art that I did not put an end to my life by suicide — Farewell and love one another — I thank all my friends, and especially *Prince Lichnowsky* and *Professor Schmidt*. I would like Prince L[ichnowsky]'s instruments [a quartet set of two violins, a viola and cello, now in the Beethoven-Haus, Bonn] to be preserved by one of you, provided this does not lead to a quarrel between you. But as soon as they can serve a more useful purpose, just sell them; and how glad I shall be if in my grave I can still be of some use to you both — Well, that is al! — Joyfully I go to meet Death — should it come before I have had an opportunity of developing all my artistic gifts, then in spite of my hard fate it would still come too soon, and no doubt I would like it to postpone its coming — Yet even so I should be content, for would it not free me from a condition of continual suffering? Come then, Death, *whenever* you like, and with courage I will go to meet you — Farewell; and when I am dead, do not wholly forget me. I deserve to be remembered by you, since during my lifetime I have often thought of you and tried to make you happy — Be happy —

LUDWIG VAN BEETHOVEN

The end of the so-called Heiligenstadt Testament (Staats/Universitäts-bibliothek, Hamburg). It was Karlheinz Stockhausen who incorporated parts of this document in his bicentenary tribute to Beethoven, *Kurzwellen mit Beethoven* ('Stockhoven-Beethausen Opus 1970')

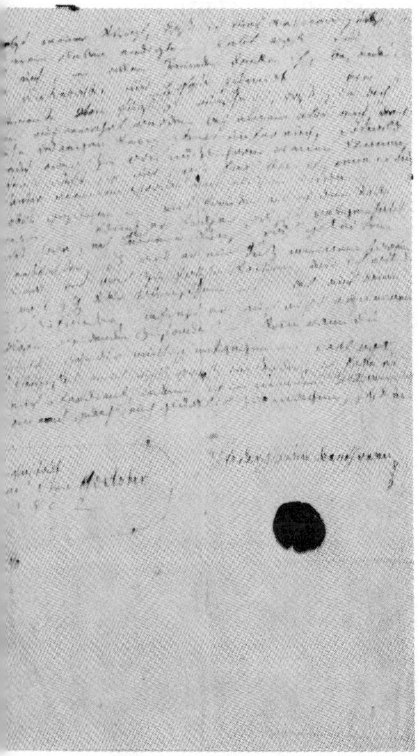

For my brothers Carl and [Johann]
To be read and executed after my death —
HEILIGENSTADT, 10 October 1802 — Thus I take leave of you — and, what is more, rather sadly — yes, the hope I cherished — the hope I brought with me here of being cured to a certain extent at any rate — that

hope I must now abandon completely. As the autumn leaves fall and wither, likewise — that hope has faded for me. I am leaving here — almost in the same condition as I arrived — Even that high courage — which has often inspired me on fine summer days — has vanished — Oh Providence — do but grant me one day of *pure joy* — For so long now the inner echo of real joy has been unknown to me — Oh when — oh when, Almighty God — shall I be able to hear and feel this echo and again in the temple of Nature and in contact with humanity — Never? — No! — Oh, that would be too hard.

Writing this traumatic document (discovered by Schindler after Beethoven's death and first published in the *Allgemeine Musikalische Zeitung* for 17 October 1827) proved to be the turning point. Beethoven had crossed the Rubicon, he had faced up to the disaster in his life, and he had somehow managed to see beyond it. He felt himself near death, yet paradoxically he also re-discovered life again. Within days, he was back in Vienna, writing to his publishers, working on his music, and preparing for the coming year. With the Heiligenstadt Testament, he became more than ever a philosopher, he had overcome the greatest crisis of his mortal span, and his spirit had found its ultimate salvation not in materialism, earthly consolation, but in those Elysian fields of music that were to be his lifeblood and hunting ground for another twenty-five years.

The immediate celebration of that salvation was, of course, the remarkably buoyant Second Symphony, a work that H. C. Robbins Landon rightly suggests nevertheless should be seen as 'a warning to those who will insist on seeing a *constant* parallel between Beethoven's life and music [our italics]. We do not need to go so far as W. H. Auden in condemning Beethoven's letters, but,' Landon continues, 'it is obvious that his muses always existed on a higher level, often isolated from his physical and mental agonies'. No less representative were the three piano sonatas, Op 31, and the three violin sonatas, Op 30 dedicated to Tsar Alexander I. The G major works from both sets offer much the same kind of classico-romantic, bucolic brilliance as the symphony, but the D minor Piano Sonata and the C minor Violin Sonata look to the future with a new-found identity and personality that at once proclaims the advent of an original and fresh creative direction — Beethoven's so-called second period, no less — what d'Indy called his period of 'externalization'.

Life in Vienna in the meantime continued on its unhurried, fashionable way. A report on 'Amusements of the Viennese after Carnival', published in the Berlin *Freymüthige* for 12 April 1803, gives an evocative idea of the musical pulse of the city and is interesting for the incidental but important light it throws on Beethoven's own activities:

. . . Amateur concerts at which unconstrained pleasure prevails are frequent. The beginning is usually made with a quartet by Haydn or Mozart; then follows, let us say, an air by Salieri or Paër, then a pianoforte piece with or without another instrument *obbligato*, and the concert closes as a rule with a chorus or something of the kind from a favourite opera. The most excellent pianoforte pieces that won admiration during the last carnival were a new quintet [Op 16] by Beethoven, clever, serious, full of deep significance and character, but occasionally a little too glaring, here and there *Odensprünge* in the manner of this master; then a quartet by Anton Eberl, dedicated to the Empress, lighter in character, full of fine yet profound invention, originality, fire and strength, brilliant and imposing. Of all the musical compositions which have appeared of late these are certainly two of the best. Beethoven has for a short time past been engaged, at a considerable salary, by the Theater an der Wien, and will soon produce at that playhouse an oratorio of his composition entitled *Christus am Ölberg*. Amongst the artists on the violin the most notable are Clement, Schuppanzigh (who gives the concerts in the Augarten in the summer) and Luigi Tomasini. Clement (Director of the Orchestra an der Wien) is an admirable concerto player; Schuppanzigh performs quartets very agreeably.

One of the first fruits of Beethoven's association with Schikaneder's Theater an der Wien was a concert on 5 April 1803 which included the first performance of the new oratorio *Christus am Ölberg*, as well as the recently finished Third Piano Concerto*. In keeping with the insatiable musical appetite of early 19th century audiences the programme also included the First and Second Symphony as well as other vocal pieces. Ries reports that the rehearsal began at eight in the morning; 'it was a terrible rehearsal, and at half past two everybody was exhausted and more or less dissatisfied'. He then continues:

Prince Karl Lichnowsky, who attended the rehearsal from the beginning, had sent for bread and butter, cold meat and wine, in large baskets. He pleasantly asked all to help themselves, and this was done with both hands, the result being that good nature was restored again. Then the Prince requested that the oratorio be rehearsed once more from the beginning, so that it might go well in the evening and Beethoven's first work in this genre be worthily presented. And so the rehearsal began again. The concert began at six o'clock, but was so long that a few pieces were not performed.

* The recently re-discovered autograph, lost since World War II, appears to be dated 1803 and not 1800 as once thought, a fact that could account for the sketchiness of the work as reported by Seyfried.

Plentiful reports have survived about this concert. Ignaz Ritter von Seyfried in particular said that in the concerto he turned the pages for Beethoven:

but — heaven help me! — that was easier said than done. I saw almost nothing but empty leaves; at the most on one page or the other a few Egyptian hieroglyphs wholly unintelligible to me scribbled down to serve as clues for him; for he played nearly all of the solo part from memory, since, as was so often the case, he had not had time to put it all down on paper. He gave me a secret glance whenever he was at the end of one of the invisible passages and my scarcely concealable anxiety not to miss the decisive moment amused him greatly and he laughed heartily at the jovial supper which we ate afterwards.

Press comments suggest that the concert was nevertheless received coolly, even disastrously, by the Viennese public. The *Freymüthige* wrote:

Even our doughty Beethofen, whose oratorio *Christus am Ölberg* was performed for the first time at suburban Theater an der Wien, was not altogether fortunate, and despite the efforts of his many admirers was unable to achieve really marked approbation. True, the two symphonies and single passages in the oratorio were voted very beautiful, but the work in its entirety was too long, too artificial in structure and lacking expressiveness, especially in the vocal parts. The text, by F. X. Huber, seemed to have been as superficially written as the music. But the concert brought

The Theater an der Wien. Anonymous coloured engraving

1800 florins to Beethofen and he, as well as Abbé Vogler, has been engaged for the theatre. He is to write one opera, Vogler three; for this they are to receive 10 per cent of the receipts at the first ten performances, besides free lodgings.

The *Zeitung für die Elegante Welt* observed:

. . . the first symphony is better than the later one [in D] because it is developed with a lightness and is less forced, while in the second the striving for the new and surprising is already more apparent. However, it is obvious that both are not lacking in surprising and brilliant passages of beauty. Less successful was the following Concerto in C minor which Hr. v. B., who is otherwise known as an excellent pianist, performed also not completely to the public's satisfaction.

Christus was not published until October 1811 and Beethoven seems to have been fairly dissatisfied with it; it nevertheless enjoyed a measure of success in his later years.

Rather more immediately successful was another concert at one of the Augartensaal 8 o'clock morning functions on 24 May, when Beethoven and the mulatto violinist, George Augustus Polgreen Bridgetower, gave the first performance of the concerto-like Op 47 Violin Sonata, the so-called *Kreutzer* Sonata. Though dedicated to Rodolphe Kreutzer, the eminent French violinist and composer, an incomplete manuscript, auctioned in 1965 and now in the Beethoven-Haus, Bonn, bears the heading 'Sonata mulattica Composta per il Mulatto Brischdauer'. According to Bridgetower, an extraordinarily gifted player for whom Beethoven had a high regard, a quarrel over a girl prompted the re-dedication.

Following a few recuperative weeks at Baden, the summer was spent at Öberdöbling, in a house surrounded by vineyards in 'the street to the left where you go down the mountain to Heiligenstadt'. It was in this house that Beethoven spent the entire summer working on the symphony that was destined to become the *Eroica*. Together with the *Kreutzer* and *Christus* it was clearly the most substantial creative achievement of the year. Nothing else, even the not uninteresting sets of variations on *Rule Britannia* and *God Save the King* or a projected opera, *Vestas Feuer*, can begin to approach it.

George Augustus Polgreen Bridgetower (*c.* 1779-1860). Unsigned watercolour (William E. Hill & Sons, London)

The *Eroica*, then the largest symphony ever written and easily the first great symphony of the 19th century, was completed in score by the spring of 1804. The well-known story about its inspiration and original dedication is found in Ries's *Notizen:*

In this symphony Beethoven had Buonaparte in his mind, but as he was when he was First Consul. Beethoven esteemed him greatly at the time and

Manuscript for introduction to first movement of the "Kreutzer" Sonata

Manuscript for beginning of first movement and last page of the "Waldstein" Sonata

> likened him to the great Roman Consuls. I, as well as several of his more intimate friends, saw a copy of the score lying upon his table with the word 'Buonaparte' at the extreme top of the title page, and at the extreme bottom 'Luigi van Beethoven', but not another word. Whether, and with what the space between was to be filled out, I do not know. I was the first to bring him the intelligence that Buonaparte had proclaimed himself Emperor, whereupon he flew into a rage and cried out: 'Is he then, too, nothing more than an ordinary human being? Now he, too, will trample on all the rights of man and indulge only his ambition. He will exalt himself above all others, become a tyrant!' Beethoven went to the table, took hold of the title page by the top, tore it in two and threw it on the floor. The first page was rewritten and only then did the symphony receive the title: *Sinfonia eroica*.

The first published edition (October 1806) appeared with a dedication to Prince Franz Joseph von Lobkowitz and the telling words, 'To celebrate the memory of a great man'.

Apart from the *Eroica*, 1804 was a year notable, too, for the completion of the C major Triple Concerto for piano, violin, cello and orchestra (the concept of which had been contemplated in the form of a Sinfonia Concertante in D major as early as the first months of 1802), and the grandiose C major Piano Sonata, Op 53, dedicated to Beethoven's friend of the later Bonn years, Count Waldstein. The sketchbooks, also reveal the gradual birth of another opera — this time *Fidelio*.

A further work in gestation was the F minor Piano Sonata, Op 57, the so-called *Appassionata*. Ries says that during the summer of that year he and Beethoven went on a long walk during

The corrected title page of the *Eroica* with emendations in Beethoven's hand (Gesellschaft der Musikfreunde, Vienna)

Beethoven's Érard piano of 1803, a picture that shows clearly its extended compass and pedal options (Kunsthistorisches Museum, Vienna)

which we went so far astray that we did not get back to Döbling, where Beethoven lived, until nearly 8 o'clock, he had been all the time humming and sometimes howling, always up and down, without singing any definite notes. In answer to my question what it was he said: 'A theme for the last movement of the sonata has occurred to me' . . . When we entered the room he ran to the pianoforte without taking off his hat. I took a seat in the corner and he soon forgot all about me. Now he stormed for at least an hour with the beautiful finale of the sonata. Finally he got up, was surprised still to see me and said: 'I cannot give you a lesson today, I must do some more work.'

The publications of the year included the *Prometheus* Overture, the Second Symphony and (in the summer) the Third Piano Concerto, dedicated to Prince Louis Ferdinand of Prussia, himself a composer of no mean ability. By then Beethoven had already received from Érard in Paris a new piano (sent to him as a gift some time in August or September 1803) which featured an increased compass beyond the customary five octave keyboard range of the period: the extended range of the piano writing in the published edition of the concerto almost certainly reflects the advantages of this new development. Ries played it at an Augarten Thursday concert on 19 July 1804:

Beethoven had given me his beautiful Concerto in C minor (Op 37) in manuscript so that I might make my first public appearance *as his pupil* with it; and I am the only one who ever appeared as such while Beethoven was alive . . . Beethoven himself conducted, but he only turned the pages and never, perhaps, was a concerto more beautifully accompanied. We had two large rehearsals. I had asked Beethoven to write a cadenza for me, but he refused and told me to write one myself and he would correct it. Beethoven was satisfied with my composition and made few changes; but there was an extremely brilliant and very difficult passage in it, which, though he liked it, seemed to him too venturesome, wherefore he told me to write another in its place. A week before the concert he wanted to hear the cadenza again. I played it and floundered in the passage; he again, this time a little ill-naturedly, told me to change it. I did so, but the new passage did not satisfy me; I therefore studied the other, and zealously, but was not quite sure of it. When the cadenza was reached in the public concert Beethoven quietly sat down. I could not persuade myself to choose the easier one. When I boldly began the more difficult one, Beethoven violently jerked his chair; but the cadenza went through all right and Beethoven was so delighted that he shouted 'Bravo!' loudly. This electrified the entire audience and at once gave me a standing among the artists. Afterwards, while expressing his satisfaction he added: 'But all the same you are wilful! If you had made a slip in the passage I would never have given you another lesson.'

Beethoven. A miniature on ivory by C. Horneman, 1803, sent by the composer to his friend Stephan von Breuning as a peace offering after an argument

By the end of 1804, with his music widely known and performed throughout Europe and with a reputation that extended from St. Petersburg to Paris and Edinburgh, Beethoven, it is clear, enjoyed an especially privileged position, confirmed by the publication, in the *Wiener Zeitung* of 30 January 1805, of a complete classified catalogue of his works, an event unparalleled in the Austro-German press for the period. As Thayer puts it:

Beethoven . . . though almost unknown personally beyond the limits of a few Austrian cities — unaided by apostles to preach his gospel, owning nothing to journalist or pamphleteer, disdaining, in fact, all the arts by which dazzling but mediocre talent pushes itself into notoriety — had, in the short space of eight years, by simple force of his genius as manifested in his published works, placed himself at the head of all writers for the pianoforte, and in public estimation had risen to the level of the two greatest of orchestral composers. The unknown student that entered Vienna in 1792 was now in 1804 a recognized member of the great triumvirate, Haydn, Mozart and Beethoven.

Chapter 8

Hero and Heroine

'*I shall never crawl* — My world is the universe' — Beethoven

The winter of 1804-05 witnessed the first semi-public performance of the *Eroica*, given at one of the Sunday morning invitation concerts organised by the bankers Würth and Fellner. The *Allgemeine Musikalische Zeitung* (13 February 1805) reported:

This long composition extremely difficult of performance, is in reality a tremendously expanded, daring and wild fantasia. It lacks nothing in the way of startling and beautiful passages, in which the energetic and talented composer must be recognised; but often it loses itself in lawlessness. The symphony begins with an *Allegro* in E flat that is vigorously scored; a Funeral March in C minor follows which is later developed fugally. After this comes an *Allegro* scherzo and a Finale, both in E flat. The reviewer belongs to Herr van Beethoven's sincerest admirers, but in this composition he must confess that he finds too much that is glaring and bizarre, which hinders greatly one's grasp of the whole, and a sense of unity is almost completely lost.

Beethoven: 'For anyone who can survey [those] campaigns of the soul from which stand out the victories of the *Eroica* and the *Appassionata*, the most striking thing is not the vastness of the armies, the floods of tone, the masses flung into the assault, but the spirit in command, the imperial reason' (Rolland). A stylised portrait in oils by J.W. Mähler, *c.* 1804-05 (Historisches Museum Vienna)

The first public performance, conducted by Beethoven himself, took place shortly afterwards at the Theater an der Wien on the evening of Sunday 7 April. The *Allgemeine Musikalische Zeitung* still thought it would be 'better if it were shorter, and if the story will but stop!' According to his brother Carl, Beethoven himself actually 'thought at first that the Symphony would prove too long if the first part [the exposition] of the first movement was repeated, but then on repeated performance it was found that the omission of the repeat was harmful to the work'; and if the story is to be believed, at least one member of that privileged audience could not resist exclaiming, 'I'll give another kreutzer if the thing will but stop!'. The *Freymüthige* printed a valuable and observant review (26 April):

Beethoven's particular friends assert that it is just this symphony which is his masterpiece, that this is the true style for high-class music, and that if it does not please now, it is because the public is not cultured enough, artistically, to grasp all these lofty beauties; after a few thousand years have

Joseph Ferdinand von Sonnleithner (1776-1835), Court Secretary and editor of the *Court Calender*. Portrait in oils by A. Karner (Gesellschaft der Musikfreunde, Vienna)

passed it will not fail of its effect. Another faction denies that the work has any artistic value and professes to see in it an untamed striving for singularity which had failed, however, to achieve in any of its parts beauty or true sublimity and power. By means of strange modulations and violent transitions, by combining the most heterogeneous elements, as for instance when a pastoral in the largest style is ripped up by the basses, by three horns, etc., a certain undesirable originality may be achieved without much trouble; but genius proclaims itself not in the unusual and the fantastic but in the beautiful and the sublime. Beethoven himself proved the correctness of this axiom in his earlier works. The third party, a very small one, stands midway between the others — it admits that the symphony contains many beauties, but concedes that the connection is often disrupted entirely, and that the inordinate length of this longest, and perhaps most difficult of all symphonies wearies even the cognoscenti, and is unendurable to the mere music-lover; it wishes that H.v.B. would employ his acknowledgedly great talents in giving us works like his Symphonies in C and D, his ingratiating Septet in E flat, the intellectual Quintet in D [C major?] and others of his early compositions which have placed B. forever in the ranks of the foremost instrumental composers. It fears, however, that if Beethoven continues on his present path both he and the public will be the sufferers. His music could soon reach the point where one would derive no pleasure from it, unless well trained in the rules and difficulties of the art, but rather would leave the concert hall with an unpleasant feeling of fatigue from having been crushed by a mass of unconnected and overloaded ideas and a continuing tumult by all the instruments. The public and Herr van Beethoven, who conducted, were not satisfied with each other on this evening; the public thought the symphony too heavy, too long, and himself too discourteous because he did not nod his head in recognition of the applause which came from a portion of the audience. On the contrary, Beethoven found that the applause was not strong enough.

Thus the *Eroica*, that symphony of 'antique grief' that Berlioz found 'so spirited and at the same time noble in style', that work which Wagner felt charted some fateful 'progress towards fulfilment', was consecrated in performance.

* * *

The most dramatically significant event of 1805, however, was less the first public performance of the *Eroica* than the première of the opera *Fidelio,* given at the Theater an der Wien on 20 November under the direction of Seyfried. *Fidelio* had been commissioned by the theatre and the so-called *Leonore* sketchbooks in the Berlin State Library show that Beethoven devoted most of 1804 working on it, as well as the bulk of 1805, including the summer months spent at Hetzendorf.

Fidelio was based on a three-act libretto by Joseph Ferdinand von Sonnleithner adapted from a French original by Bouilly — *Léonore, ou l'amour conjugal.* Bouilly tells us in his *Memoirs* (Paris 1836-37) that his stories all derived from real events in which he himself had been involved in some capacity or other. In the case of *Fidelio*, the inspiration was initially the heroic self sacrifice and the devoted loyalty of a wife to save her husband from the guillotine. Bouilly's story not only achieved popularity, it established his fame, and it caught the imagination of composers who saw in it likely material for operatic development. Gaveaux was the first to set it as an opera — staged in Paris in 1798. Paër's version then followed in Dresden in 1804, and Mayr's in Padua in 1805. Of these, Paër's *Léonore* provided, in at least some respects, a model for Beethoven's own attempt (a vocal score of it in Beethoven's possession was auctioned after his death). So too did Gaveaux's, and it seems that Beethoven also gained traceable inspiration (to the extent of arguable plagiarism) from Cherubini (whom he met for the first time in July 1805) and Méhul, both operatic and stage masters who 'fascinated' him. It is not irrelevant to note that Cherubini's successful *Lodoïska*, a 'rescue' opera like *Fidelio*, had been given at the Theater an der Wien in March 1803, while Méhul's particularly striking and dramatically original *Ariodante* was later produced there in February 1804. Beethoven, a lover of opera since his Bonn days and an avid opera-goer in the first decade of his Vienna period, must have rejoiced in the opportunity to get to know such works at first hand. Yet another influence could have been Gluck: Beethoven played part of *Iphigenia in Tauris* to French officers during the occupation of Vienna at the end of 1805.

Fidelio has been described as the greatest of all the 'Terror' or 'Rescue' operas written in that twenty or so year period which followed the performance of Berton's *Les Rigueurs du Cloître* in Paris in 1790, often regarded as the first genuine example of the genre. In his adaptation, Sonnleithner acknowledged much of the essence of Bouilly's story, though in view of the censor he found it politely prudent to shift the scene from France and the Revolution to Spain and the 16th century. The chief *dramatis personae* comprise Florestan, a fighter of tyranny who has been imprisoned, and his wife, Leonore, who plans to rescue him. Disguised as a boy, 'Fidelio', she goes to the prison as an assistant to the jailor, Rocco. Pizarro, the governor, decides in the meantime to kill Florestan, his political opponent. Rocco and Leonore go to the dungeon where Florestan is chained and prepare to dig his grave. Pizarro attempts to kill Florestan but Leonore prevents him at pistol point — a hair-breadth scene straight from the Reign of Terror. Distant trumpets signal the arrival of the inspecting minister. The prisoners are released, Pizarro is arrested, and Leonore frees her Florestan.

Superficially, the story presented Beethoven with a fashionable theme of current topicality and theatrical potential which fitted in well with the innumerable French post-Revolutionary operas that were then the rage in Vienna. But in reality it meant much more to him. Just as in the vineyards of Öberdöbling, he had enshrined his ideal hero in the *Eroica*, so in the Schönbrunn woods Leonore became his ideal heroine, his ideal woman full of lofty sentiments and humanitarian principles. For Beethoven, Lessing's assertion, 'Nature meant woman to be her masterpiece', was a very real philosophy and in the morality of Leonore he found its pedestalled embodiment.

The production of *Fidelio* (a title insisted on by the authorities — Beethoven always wanted *Leonore*) was anticipated by months of increasing tension as the war with Napoleon escalated. A remarkably observant *Diary* kept by Joseph Carl Rosenbaum (the manuscript of which is in the Austrian National Library) reveals the atmosphere in the Viennese capital in particularly vivid terms. As early as July the city was already tense. Here Rosenbaum sums up three days, from Sunday the 7th to Tuesday the 9th:

Sunday, July 7th. We came to the bakery 'At the Peacock'. The whole shop and all the rooms were robbed clean . . . The mob had broken the fence, the iron gate, the house door and the inner door . . . The riot was started by a baker's wife refusing to sell to a young apprentice a groschen worth of bread while she still had some. The tumult began at five o'clock and lasted the whole night through . . . The Court is in Baden. The news won't be exactly pleasant to them.

Monday, July 8th. A bunch of demonstrators came along, boys carrying whole bags full of bread. Others carried clubs and bedslats. As soon as we arrived the grenadiers began to shoot . . . Some rowdies took a baker's stick with a rag of linen and used it as a flag. Another an old drum. They proceeded furiously to pelt the soldiers with a hail of stones. A cavalryman split the head of the flag carrier, another slashed the armpit of the drummer, a grenadier plunged his bayonet into his body. Then the grenadiers had to seek refuge in the Cadet-School. They closed the door, the mob threw stones and threatened to force the doors. The grenadiers fired on the people from the windows. More than a hundred were injured or killed.

Tuesday, the 9th. Soldiers are quartered in all the suburbs. War preparations. Hordes of demonstrators are rounded up. The order is that at nine o'clock all houses in the suburbs are to be locked and all inns cleared out.

The arrival of the French in Vienna, 1805 (Osterreiche National-bibliothek, Vienna). 'As long as the Austrian still has brown beer and sausages,' Beethoven once mused, 'he will never revolt.'

At Ulm on 20 October the Russians conceded defeat to the French. Ten days later, Bernadotte and the French army entered Salzburg. Rosenbaum chronicled the scene in Vienna:

Monday, November 4th. Every moment one sees baggage and travel-carriages passing. In the afternoon I went with TH[erese] to the Danube. We saw the possessions of the Court [being shipped off] . . . The Court is sending everything away, even bedwarmers and shoetrees. It looks as if they have no intention of ever coming back to Vienna.

Wednesday the 6th. After lunch Eppinger came with the devastating news that the Russians have retreated as far as St. Pölten. Vienna is in great danger of being swept over by marauding Chasseurs . . .

Poster announcing the first performance of *Fidelio*, 20 November 1805

On the Josephsplatz 100 horses were standing, ready to be hitched to transport carriages . . . [The carriages] are loaded with kegs of gold, the Treasury, Medallion and Natural History Collections, Silver, Linen etc. Many people gathered who resented this removal of all movable objects . .

Sunday the 10th. All three Tabor Bridges will be burned. Ships loaded with firewood are placed under their vaults . . . Wrbna summoned the entire magistracy to City Hall and announced: His Majesty has determined not to permit a single shot to be fired on the city and therefore has sent a deputation to the enemy to negotiate the question of how Vienna can be spared. His Majesty expects, however, that all citizens of Vienna will avoid excesses and behave in a quiet and friendly manner.

Wednesday the 13th. At half past eleven a mass of people pressed through the portals of the Burg. Everybody screamed 'The French are coming'. The cavalry was in the vanguard. Some of them had beards like Jews. In their midst rode Prince Murat, surrounded by generals, a tall, strong, handsome man . . . The infantry looked very sloppy, not uniformed alike. One wore a hat, another a cap, a shako, one a silk scarf, another mousseline cloth, boots, shoes, slippers, linens, Manchester trousers; everything topsy-turvy. The troops look quite wild. Nothing is known of our army. They have retreated far from Spitz. The French are the masters of the whole region.

Friday the 15th. Nothing is to be found in the market. Yesterday a pound of butter cost two, even three florins. Nobody dares to bring anything here because they [the French] take everything; even the horses are unharnessed . . . On the Laimgrube at noon a French soldier who had torn shoes grabbed an apprentice and wanted to take his boots by force. When he struggled, the soldier hit him in the mouth with his sword and cleaved his mouth. Then our people came running to help the boy, disarmed the Frenchman, and took him to the next guard-station . . . Women are hardly to be seen in the theatres, except the whores.

Sunday the 17th. Every day the Magistrate has to deliver 50,000 measures of bread, meat, wine, grain and hay. Everybody is scared of famine. The burden of the billeting is unbelievable . . . In an Extra Edition I read that Tirol has been conquered. Archduke Johann has fled into the mountains, and Prince Carl in Italy has retreated. Terrible loss!

Georg Friedrich Treitschke (1776-1842). Lithograph by J. Kriehuber, 1830

Three days later, on the 20th, in the midst of occupation and pandemonium, and with General Hulin, the French Commanding General of Vienna esconced in the Palace of Beethoven's patron, Prince Lobkowitz, the Theater an der Wien bravely opened its doors to anyone inclined to come and hear the latest fruit of Beethoven's muse. Rosenbaum says that for him it 'contained beautiful, artful, heavy music, a boring, uninteresting book. It had no success and the theatre was empty'. In the *Freymüthige* for 26 December, the review was similarly dismissive, overshadowed as it was by an account of other, more immediate, activity in the city.

With most of Beethoven's friends and patrons away, with rehearsals troubled by intrigue and argument, and with very little to encourage attendance, *Fidelio* ran for a further two performances on November 21 and 22. It was then withdrawn. Days later at the beginning of December, the Battle of Austerlitz robbed of life nearly 30,000 Austrians and Russian in the field. The Emperor Franz called for an armistice, and 'that bastard' Napoleon (as Beethoven was to describe him) returned to Vienna. A peace treaty was signed on the 26th, and Napoleon left the capital on the 28th: relative peace returned.

By then Beethoven had had an important meeting with Prince Lichnowsky and his wife, his brother Carl, Stephan von Breuning, the poet Heinrich von Collin, the actor Lange, Georg Friedrich Treitschke, stage manager of the Court Opera, Franz Clement, leader of the orchestra, and others. At this meeting it was decided to revise and shorten *Fidelio*. Von Breuning was entrusted with remodelling Sonnleithner's libretto, transposing some scenes, altering passages in the text, and reducing the three acts to two. The original overture (*Leonore* No 2) was replaced with a new one (*Leonore* No 3) conceived on an even grander symphonic scale that distilled the essence of the opera into a kind of tone-poem, but which was still far from satisfactory as a *theatrical* curtain-raiser*. In spite of this the opera was markedly improved and in this form was given its first performance at the Theater an der Wien on Saturday 29 March 1806, with a repeat performance on 10 April. It had, however, been staged again in some hurry, and while the public liked it better, Beethoven was increasingly dissatisfied. To Friedrich Sebastian Mayer, creator of Pizarro's rôle, Beethoven wrote:

> Baron Braun informs me that *my opera* is to be performed on *Thursday*. When I see you I will tell you why — But I do earnestly beseech you to see that the choruses are still better rehearsed, for the last time they made *dreadful* mistakes. Furthermore, on *Thursday* we must have one more rehearsal with *full orchestra in the theatre* — True, the *orchestra* did not go wrong, but the *performers on the stage did several times* — Still, that was to be expected, for the time was too short.

Further performances in the 1806 season seem to have been expected. But they were not forthcoming. The owner of the theatre, the Baron Peter von Braun, sometime associate, but a distrusted figure in Viennese theatrical circles, had aroused Beethoven's anger. Joseph August Röckel, the new Florestan, remembered the scene:

* *Leonore* No 1, published in 1838, was discarded at the rehearsal stage from the original 1805 production.

While I accidentally chanced to be waiting in the anteroom to the Baron's business office, I heard a violent altercation which the financier was carrying on with the enraged composer in the adjoining room. Beethoven was suspicious and thought that his percentage of the net proceeds was greater than the amount which the Court Banker, who was at the same time director of the Theater an der Wien, had paid him. The latter remarked that Beethoven was the first composer with whom the management, in view of his extraordinary merits, had been willing to share profits, and explained the paucity of the box-office returns by the fact that the boxes and front row seats all had been taken, but that the seats in which the thickly-crowded mass of the people would have yielded a return as when Mozart's operas were given, were empty. And he emphasized that hitherto Beethoven's music had been accepted only by the more cultured classes, while Mozart with his operas invariably had roused enthusiasm in the multitude, the people as a whole. Beethoven hurried up and down the room in agitation, shouting loudly: 'I do not write for the multitude — I write for the cultured!'

'But the cultured alone do not fill our theatre', replied the Baron with the greatest calmness, 'we need the multitude to bring in money, and since in your music you have refused to make any concessions to it, you yourself are to blame for your diminished percentage of return. If we had given Mozart the same interest in the receipts of his operas, he would have grown rich'.

This disadvantageous comparison with his famous predecessor seemed to wound Beethoven's tenderest susceptibilities. Without replying to it with a single word, he leaped up and shouted in the greatest rage: 'Give me back my score!'

The Baron hesitated and stared as through struck by lightning at the enraged composer's glowing face, while the latter, in an accent of the most strenuous passion repeated: 'I want my score — my score, at once!'

The Baron pulled the bell-rope; a servant entered.

'Bring the score of yesterday's opera for this gentleman', said the Baron with an air; and the servant hastened to return with it. 'I am sorry', the aristocrat continued, 'But I believe that on calmer reflection — '. Yet Beethoven no longer heard what he was saying. He had torn the gigantic volume of the score from the servant's hand and, without even seeing me in his eagerness, ran through the anteroom and down the stairs.

For the time being that was the end of *Fidelio*. In spite of various plans, it was not to be revived again until 1814.

Chapter 9
Passions and Enigmas

'There was never a time when Beethoven was not in love, and that in the highest degree' — Wegeler

If *Fidelio* enshrined something of Beethoven's dream of the ideal woman as a youthful creature of unsullied beauty, of morality, and of virtue, high-minded principle and philosophical spirituality, the reality of life held rather different prospects in store for him. Many women, great and forgotten, were to cross his path, were, for a moment in time, to become entwined in the course of his destiny, but none, it seems ever quite came up to his expectations. When they did in some respect or other, his tendency was to raise mentally another obstacle, at once to retreat into that secretive, elusive, private world of his own, into the safe domain of the mind in which the visions of his imagination and his spiritual longing could still continue to remain untarnished by what he thought to be the less exultant experiences of earthly, fleshly contact.

Nonetheless his need and capacity for the physical act of love was something from which he could not escape. But he did not like himself for it. In his late years he remarked to Karl Holz, with whom he was on intimate terms, that he always regretted when his better nature succumbed to the 'miserable necessity' of his body. For Beethoven love had to be on a higher plane: an entry in one of his journals reads that 'sensual pleasure without unity of souls is and remains bestial; after it there remains no trace of noble sentiment, regret only'. Yet physical demands continued to consume him. A fragment of a letter from Josephine Deym, *née* Brunsvik, the great love of Beethoven's life around the years 1804-1806 (the period of the *Eroica, Fidelio,* the *Appassionata* and the lyrical ecstacy of the Fourth Symphony, the Fourth Piano Concerto and the Violin Concerto), says: 'the distinction you bestowed on me, the pleasure of your company, could have been the greater adornment of my life if you could love me in a less sensual way — Because I cannot satisfy this sensual love — you are angry with me — I would have to tear holy bonds if I acceded to your desire. . .'

Beethoven's attitude towards women was determined, ostensibly anyway, by clear-cut philosophies: 'One of my chief principles', he wrote to Marie Bigot in March 1807, is '*never to be in any other relationship than that of friendship with the wife of another man. For I should not wish by forming any other kind of relationship to fill my heart with distrust of that woman who some day will perhaps share my fate* — and thus by my own action to destroy the loveliest and purest relationship'. Such attitude of mind can be seen further in Beethoven's very literal disgust for women with lesser ideals than himself. Later in life he was to abhor the wives of his two brothers because they followed a loose moral code. He had little time, too, for the whores of Vienna who used to so amuse and entertain his friends. 'Be on your guard against the whole tribe of bad women', he wrote to Johann on 19 February 1796 — he was still only twenty-five. Yet, paradoxically, he seems at the same time to have been fascinated by the corruption of morality — in a furtive kind of way. What, one wonders, were his thoughts in this scene of the last years that Grillparzer described:

Opposite my grandmother's windows stood the dilapidated house of a peasant named Flohberger, notorious for his profligate life. Besides his nasty house, Flohberger also possessed a pretty daughter, Lise, who had none too good a reputation. Beethoven seemed to take a great interest in this girl. I can still see him, striding up the Hirschgasse, his white handerchief dragging along the ground in his right hand, stopping at Flohberger's courtyard gate, within which the giddy fair, standing on a hay or manure-cart, would lustily wield her fork amid incessant laughter. I never noticed Beethoven spoke to her. He would merely stand there in silence, looking in, until at last the girl, whose taste ran more to peasant lads, roused his wrath either with some scornful word or by obstinately ignoring him. Then he would whip off with a swift turn yet would not neglect, however, to stop again at the gate of the court the next time.

Ferdinand Ries wrote that 'Beethoven loved to see women, particularly pretty youthful faces; and usually when we passed a reasonably charming girl on the street, he turned around, looked at her sharply through his glasses, and laughed or grimaced if he saw that I had observed him'. He contemplated marriage on several occasions. 'Now you can help me to look for a wife', he writes humorously to the Baron Ignaz von Gleichenstein in March 1809: 'Indeed you might find some beautiful girl at F[reiburg] where you are at present, and one who would perhaps now and then grant a sigh to my harmonies . . . But she must be beautiful, for it is impossible for me to love anything that is not beautiful — or else I should have to love myself'. His feelings on the subject, however, remained mixed. He told Nanni Giannatasio del Rio that he knew 'of no marriage in which one or the other did not regret the step after a time and that he was glad that none of the few women whose capture he might once have considered the greatest bliss became his wife: it was good that mortal wishes often remained unfulfilled.'

To go through Beethoven's letters and various other documents that have come down to us is to witness curious, often irrational kaleidoscopic shifts of mood and emotional response. Sometimes, one thinks, he was only ever in love with the *idea* of love, that he lived in a dream-world, that deep down he was a confirmed bachelor, that early on perhaps he had had a repelling experience. In his maturity his character seems to have developed a dominating element of almost Svengali-like implication. His women were very often little more than girls, years younger than himself, impressionable, and of an intellectual ability that for the most part remained agreeable rather than challenging. In his later years Beethoven was in search of neither challenges nor arguments — he had enough of his own to contend with.

Then one becomes conscious of an element motivating him in his quests of the heart that seems to have been almost willfully doomed to self-destruction. 'So far as I know', Wegeler believed, 'every one of his sweethearts belonged to the higher social stations'. Considering the circle that Beethoven moved in this was not surprising: beyond the realm of art the class distinctions of the day, however, made the fulfilment of any long-term relationship ultimately impossible if the woman herself wanted to retain a status and position in Habsburg society — even if her lover *was* Beethoven. As Marek puts it, 'the women Beethoven knew were not women who would proclaim a passion publicly'. Elsewhere Marek says that

> 'Uncertainty' is the word to describe Beethoven's search for love. That proud heart needed love, needed it very much, and sought it often. But when he did find it, he sooner or later turned away as if in fear. He could not bind himself. It was not the practical difficulties, not the social status of the woman, not his deafness, his illness, nor his disorderly household which wholly prevented lasting attachments or marriage plans; but an inner hesitancy, as if he were loath to give love house-room in his heart, letting it share the lodging with music. Perhaps he never found the right woman. More likely he subsonsciously did not want to find her. He flamed high, but the flames died down quickly.

In 1814 Alois Weissenbach, a surgeon, dilletante and would-be-author, said that 'As to the sin of lust — [Beethoven] is unspotted'. Nine years later a young writer, Johann Chrysostomus Sporschil, claimed that 'towards women [Beethoven] harbours a tender respect, and his feelings for them are of virginal purity'. Nine years again

Beethoven: 'I need a text which stimulates me; it must be something moral, uplifting. Texts such as Mozart composed I should never have been able to set to music. I could never have got myself into a mood for licentious texts'. Portrait in oils by I. Neugass, *c.* 1806

after that, Seyfried came up with the categoric statement that Beethoven 'never had a love affair'. In the light of both direct and circumstantial evidence we know how much value can now be attributed to these opinions. Their significance nevertheless remains undiminished for what they can tell us about how closely Beethoven guarded his personal emotions and how his affairs were very much a matter of private rather than public concern.

Of all the women in Beethoven's life — and he was 'generally involved in one entanglement or the other' up to around 1820-21, when he was fifty — several of particular importance stands out. Countess Giulietta Guicciardi (1784-1856) was the first. She was related to the Brunsvik family, married Count Wenzel Robert Gallenberg in 1803, and subsequently went to live in Naples. Beethoven became involved in 1801 and dedicated the so-called *Moonlight* Sonata to her. His letter to Wegeler of 16 November 1801 is believed to contain a significant but characteristically veiled reference to her:

> This change has been brought about by a dear charming girl who loves me and whom I love. After two years I am again enjoying a few blissful moments; and for the first time I feel that — marriage might bring me happiness. Unfortunately she is not of my class — and at the moment — I certainly could not marry — I must still bustle about a good deal.

It does seem nevertheless that Beethoven did actually offer her marriage and that she was prepared to accept but that her father opposed the match on the grounds that Beethoven was 'without rank, fortune, or permanent engagement'. Beethoven kept an ivory miniature of her in his desk, and in one of the conversation books for 1823 (at which time she and her husband were on a visit to Vienna) we find him saying to Schindler: 'She loved me much more than she ever did her husband. However, he was her lover more than I was'.

Then there was Therese (1775-1861) and Josephine (1779-1821) Brunsvik. The Brunsviks were one of the noted aristocratic land-owning families of Hungary and Beethoven was closely associated with them. Therese never married, Josephine did — firstly to Count Joseph Deym, a man nearly thirty years older than herself who died in 1804, and then, in 1810, to Baron Christoph von Stackelberg. Both sisters played the piano and were intensely musical: Beethoven wrote his *Ich denke dein* duet variations for them, and in 1809 dedicated the Op 78 Piano Sonata to Therese. She was clearly very attracted and gave him her portrait inscribed with the words 'To the rare genius, the great artist, the good human being, from T.B.' He kept it in a secret drawer of his writing bureau. A story that he proposed to her by moonlight in May 1806 is however, almost certainly apocryphal.

The years 1804-06 saw rather a blossoming of Beethoven's love for her sister. She had married Count Deym against her wishes, he 'detested music', and she had got into financial difficulties. Widowed in January 1804, she renewed her friendship with Beethoven in the summer of that year. He enjoyed her company,

Countess Guilietta Guicciardi (1784-1856). Miniature on ivory (Bodmer Collection, Beethoven-Haus, Bonn)

Countess Therese Brunsvik (1775-1861). Oil copy after J.B. Lampi the Elder (Beethoven-Haus, Bonn)

and gave her free lessons. By the spring of 1805 his feelings for her were clearly reaching a peak:

Oh, Beloved J[osephine], it is no desire for the other sex that draws me to you, no, *it is just you, your whole self* with all your individual qualities — this has compelled my regard — this has bound all my feelings — all my emotional power to you — When I came to you — it was with the firm resolve not to let a single spark of love be kindled in me. But you have conquered me — The question is, whether *you wanted to do so?* or whether *you did not want to do so?* — No doubt J[osephine] could answer that question for me sometime — Dear God, there are so many more things I should love to tell you — how much I think of you — what I feel for you — but how weak and poor are those words — at any rate, my words.

Long — Long — of long duration — may our love become — For it is so noble — so firmly founded upon mutual regard and friendship — Even the great similarity between us in so many respects, in our thought and feelings — Oh you, you make me hope that *your heart* will long — beat for me — *Mine* can only — cease — to beat for you — when — *it no longer beats.*

Untended, the passion died and by the autumn of 1807 we find Beethoven writing to her that 'it is better for your peace of mind and mine not to see you'. A decade later Therese wrote wistfully in her *Diary*: 'I wonder if J[osephine] does not suffer punishment because of Luigi's hurt! His wife — what could she not have made out of this hero!' Years later on 4 February 1846 she says:

Speech is silver, but silence, silence at the right time, is pure gold. This beautiful proverb was set to music by Beethoven [in 1815]. Beethoven! It is like a dream that he was the friend, the confidant of our house — a magnificent spirit! Why didn't my sister J take him as her husband when she was the widow Deym? She would have been happier with him than with S[tackelberg]. Mother-love decided her to renounce her own happiness.

Then in 1848 she can only think of Josephine and Beethoven as having been 'born for each other'.

The Countess Anna Marie Erdödy (1779-1837), again from a distinguished Austro-Hungarian line, was a fine pianist, an admirer of Beethoven's work, and another devoted friend. Married to a Hungarian in 1796, she settled in Croatia in 1815 and seems to have left Austria itself sometime after 1820. Beethoven had rooms in her apartment in the autumn and winter of 1808-09, and was on close terms with her for about ten years from 1807 to 1817. Marek finds Erdödy 'the most enigmatic, the least decipherable' woman that Beethoven knew. No letters from her survive, no diary, merely contradictory reports and the scandal of an unproven crime (that of allegedly having a hand in the killing of her son). Like many other

Hungarian aristocrats, she was in the end a victim of the police-state that Austria was to become under Metternich.

Less tragic than the Brunsviks and less disturbing than the Countess Erdödy, was the bizarre German-Italian figure of Bettina Brentano (1785-1859), that gushingly expressive, well-proportioned, dark-eyed, over-imaginative friend of Goethe's who was more than given to exaggeration and lies, and who *seems* to have been besotted with Beethoven in the period 1810-12. The poet Varnhagen wrote of her in his *Diary:*

Countess Josephine Deym, *née* Brunsvik (1779-1821). Anonymous miniature (Count Joseph Deym)

> If I didn't resist, Bettina would turn me entirely into her slave; it is incredible how she captures and spins her web around people . . . She makes you feel that you have nothing more important to do than to please her. . . She always wants something from the man who is with her, she wants to admire him and use him and tease him, or be admired, used, teased by him.

After Beethoven's death, Bettina published three letters purporting have been sent to her by him. Of them, the only genuine one is probably the second, dated 10 February 1811, for which an autograph survives. A light-hearted document ('I did not get home until four o'clock this morning from a bacchanalia, when I really had to laught a great deal, with the result that today I have had to cry as heartily'), it suggests that Beethoven saw through the flippancy of Bettina. If attracted to her for a time, it seems unlikely that he had the same kind of deep feelings that he had for Josephine Brunsvik.

Count Joseph Deym (1752-1804). Anonymous miniature (Count Joseph Deym)

Therese Malfatti (1792-1851) was the niece of Johann Malfatti who founded the Vienna Medical Society and who was to attend Beethoven in his last illness. Therese and her sister Anna were thought by the striking Antonie Adamberger (who played the part of Klärchen in the 1810 Vienna production of *Egmont* with Beethoven's music) to be 'the two most beautiful girls in Vienna'. Beethoven fell for the eighteen-year-old Therese with her brunette locks, her dark eyes, and determined temperament, and suddently began to take notice of his appearance and his wardrobe. Bengal cotton shirts and clothes from the best tailor in Vienna were ordered. Wegeler was asked to obtain his baptismal certificate from Bonn. Hot-headedly, marriage was suddently contemplated again. Marion Scott, who always had sympathy for Therese *Brunsvik*, has written of Beethoven's eventual humiliation:

> His infatuation for the young minx was absolutely foolish; her family were furious, and she, after playing with him, turned down his proposal of marriage. Therese Malfatti, without meaning it, revenged Therese von Brunsvik.

Galerie Müller, 'am Rothen Turm', near the Danube. A popular meeting place for artists, The Brunsvik sisters ran it together after 1804

Another romance of a superficial nature followed with Amalie Sebald (1787-1846), a singer whom Beethoven met at Teplitz in 1811. Possibly more substantial was a long relationship with Dorothea von Ertmann (1781-1849), who married an Austrian army officer in 1798, and who began taking piano lessons from Beethoven five years later. She became one of the most famous pianists of her time, and was a powerfully distinguished interpreter of Beethoven's piano works. The big A major Sonata, Op 101 was dedicated to her in 1815-16. Towards the end of her life she remembered that

During a long series of years, Beethoven was a daily guest in our house. Often he would complain that he had no appetite at all; then he would suddenly remember that he had already partaken of an excellent meal. Other times he forgot, though plagued by bitter hunger, that in his peregrinations of many hours, he had partaken of no nourishment whatever. He was very irritable, very jumpy, very sensitive and therefore often unjust to and suspicious of his best friends. But who could have been angry with the unfortunate man and his everincreasing deafness? One had to remember his physical and moral suffering and forgive everything. Thus did we live for many years in unclouded friendship.

Countess Anna Marie Erdödy (1779-1837), Beethoven's 'father confessor'. Miniature on ivory (Bodmer Collection, Beethoven-Haus, Bonn)

Dorothea's relationship with Beethoven seems to have been entirely platonic, a warm genuine association. Marek, however, has put her forward as a possible candidate for the 'Immortal Beloved' letter than Beethoven wrote in 1812. The evidence he offers is plausible enough to add a completely new dimension to the story of this famous, much discussed document. Whether it can be entirely proved, however, still remains in doubt. The 'Immortal Beloved'

letter, found in that same secret drawer of Beethoven's bureau that contained the portrait of Therese Brunsvik, was unaddressed, partially undated, and possibly never even sent to its intended recipient. If indeed it was never sent, Marek asks interestingly, was Beethoven perhaps in an excess of emotion motivated to write it 'by the same sort of self-confessing impulse that made him write and then preserve the Heiligenstadt Testament?' The autograph, now in the Deutsche Staatsbibliothek, Berlin, covers the twenty-four hours from the morning of Monday 6 July to the morning of Tuesday 7 July. It begins, 'My Angel, my all, my very self'. It ends, 'Be calm; for only by calmly considering our lives can we achieve our purpose to live together — Be calm — love me — Today — yesterday — what tearful longing for you — for you — you — my life — my all — all good wishes to you — Oh, do continue to love me — never misjudge your lover's most faithful heart. Ever yours, ever mine, ever ours'. In between are such lines as 'Love demands all, and rightly so', 'To face life I must live altogether with you or never see you', 'You will become composed, the more so as you know that I am faithful you you; no other woman can ever possess my heart — never — never — Oh God, why must one be separated from her who is so dear'. Elsewhere he overflows with this intense torrent of passionate declamation:

Interior of the Burgtheater. Anonymous coloured engraving

Dorothea, Baroness von Ertmann, *née* Graumann (1781-1849). Miniature on ivory by J. D. Oechs

What a life!!!! as it is now!!!! without you — pursued by the kindness of people here and there, a kindness that I think — that I wish to deserve just as little as I deserve it — man's homage to man — that pains me — and when I consider myself in the setting of the universe, what am I and what is that man — whom one calls the greatest of men — and yet — on the other hand therein lies the divine element in man — I weep when I think that probably you will not receive the first news of me until Saturday — However much you love me — my love for you is even greater — but never conceal yourself from me.

Besides Dorothea von Ertmann, candidates for this letter have included several of the other women we have mentioned, as well as a few more. No doubt the controversy, begun by Schindler who favoured Giulietta Giucciardi, will continue. Suffice to note that in his revision of Thayer, Elliot Forbes concludes categorically that no success 'can be claimed for the question of the identity of the intended recipient of this letter. There is voluminous material on this subject, but no proof'.*

In her *Memoirs* (1857) Fanny Giannatasio del Rio said: 'My sister who had observed a gold ring on [Beethoven's] finger asked him jocularly whether he had any other loves than the *Distant Beloved*. He did not seem to have vouchsafed her any information'. Neither did he to anyone else. The enigma of his life, his great secret, went to the grave with him.

*Even Maynard Solomon, whose persuasively documented opinion that Antonie Brentano (the sister-in-law of Bettina and the future dedicatee of the *Diabelli* Variations) was the actual recipient—'the weight of the evidence in her favour is so powerful that it is not presumptuous to assert that the riddle of Beethoven's Immortal Beloved has now been solved'—has found wide acceptance in current academic circles, does not deny such a view: 'There is still room,' he says, 'for . . . *reasonable doubt*' in reaching any kind of positive identification (our italics; see the *New York Times*, 21 May 1972, and 'New Light on Beethoven's Letter to an Unknown Woman', *Musical Quarterly*, LVIII [1972]).

Chapter 10

'A pure romantic': 1806-08

'I do not like or want to have anything to do with people who refuse to believe in me because I have not yet achieved a wide fame for myself' — Beethoven

If 1805 had been a year of storms and epoch-making statements, of *Fidelio* and the completion of the Op 57 Piano Sonata, 1806 was a year of supremely lyrical outpouring and consolidation. The three great String Quartets, Op 59, the Fourth Piano Concerto, the Fourth Symphony, and the Violin Concerto were all finished in 1806, each a testament of supremacy in art that future generations, if not always Beethoven's contemporaries, were to recognise to the full.

The Quarters were commissioned by Count Andreas Kyrillowitsch Rasumowsky, the Russian ambassador to Vienna who had been one of the original subscribers to the Op 1 Piano Trios. Rasumowsky was a colourful character whose reputation in diplomatic circles had been achieved 'less through his skill in diplomacy than through his lavish expenditure and his love affairs with ladies of the highest standing, not excluding the Queen of Naples'. A contemporary reported that he 'lived in Vienna like a prince, encouraging art and science, surrounded by a luxurious library and other collections and admired and envied by all; what advantages accrued from all this to Russian affairs is another question'. His magnificent new palace near the Prater was to become a renowned centre of artistic activity, offering a platform to some of the most distinguished musicians of the day. Towards the end of 1808 he could afford to establish a private string quartet of his own, led by Schuppanzigh, by then one of Vienna's most renowned chamber musicians, and he enjoyed links with all the Viennese nobility, and especially with Karl Lichnowsky: he was married to Elizabeth, Countess Thun, the Prince's elder sister.

Count (later Prince) Andreas Kyrillowitsch Rasumowsky (1752-1836). Oil painting by J.B. Lampi the Elder (Historisches Museum, Vienna)

By way of acknowledging Rasumowsky's Russianness, Beethoven, according to Czerny, 'pledged himself to weave a Russian melody into every quartet'. At the time there was much interest in Vienna in Russian popular music, and several articles

Prince Karl Lichnowsky's castle at Grätz, near Troppau, as Beethoven knew it. Detail from an oil painting by F. Amerling

had been written on the subject. Whether Beethoven actually did incorporate such tunes into *every* quartet is however debatable. On their first performance they were accorded a particularly hostile reception. According to Czerny again, 'when Schuppanzigh first played the *Rasumowsky* Quartet in F[No 1], they laughed and were convinced that Beethoven was playing a joke and that it was not the quartet which had been promised'. Others found it 'crazy music'. The *Allgemeine Musikalische Zeitung* (27 February 1807) referred, on the other hand, to the fact that 'three new, very long and difficult Beethoven string quartets . . . are . . . attracting the attention of all connoisseurs. The conception is profound and the construction excellent, but they are not easily comprehended'. A later comment (5 May), says that 'In Vienna Beethoven's most recent, difficult but fine quartets have become more and more popular'. Not everyone, clearly, dismissed them without thought. The Bureau des Arts et d'Industrie published the set in January 1808.

A postscript to a letter sent to Breitkopf & Härtel on 3 September records that 'I am staying on here in Silesia as long as the autumn lasts — and at the resident of Prince Lichnowsky — who sends you his greetings — My address is: To L. v. Beethoven at Troppau —'. Beethoven in fact spent the September and October of 1806 at

Lichnowsky's country seat at Grätz, then an area still occupied by the French.

Theodor van Frimmel related how the stay ended on the authority of a grandson of Lichnowsky's personal physician, Anton Weiser:

In order to humour [the French officers], it was promised that after dinner they would have the pleasure of hearing the famous Beethoven, who was then a guest at the castle, play. 'They went to table; one of the French staff officers unhappily asked Beethoven if he also knew the violin.' Weiser, who was also at table, 'saw at once how this outraged the artist . . . Beethoven did not deign to answer his interlocutor.' Weiser could not attend the rest of the dinner since, as Director of the Troppau Hospital, he had to make a professional call there. He heard the rest of the story from Beethoven himself. When the time came for Beethoven to play, he was nowhere to be found. He was looked for. The Prince wanted to persuade him — to cajole him — into playing. No use. An unpleasant, even vulgar, scene took place. Beethoven immediately had his things packed, and hastened, despite the pouring rain, on foot to Troppau, where he spent the night at Weiser's. It was because of the rain that the Sonata in F minor, Op 57, the *Appassionata* which Beethoven was carrying with him was damaged by water . . . Weiser tells further that the next day it was difficult, without the Prince, to get a passport to return to Vienna. Finally it was procured. Before he left, Beethoven wrote a very self-willed letter to Lichnowsky, which is supposed to have read as follows: 'Prince! What you are, you are by circumstance and by birth. What I am, I am through myself. Of princes there have been and will be thousands. Of Beethovens there is only one.' Unfortunately, it seems that the march from Grätz to Troppau induced a considerable worsening of Beethoven's deafness.

One fruitful outcome of the Silesian trip, however, was the completion of the Fourth Symphony, that radiantly buoyant Elysian essay which Schumann likened to 'a slender Grecian maiden between two Nordic giants'. Count Franz Von Oppersdorff, whom Beethoven visited at about this time, and whose orchestra apparently played the Second Symphony in honour of the occasion, paid Beethoven 500 florins (£50) for the privilege of commissioning the Fourth.

Back in Vienna, Beethoven — now an uncle: a son, Karl, had been born to his brother Carl and his wife of not yet four months, Johanna Reiss, on 4 September — gave some further thought to his recently re-opened correspondence with the publisher George Thomson of Edinburgh. Thomson had requested some folk song settings for voice and piano trio of a kind that Pleyel, Koželuh and Haydn had already done for him. In a letter, dated 1 November, and written in another hand in French, Beethoven remarked that 'I will take care to make the composition easy and pleasing, as far as I can and as far as is consistent with that elevation and originality of

Heute Dienstag den 23. Dezember 1806
Wird in dem k. k. priv. Schauspielhaus an der Wien
gegeben
Eine große
musikalische Akademie
mit Verstärkung des Orchesters
Zum Vortheil des Franz Klement,
Musikdirektor dieses Theaters.

Erste Abtheilung.

1. Eine grosse neue *Overture* von Herrn *Mehul*
2. Ein neues *Violin-Concert* von Herrn Ludwig *van Beethoven*, gespielt von Hrn. Clement.
3. Eine *Aria* von Herrn W. Mozart, gesungen von Mad. Campi.
4. Eine *Overture* samt einen grossen *Chor* von Herrn *Hendel*, aus der *Ode auf St. Cäcilia*, instrumentirt von Herrn W. Mozart.

Zwente Abtheilung.

1. Eine neue *Overture* von Herrn *Cherubini*.
2. Ein neues *Quartetto* von Herrn *Cherubini*, gesungen von Mad. Campi, Hrn. Ehlers, Herrn Meier und Herrn Frankopl.
3. Wird Herr Clement auf der *Violine phantasiren* und auch eine *Sonate* auf einer einzigen Saite mit umgekehrter *Violin* spielen.
4. Ein grosser *Chor* von Herrn *Hendel*, aus der *Ode auf St. Cäcilia* instrumentirt von Herrn W. Mozart.

Die Logen und gesperrten Sitze sind in seiner Wohnung beym schwarzen Bären an der Wien Nro. 456 im 1ten Stock, von 9 Uhr früh bis Nachmittag um 5 Uhr zu haben.

Der Anfang um halb 7 Uhr.

Programme of Franz Clement's benefit concert on 23 December 1806, at which Beethoven's Violin Concerto was played for the first time

style which, as you yourself say, favourably characterises my works and from which I shall never stoop'.

A final event of the year took place on 23 December at a benefit *Akademie* given at the Theater an der Wien by Franz Clement — the first performance of the newly completed Violin Concerto. Destined to occupy a place in history as the first great fiddle concerto of the 19th century, its reception was at first cool. In spite of Czerny's view that it 'was produced with very great effect', The Viennese *Zeitung für Theater, Musik und Poesie* (8 January 1807) commented that 'the verdict of the cognoscenti is unanimous: they concede that it has some beauty, but maintain that the continuity is often completely fragmented, and that the endless repetition of some commonplace passages might easily prove wearisome'. What attracted the public more was Clement's playing, said to have been at sight without previous rehearsal — the hastily written and heavily corrected autograph in the Nationalbibliotek, Vienna, suggest that, as usual, Beethoven had left the completion of the work to the very last moment. In keeping with the day, the first movement was played in the first half, the remaining two in the second. In between Clement offered other pieces, including a work of his own played on one string with the violin turned upside down, a popular trick. In spite of various attempts to resurrect the Concerto, including an adaptation for piano and orchestra published with the original version in 1808 (and including a remarkable cadenza for piano and timpani), its early career proved to be dubious. Alan Tyson, indeed, has observed that during the ensuing thirty years or so its received no more than 'about half a dozen further performances'.

The Music Room of the Rasumowsky Palace following its restoration after the fire of December 1814. Photograph (Fischer & Kock)

Marathon concerts, no less than the almost overwhelming patronage of a band of nobility thirsting for cultural enlightenment, were almost as much a part of early 19th century Viennese life as the stocky, Napoleon-like figure of Beethoven himself. One obvious, all-embracing example took place in the first week of March 1807. The *Jounal des Luxus und der Modern* reported in April:

Beethoven gave two concerts at the house of Prince L[obkowitz] at which nothing but his own compositions were performed; namely his first four symphonies, an overture to the tragedy *Coriolan*, a pianoforte concerto and some airs from the opera *Fidelio*. Richness of ideas, bold originality and fullness of power, which are the particular merits of Beethoven's muse, were very much in evidence to everyone at these concerts...

Beethoven's hasty bad feeling with Lichnowsky now sufficiently abated, the *Coriolan* overture was also included at this time in one of Lichnowsky's own concerts. Recently completed (the manuscript bears the date 1807), associated with Heinrich von Collin's tragedy *Coriolan* first staged in Vienna in November 1802, symphonic-poem-like, and in Beethoven's archetypally tragic key of C minor, it at once created the kind of favourable early impression that had been denied to the Violin Concerto. The *Allgemeine Musikalische Zeitung* spoke of 'fire and power'.

On 20 April 1807 Beethoven signed an important contract with the London publisher, Muzio Clementi, which had the effect of authorising at last the official (rather than pirated) publication of Beethoven's work in England. Two days later Clementi wrote to his business partner, Collard, in terms that suggest he was more than well-pleased with his coup:

Muzio Clementi (1746-1832). Engraving by E. Scriven from a painting by J. Lonsdale, 1819 (Gesellschaft der Musikfreunde, Vienna)

By a little management and without committing myself, I have at last made a complete conquest of the *haughty beauty*, Beethoven, who first began at public places to grin and coquet with me, which of course I took care not to discourage; then slid into familiar chat, till meeting him by chance one day in the street — 'Where do you lodge?' says he; 'I have not seen you this *long* while!' — upon which I gave him my address. Two days after I found on my table his card brought by himself, from the maid's description of his lovely form. This will do, thought I. Three days after that he calls again, and finds me at home. Conceive then the mutual ecstasy of such a meeting! I took pretty good care to improve it to our *house's* advantage, therefore, as soon as decency would allow, after praising very handsomely some of his compositions: 'Are you engaged with any publisher in London?' — 'No' says he. 'Suppose, then, that you prefer *me*?' — 'With all my heart.' 'Done. What have you ready?' — 'I'll bring you a list'. In short I agreed with him to take in MSS three quartets, a symphony, an overture and a concerto for the violin, which is beautiful and which, at my request he will adapt for the pianoforte with and without additional keys; and a concerto for the pianoforte, for *all* which we are to pay him two hundred pounds sterling. The property, however, is only for the British Dominions. To-day sets off a courier for London through Russia, and he will bring over to you two or three of the mentioned articles.

Remember that the violin concerto he will adapt himself and send it as soon as he can.

The quartets, etc, you may get Cramer or some other very clever fellow to adapt for the Pianoforte. The symphony and the overture are wonderfully fine so that I think I have made a very good bargain. What do you think? I have likewise engaged him to compose two sonatas and a fantasia for the Pianoforte which he is to deliver to our house for sixty pounds sterling (mind I have treated for Pounds, not Guineas). In short he has promised to treat with no one but me for the British Dominions.

The summer months were spent in Baden and Heiligenstadt working on another symphony, the Fifth in C minor, and on a Mass in C which had been commissioned by Prince Nikolaus Esterházy to mark the name day of his wife. The new Mass was duly conducted by Beethoven himself at Eisenstadt on 13 September. The experience was not cherished. Instead of being treated as a social equal and given quarters in Esterháza itself, he found himself instead in some damp, sub-standard room in the apartments of the Court Secretary of Music. There was more humiliation to come, as Schindler says:

It was the custom at this court that after the religious service the local as

Baden, a view of the Helenental, a summer spot of Beethoven's. Oil painting by F. Scheyerer (Niederösterreichisches Landesmuseum, Vienna). Life in Vienna during the hot months was not pleasant. There were over a thousand horse-drawn cabs and over 300 coaches for hire. Travelling across granite cobbles they raised, according to one visitor, 'a terrible dust which hovered in the air the whole summer and even during part of the winter . . . It was like a dirty fog.'

well as foreign musical notabilities met in the chambers of the Prince for the purpose of conversing with him about the works which had been performed. When Beethoven entered the room, the Prince turned to him with the question: 'But my dear Beethoven, what is this that you have done again?' The impression made by this singular question, which was probably followed by other critical remarks, was the more painful on our artist because he saw the *Kapellmeister* [Hummel] standing near the Prince laugh. Thinking that he was being ridiculed, nothing could keep him at the place where his work had been so misunderstood, and besides, as he thought, where a brother in art had rejoiced over his discomfiture.

In spite of such response and the fact that this was his first attempt at writing in a genre that had been so perfected by Mozart and Haydn, Beethoven was by no means displeased with the music itself. He wrote to Härtel (8 June 1808): 'I think I have treated the text in a manner in which it has rarely been treated'. Härtel, however, felt uneasy about publishing it (religious feeling was then at a low ebb) and a month later Beethoven felt it necessary to suggest that a German translation of the Latin text be made available for performance, so widening the work's scope. Some time later Härtel commissioned Christian Schreiber to do just this, and Beethoven's reactions in an interesting letter dated 16 January 1811 are revealing for what they tell us about his views and beliefs:

The translation of the Gloria I consider very suitable, but that of the Kyrie not so good. Although the beginning 'tief im Staub anbeten wir' is very appropriate, yet several expressions, such as 'ew'gen Weltenherrscher' and 'Allgewaltigen' seem to fit the Gloria better. The general character of the Kyrie (I consider that in a translation of this kind only the general character of each movement should be indicated) is heartfelt resignation, deep sincerity of religious feeling, 'Gott erbarme dich unser', yet without on that account being sad. Gentleness is the fundamental characteristic of the whole work. And here the expressions 'Allgewaltiger' and so forth do not seem to convey the meaning of the whole work. Apart from 'Eleison erbarme dich unser' — cheerfulness pervades this Mass. The Catholic goes to church on Sunday in his best clothes and in a joyful and festive mood. Besides, the Kyrie Eleison is the introduction to the whole work. If such strong expressions were used here, few would be left for those portions where really strong expressions are required.

The Mass was eventually published in October 1812.

At the end of 1807, a Society of Cavaliers, comprising among others the Princes Lobkowitz, Esterházy and Schwarzenberg, was formed to take over the running of the Theater an der Wien and the two court theatres. Beethoven, strangely enough for one so independent, saw this as a possible opportunity for gainful employment, and took it upon himself to apply for the post of opera

Vienna, the old University. Coloured engraving by C. Schütz, 1790

composer, guaranteeing (amazingly) 'to compose every year at least one grand opera . . . a small operetta or a *divertissement, choruses* or occasional pieces', all in return for 'a fixed remuneration of 2400 florins per annum [£240] and the gross receipts of the third performance of each such opera' and 'at least one day per year for a benefit concert in the theatre building.' The nature of this proposition demanded some believing. Beethoven may have dreamed of himself as *the* opera composer of the day, but he had scarcely proved himself artistically or commercially with *Fidelio*, and his aspirations were renowned for being too lofty for the public at large. Perhaps what he really wanted was a salary and the guarantee of a free venue for the kind of music he knew best how to write. The Directorate of Princes, neither innocently gullible nor charitably sentimental, rejected the application.

The latter half of 1807 witnessed a number of performances of Beethoven's work in the so-called *Liebhaber-Konzert* series held in the Great Hall of the University. Mostly conducted by the composer himself, the Second, Third and Fourth Symphonies were included, as well as the *Prometheus* and *Coriolan* overtures. The Fourth Symphony was additionally played at the Burgtheater in November at a charity function. The trend continued in 1808 with a series of concerts in April which again included (in spite of its apparent unpopularity) the *Eroica*, as well as the Fourth Symphony, the Third Piano Concerto and the *Coriolan* Overture — all once more under Beethoven's direction.

Then in May, at the Augartensaal, came the first public performance in Vienna of the Triple Concerto, which had been published in the previous summer with a dedication to Prince Lobkowitz. Originally written for the Archduke Rudolph and almost certainly played privately at his home some time in 1805 or 1806, with him at the keyboard, it had already been performed in public in Leipzig some time before the Easter of 1808.

According to Schindler the work fell out of favour and did not gain its proper due until 1830. Even so, the evidence of such concerts as a whole does offer, perhaps, some proof that contrary to a widely-held view there was indeed a demand for Beethoven's music in the Vienna of these years. He was, it is clear, by no means neglected, he was recognised, and, as Thayer says, it seems that 'few as his published orchestral compositions then were, none were more likely to fill the house'.

The summer of 1808 was spent again at Heiligenstadt. Back in Vienna, Beethoven prepared himself once more for another marathon *Akademie* to be given again at the Theater an der Wien, this time on Thursday evening, 22 December. In importance and substance, if not in critical or popular aclaim, it was to prove an event of extraordinary historical significance. The programme included the first public performances of no less than the Fifth Symphony (described as No 6), the Sixth Symphony (correspondingly labelled No 5), the Fourth Piano Concerto in G major, the hybrid Choral Fantasia for piano, chorus and orchestra, and the improvisatory Fantasia in G minor for piano, as well as sundry items, among them extracts from the Mass in C.

Faced with such a programme, it is not difficult to sympathise with those who found the experience overlong and musically indigestible. Yet there is no denying its remarkable impact, nor the fact that it constituted the birth in sound of masterpieces that were to influence the direction of western musical thinking for a century to come. Of the two symphonies, No 5 in C minor, dedicated jointly to Prince Lobkowitz and Count Rasumowsky, had been completed in the spring. To Romantic minds it was an even more overtly programmatic essay than its companion, the Sixth, and following its publication in April 1809 it became the subject of a powerfully committed, intensely personal, often highly perceptive article contributed by E. T. A. Hoffmann to the *Allgemeine Musikalische Zeitung* in July 1810. His words were to be an emotive inspiration for generations to come:

This reviewer has before him one of the important works of the master whose position in the first rank of composers of instrumental music can now be denied by no one. So imbued is he with the subject at hand that he hopes that no one will take it amiss if he oversteps the boundaries of run-of-the-mill reviewing in an attempt to put into words the profound feelings which this composition has stirred within him. When one considers music as an independent art, one should always mean instrumental music which, avoiding all assistance, any interference from any of the other arts, exclusively expresses its own individual artistic essence. It is the most romantic of all the arts — in fact one might almost say the only purely romantic one . . . Haydn and Mozart, the creators of the newer instrumental music, first revealed this art to use in the fullness of its glory. He who looked upon it filled with love and who penetrated its innermost substance is — Beethoven. Although the instrumental compositions of all three masters breathe the same romantic spirit which lies precisely in the same intimate ability to comprehend the individual essence of this art, the nature of their compositions differs markedly. In Haydn's compositions the expression of a youthful, light-hearted spirit is dominant. His symphonies lead us into an infinite green grove, in a cheerful, gaily coloured throng of merry people. Mozart leads us into the depths of the spiritual world. Fear grips us, but without torment; it is more a foreboding of the eternal . . . Beethoven's instrumental music also opens up to us the world of the immense and infinite. Glowing rays of light blaze through the dark night of this world and we are made conscious of gigantic shadows which surge up and down,

Johann Wolfgang von Goethe (1749-1832)

E. T. A. Hoffmann (1776-1822)

BOSTON, SUNDAY MORNING, OCT. 27.

MUSIC.

The Symphony Concert.

The second symphony concert of the season was given last evening, at Music Hall, with the following programme:

Overture, "The Flying Dutchman" ....Wagner
Mad Scene from "Hamlet"........ .....A. Thomas
Mme. De Vere Sapio.
Suite A-minor, op. 42....................MacDowell
Aria, "Ah perfido"......................Beethoven
Mme. De Vere Sapio.
Symphony, No. 5, op. 69.................Beethovén

"Old friends, old wines, old memories." Mr. Paur has the happy knack of realizing two thirds of this proverb; he gives us old friends and old memories, and he loses none of his old and exuberant enthusiasm in introducing them to us. The world may grow older, taste may change; novelties may be abundant; but what better company can one have than Beethoven and Wagner. Fate eloquently tapping on the door and Legend pathetically blowing in a bass tuber? The new æsthetic Hoyle solemnly insists that when a conductor is in doubt he must lead Beethoven. Novelties in music are always ticklish things to deal with; one can never tell if they are classic or if they have the proper educational value and have the unimpeacheable morality which will allow of them being played before our daughters and sweethearts. Even the most exacting of plaguey critics cannot deny that Beethoven's fifth symphony is a most excellent and approved work, and that it deserves from its conductor all the superfluity of energy and excess of perspiration that he gives to present day works when he serves them up. A less careful conductor than Mr. Paur would give his orchestra the credit of knowing something of their Beethoven by this time, and content himself with beating time in a quiet and conventional manner; but Mr. Paur has faith in gesture and energy, and he is as conscientiously gym nastic with the works of the old masters as if they had been written only yesterday. Aside from ts æsthetic worth there is a practical value in this system of treatment, for if the hearer is in danger of neglecting Beethoven, he cannot banish Mr. Paur from his sight or memory. Aside from their reverence for what is old there is another merit in the symphony programmes, and that is, every week they present a problem in the nature of an unanswerable puzzle. Last week the audience amused itself by trying to discover why the theatrical scherzo of Dvorak was tagged on the end of a classical programme, and this week lovers of charades and rebuses lost themselves in the mazes of conjecture, seeking for the link that connected the Flying Dutchman overture with the fifth symphony. Mr. Paur's programmes are always orthodox, but at the same time they have the peculiarity of shocking in some way orthodox taste; they unaccountably suggest the incon. sistency of improving the statue of Apollo with a pair of Wellington boots or of affixing Gothic gargoyles to the Parthenon. One regrets these little lapses in taste, for of all the conductors yet vouchsafed to Boston, Mr. Paur is the most able, the most catholic in taste, the most conscientious in execution. The symphony was superbly read, and, of course, superbly played—color, power, finish could go no further.

The MacDowell suite is well worth the rehearing. It is a most artistic and most dainty piece of work; learned without ostentation. It is not the work of an inspired giant who hurls out his ideas in passion, and fashions them while they are white-hot; but it is marked with careful poetic daintiness, super-excellent in taste, and reserved in treatment. There is no wearing of the subject threadbare through over-elaboration. Of all our composers, Mr. MacDowell possesses in the highest degree the gift of knowing when to stop. He is also melodious, a demonstration that he is gifted with ideas, and he does not beat the gold of his imagination too thin, nor rigidly compress it into one unyielding form. The suite is a most charming work, one of several of a composer who in imagination and fertility of ideas holds a very high, if not the highest place in American musical art.

The soloist of the evening did not interfere with Mr. Paur's intentions by adding anything new to the programme; both her contributions are only too well known to concert goers and those gave an opportunity for comparison that did not tell always in favor of the soloist. Mme, De Vere Sapio was most effective in Hamlet selection the Beethoven Scena and aria being, seemingly beyond her power. She sings always like an artist, but at times overestimates her endurance and so loses control over her voice at critical moments. In listening to her one feels a sense of effort, the machinery producing singing is more prominent than feeling and interpretative imagination, and when the singer is at her best, one listens unmoved. Mme. De Vere Sapio has a voice of pleasant quality, particalarly pleasant in its lower portion, and it may be that such faults as were revealed last evening are due to our treacherous Boston climate and not to lack of skill in the singer, who aroused a large amount of enthusiasm, and was recalled after each song.

Boston Gazette clipping of October 27, 1895, referring to a performance of Beethoven's Fifth Symphony

gradually closing in on us more and more and annihilating everything within us, except the torment of endless longing . . . Beethoven is a pure romantic and because of this a truly musical composer. That may be the reason why he is less successful in vocal music (which does not allow undefined longings, but represents only those passions, expressed through words, which are experienced as if in the realm of the eternal), and his instrumental music rarely appeals to the crowd . . . Beethoven bears deep within his nature the romantic spirit of music, which he proclaims in his works with great genius and presence of mind. Your reviewer has never felt this so clearly as in this particular symphony which, more than any other of his works, unfolds Beethoven's romantic spirit in a climax rising straight to the end and carries the listener away irresistibly into the wondrous spirit world of the infinite . . .

Subsequently, the almost certainly apocryphal story about 'destiny knocking at the door' (attributed variously to Ries or Schindler) gained wide currency, so much so in fact that the Fifth, and its opening motif in particular is still, for many, *the* 'Fate' Symphony above all others. The idea of it, too, expressing that Romantically dramatic notion of triumph over tragedy was similarly to catch the imagination of millions, as did the finale with its magnificent introduction of trombones (not for the first time in a classico-romantic

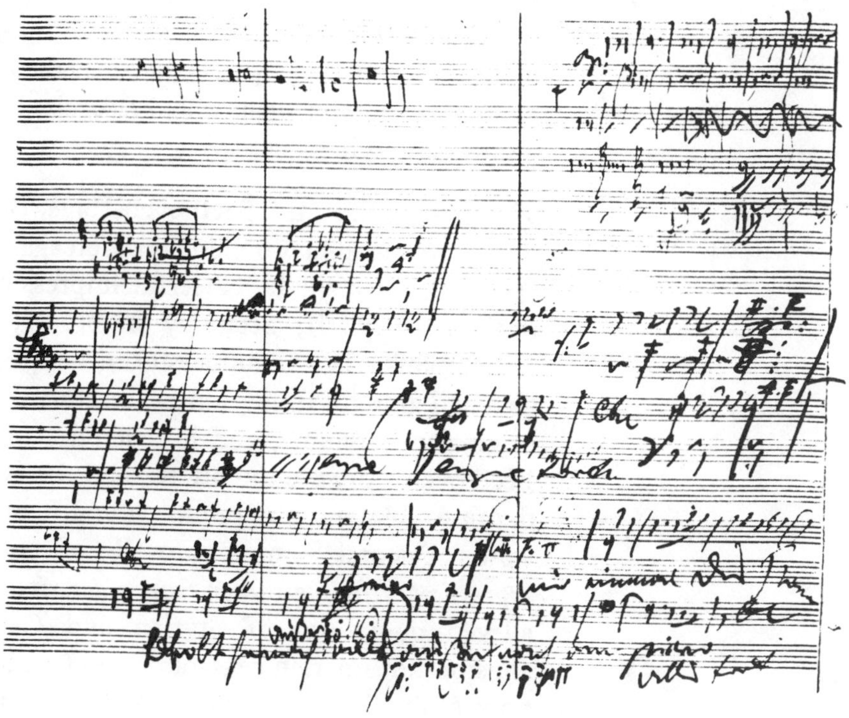

Sketches for the Fifth Symphony (Gesellschaft der Musikfreunde, Vienna): 'Though I am well aware of the value of my *Fidelio*, I know just as well that the symphony is my real element. When sounds ring in me I always hear the full orchestra' (Beethoven, *c.* 1823-24)

symphony, but certainly for the first time with such theatrical effect and splendour) and its Titanic C major peroration of ascending white light. Today we can view the Fifth more objectively, we can study the sketchbooks, we can point to Czerny's less romantically-inflamed view that the 'Fate' motto was nothing but the rhythmic call of the yellowhammer, we can dismiss the alleged tragedy-triumph 'programme' by saying that Beethoven had originally planned a very different, less martial 6/8 finale in C *minor* — yet the connotations of it as it stood at the time of its first performance, the subjective implications of its final ground plan, and the audibly apparent concept of Beethoven shaking his fist metaphorically at the adversary, still seem powerfully evocative conditioning factors. It is difficult in fact to escape the feeling that just as the *Eroica* had bidden farewell to the classical age, so the Fifth unmistakably beckoned that dreamland of the future that was to come. In every respect it was a stridently defiant, progressive product of Beethoven's creative imagination. In 1808 nothing quite like it had been heard before in the Austrian capital.

Like the Fifth, the Sixth (the *Pastoral*) was also in many ways to break new ground. Similarly dedicated to Lobkowitz and Rasumowsky, its programmatic nature was noted down early on in the sketchbooks:

> The hearers should be allowed to discover the situations
> Sinfonia caracteristica — or recollection of country life
> A recollection of country-life
> All painting in instrumental music is lost if it is pushed too far
> Sinfonia pastorella. Anyone who has an idea of country-life can make
> out for himself the intentions of the composer without many titles —
> Also without titles the whole will be recognized as a matter more of feeling
> than of painting in sounds

The autograph in the Beethoven-Haus, Bonn bears the movement titles in German (a prophetic reaction again the Italian 'internationalism' of the day): I, 'Cheerful impressions awakened by arrival in the country'; II, 'Scene by the brook'; III, 'Merry gathering of country folk'; IV, 'Thunderstorm: tempest'; V, 'Shepherd's song; glad and grateful feelings after the storm'. In other sketches, in the original programme, and in a letter to Härtel (28 March 1809), Beethoven's precise intentions, and the fact that he never had any desire to follow a programme literally, are further clarified in the words 'Pastoral Symphony or Recollections of Country Life, *an expression of feeling rather than a description'* (our italics). With its alleged quotations of Styrian and Carinthian folk tunes, its allusions to Austrian peasant dances (not least in the metric alternations of the third movement), and the imagery of a rural landscape born within the summer fields, by the murmuring mountain streams, beneath the trees and among the villagers of Heiligenstadt and Baden, the character of the *Pastoral* Symphony as a whole was to prove no less distinctive or well-defined than that of the Fifth. Debussy may have felt, typically, that one could learn more about Nature by watching the sun rise, but for countless others the atmosphere of the work and the strength of its connotations, summed-up an undeniably early Romantic view of elemental things which had equal validity and meaning.

Beethoven composing the *Pastoral* by a brook, a well-known coloured lithograph from the 1834 *Almanach* of the Zürich Musikgesellschaft. 'You will ask me where I get my ideas. That I cannot tell you with certainty; they come unsummoned, directly, indirectly — I could seize them with my hands — out in the open air, in the woods, while walking, in the silence of the night, early in the morning, incited by moods, which are translated by the poet into words, by me into tones that sound, and roar and storm about me until I have set them down in notes' — Beethoven to Louis Schlösser, 1822-23

In the July of 1808, Wilhelm Rust wrote to his sister and penned this description of Beethoven: 'He is as original and singular as a man as are his compositions; usually serious, at times merry, but always satirical and bitter. On the other hand he is also very childlike and certainly very sincere. He is a great lover of truth and in this goes too far very often; for he never flatters and therefore makes many enemies'. Such a manner did not endear him to orchestras: so much so that that of the Theater an der Wien reached the stage of only agreeing to rehearsals if Beethoven was not in the room at the same time. Only the leaders — Seyfried or Clement — would have anything to do with him. Reichardt attended the December *Akademie*, and what he had to say endorses the uneasy relationship that existed between Beethoven and his musicians:

I accepted the kind offer of Prince Lobkowitz to let me sit in his box with hearty thanks. There we continued, in the bitterest cold, too, from half past six to half past ten, and experienced the truth that one can easily have too much of a good thing — and still more of a loud. Nevertheless, I could no more leave the box before the end than could the exceedingly good-natured and delicate Prince, for the box was in the first balcony near the stage, so that the orchestra with Beethoven in the middle conducting it was below us and near at hand; thus many a failure in the performance vexed our patience in the highest degree. Poor Beethoven, who from this, his own concert, was having the first and only scant profit that he could find in a whole year, had found in the rehearsals and performance a lot of opposition and almost no support. Singers and orchestra were composed of heterogeneous elements, and it had been found impossible to get a single full rehearsal for all the pieces to be performed, all filled with the greatest difficulties.

Chapter 11
Entr'acte: 1809-13

'An unlicked bear' — Cherubini

The immediate net result of the 1808 *Akademie*, then, was uneven, frustrating and in at least one respect final: with it Beethoven effectively took his leave of the concert platform as a solo pianist, some thirty years after his first public appearance as a prodigy in Cologne. That he was disappointed, disillusioned and angry clearly emerges in a revealing letter to Breitkopf & Härtel, written on 7 January 1809, a letter which further alludes to the fact that he had by then already (in the previous autumn) been offered a post by Jerome Bonaparte of Westphalia which he suddenly saw as a means of possibly escaping the intrigue, gossip, jealousy and malicious smallmindedness which then riddled Vienna:

Abusive articles about my latest concert will perhaps be sent again from here to the *Musikalische Zeitung*. I certainly don't want everything that is written against me to be suppressed. But people should bear in mind that nobody in Vienna has more private enemies than I have. This is the more understandable since the state of music here is becoming worse and worse — We have *Kapellmeisters* who not only do not know how to conduct but also can hardly read a score — Conditions are worst of all, of course, at the Theater an der Wien — I had to give my concert there and on that occasion obstacles were placed in my way by all the circles connected with music — The promoters of the concert for the widows, out of hatred for me, Herr Salieri being my most active opponent, played me a horrible trick. They threatened to expel any musician belonging to their company who would play for my benefit — In spite of the fact that various mistakes were made, which I could not prevent, the public nevertheless applauded the whole performance with enthusiasm — Yet scribblers in Vienna will certainly not fail to send again to the *Musikalische Zeitung* some wretched stuff directed against me —

However honourable the position at the Westphalian court in Cassel, the notion of Beethoven with his temperament, his deafness and his self-willed creativity working within the restricting confines of a provincial court even less endowed than the one he had known in Bonn, seems today as unlikely and out of character as was his 1807 request to become opera composer to the Society of Cavaliers. Fortunately his closest, most faithful friends realised the gravity of the situation, and the loss to Vienna that his absence would mean. Accordingly the dedicatee of the Op 70 Piano Trios, the Countess Marie Erdödy, appears to have suggested that the Westphalian post be declined in exchange for a formally drawn-up contract guaranteeing both financial and artistic security. Beethoven, with the help of the Baron Ignaz von Gleichenstein, drafted a proposed contract in February 1809. He began it by saying that

The endeavour and the aim of every true artist should certainly be to win for himself a position in which he can devote himself entirely to the completion of great works and need not be debarred from this occupation by other avocations or by financial considerations.

He then went on to observe that the King of Westphalia had offered him 600 gold ducats for life plus 150 ducats for travelling expenses (totalling about 3375 gulden, or just under £350 a year). Then, by way of political necessity but scarcely in keeping with his letter of a few weeks earlier to Härtel, he says:

At the same time Beethoven's preference to reside in this city is so great, he is so grateful for the many proofs of goodwill which he has received and he cherishes such patriotic feelings for his second fatherland that he will never cease to count himself among the number of Austrian artists and will never choose to live anywhere else, provided that the advantages listed below are granted to him to a certain extent.

The advantages listed included an income of not less than 4,000 gulden (£400) a year 'in view of the present high cost of living', freedom to travel where he pleased 'in the interests of his art', the title of Imperial *Kapellmeister* which 'would make him very happy' and would encourage him to stay permanently in Vienna, and, finally, a plea with a familiar ring:

Since Beethoven desires to produce his new and greater works now and then before a large public as well, he would like to receive from the Directors of the Court Theatres on their behalf and on behalf of their successors an assurance that on Palm Sunday of every year he would be granted the Theater an der Wien for a concert to be held for his own benefit.

A formal contract was drawn up on 1 March 1809 by the Archduke Rudolph (then 21), Prince Lokbowitz (35) and Prince Ferdinand Kinsky (27). In view of 'the daily proofs which Herr Ludwig van Beethoven is giving of his extraordinary talents and genius as a musician and composer', and since they had 'decided to place Herr Ludwig van Beethoven in a position where the necessities of life shall not cause him embarrassment or clog his powerful genius', the agreed sum of 4,000 guldens was guaranteed for as long as need be.

The late spring of 1809 witnessed in the meantime another French invasion of Vienna. The Archduke Rudolph and the Imperial family left the capital on 4 May, and the defence of the city was left in the main to 16,000 soldiers, 1000 students and artists, and the civil militia. The French cannon opened fire on 11 May. A contemporary wrote:

The French bombardment of Vienna on the night of 11-12 May 1809 (Österreiche Nationalbibliothek, Vienna)

> In the morning everybody in the suburbs was as still as a mouse . . . In the city, the people tried to pass the hours and lighten their fears by swapping jokes. When night fell, it became quieter and quieter. The noise of the far-off shelling subsided. We sat down to supper with a will. As the plates for the first course were being served, we heard detonations. We looked out of the window and we saw, sailing through a starless night sky, black objects which trailed fiery tails behind them. Suddenly such a body descended from the air, danced in great hops on the granite pavement, and — whoever had stood at the window was now lying on the ground. A sixty-pound bomb had exploded. As the autumn wind shakes the tree, so did the air pressure shake the whole street. The windows shattered. We heard the chimes from the Stephansdom, ten o'clock . . . A few shadowy figures groped along the houses to escape the bombardment . . .

Beethoven took refuge in a cellar, covering his head with pillows, while in another part of the city Haydn repeatedly played his *Kaiserhymne* in a last gesture of grim defiance against the invader — he was to die on 31 May. By half-past two the following afternoon a 'white flag was sent up as notice of capitulation to the outposts of the enemy'.

Beethoven, then putting the finishing touches to a new piano concerto, the Fifth in E flat, found life more intolerable than usual. The public gardens were shut, he could not get away to the sweet, perfumed air of his customary summer haunts in the country, and the French occupation had placed colossal levies and taxes on the city: 'Normally,' Beethoven wrote to Härtel on 26 July, 'I should now be having a change of scene and air — The levies are beginning this very day — What a destructive, disorderly life I see and hear around me, nothing but drums, cannons and human misery in every form . . .'. Families were reduced to begging in the streets, and there was little fraternisation with the enemy. If Beethoven's unscrupulous brother, Johann, saw no harm in supplying medicines to both the Austrians and the French, Beethoven himself held Napoleon and his men in disgust: 'If I, as a general, knew as much about strategy as I the composer know of counterpoint, I'd give you something to do', he is said to have berated one unsuspecting officer.

At about this time the Baron de Trémont visited Beethoven and reported in his *Diary*

I wended my way to the unapproachable composer's home, and at the door it struck me that I had chosen the day ill, for, having to make an official visit thereafter, I was wearing the every-day habiliments of the Council of State. To make matters worse, his lodging was next the city wall, and as Napoleon had ordered its destruction, blasts had just been set off under his windows.

The neighbours showed me where he lived: 'He is at home (they said), but he has no servant at present, for he is always getting a new one, and it is doubtful whether he will open'.

I rang three times, and was about to go away, when a very ugly man of ill-humoured mien opened the door and asked what I wanted.

'Have I the honour of addressing M. de Beethoven?'

— 'Yes, Sir! But I must tell you,' he said to me in German, 'that I am on very bad terms with French!'

'My acquaintance with German is no better, Sir, but my message is limited to bringing you a letter from M. Reicha in Paris'. He looked me over, took the letter, and let me in. His lodging, I believe, consisted of only two rooms, the first one having an alcove containing the bed, but small and dark, for which reason he made his toilet in the second room, or salon. Picture to yourself the dirtiest, most disorderly place imaginable — blotches of moisture covered the ceiling; an oldish grand piano, on which the dust disputed the place with various pieces of engraved and manuscript music; under the piano (I do not exaggerate) an unemptied *pot de nuit*; beside it, a small walnut table accustomed to the frequent overturning of the secretary placed upon it; a quantity of pens encrusted with ink, compared wherewith the proverbial tavern-pens would shine; then more music. The chairs, mostly cane-seated, were covered with plates bearing the remains of last night's supper, and with wearing apparel, etc. Balzac or Dickens would continue this description for two pages, and then would they as many more with a description of the dress of the illustrious composer; but, being neither Balzac nor Dickens, I shall merely say, I was in Beethoven's abode.

With its fortifications razed to the ground, Vienna looked a different, altogether more exposed city. By the end of November, with peace negotiations under the control of Metternich, the Emperor Franz returned surreptitiously to his capital. By then, as Beethoven put it, the Viennese were 'enjoying a little peace after violent destruction, after suffering every hardship that one could conceivably endure . . .' The peace, however, was uneasy, in Beethoven's words, a 'dead peace': 'I no longer expect to see any stability in this age. The only *certainty* we can rely on is *blind chance*'. To ease things, to gain time, Metternich succeeded in the

The Archduke Rudolph (1788-1831), the youngest son of Leopold II and half-brother to Franz II. A staunch supporter of Beethoven to the end, he began taking lessons with him in either 1803 or 1804. Portrait in oils by J.B. Lampi the Elder, 1805

end in securing a remarkable political alliance: on 11 March 1810 he married off by proxy the pretty eighteen-year-old Princess Marie Louise, the daughter of the Emperor, to the balding, forty-year-old Napoleon. For a time, at least, Austria and France were to live in a state of armed truce. But the strain of these years, these invasions, left its mark on the 'Grand Mogul'. As Marek has said 'the winds blew harshly and the climate was inclement'. Beethoven's 'music was not time-bound, but *he* was. He could escape temporary detonations, but not the general exhaustion of Vienna, not the devaluation of the money, not the more difficult "economies of music" (his expression), not the frowns of his worried patrons, not, as he wrote in December, 1809, the "melancholy reminders of this German country which has so declined *partly through its own fault, I admit.*"

In spite of this the years up to 1814 were not to be without their moments. The summer of 1809 began with a compilation of text book instructions for the absent Archduke Rudolph (the *Materialien zum Generalbass*), and on 9 August Beethoven received a letter from Amsterdam notifying him of his appointment as 'Correspondent of the Fourth Class of the Royal Institute of Science, Literature and the Fine Arts'. Among the completed compositions of the year were the Fifth Piano Concerto (dedicated to the Archduke Rudolph), the Op 74 String Quartet, a quantity of songs and several piano sonatas, including the famous *Das Lebewohl* in E flat, Op 81a. The manuscript in the Gesellschaft der Musikfreunde bears a self-explanatory description: 'The Farewell, Vienna, 4 May 1809, on the departure of his Imperial Highness, the revered Archduke Rudolph'. The finale confirms 'The Arrival of His Imperial Highness the revered Archduke Rudolph, 30 January 1810'. The middle movement was subtitled *Abwesenheit*, 'Absence'. Publications (all by Breitkopf & Härtel in Leipzig) included the Op 69 Cello Sonata, the Op 70 Piano Trios and the two new symphonies. Towards the end of the year (23 November) negotiations were re-opened with George Thomson of Edinburgh, who on 25 September had sent Beethoven 43 Welsh and Irish melodies. In his letter Beethoven asks Thomson to 'rest assured that he is dealing with a true artist who, indeed, likes to be decently paid, but who loves fame and also the fame of art more — and who is never satisfied with himself and is always striving to make greater progress in his art.' Significantly he ends with a revealing postscript: 'Next time please send me the words of the songs along with them, as they are very necessary in order to get the correct expression'.

As for concerts, the Baroness Dorothea von Ertmann and the cellist Nikolaus Kraft had given the first performance of the Op 69

A greeting card sent by Beethoven to Dorothea von Ertmann. The inscription reads: 'To Baroness Ertmann for the New Year 1804 from her friend and admirer Beethoven' (Bodmer Collection, Beethoven-Haus, Bonn)

Sonata on 5 March. On the 8th of the 'wine month', September, the Nativity of the Virgin Mary, Beethoven conducted the *Eroica* at a charity concert for actors and their families. Then on 24 December Clement included the *Christus* oratorio in his annual *Akademie* at the Theater an der Wien.

By the end of 1809 Beethoven was, in Thayer's words, 'the master in the full vigour and maturity of his powers':

> The princes, whose generosity had just placed him, for the present at least, beyond the reach of pecuniary anxieties, may well have expected the immediate fulfilment of 'the desire that he surpass the great expectations which are justified by his past achievements.' They were [however] bitterly disappointed. Kinsky did not live to hear any new orchestral work from that recently so prolific pen; Lobkowitz, whose dissatisfaction is upon record, heard but three; while the Archduke saw the years pass away comparatively fruitless, hardly more being accomplished in ten, than formerly in two — the marvellous year 1814 excepted. The close of 1809 terminated a decade (1800-1809) during which — if quality be considered, as well as number, variety, extent and originality — Beethoven's works offer a more splendid exhibition of intellectual power than those of any other composer produced within a like term of years; and New Year, 1810, began another (1810-19) which, compared with the preceding, exhibits an astonishing decrease in the composer's productiveness.

In his revision of Thayer's *Life of Beethoven*, Elliot Forbes suggests that Thayer might have modified his conclusions if he had had access to more reliable chronological facts than were available to him in the 1850s and 60s. The appended table of major completed works nevertheless supports Thayer's view that the decrease in Beethoven's output in the years between 1810 and 1819 was a perceptible and even disturbing phenomenon, reaching a trough of particular emptiness in 1813. The fact that Beethoven was working on other lesser things, and on correcting innumerable proofs, does not invalidate conclusions that are self-evident.

1810, it seems, was a fairly depressing year for Beethoven. Early in February we find him writing to Härtel: 'My health is not quite restored. We are being supplied with bad food for which we have to pay incredible high prices — The arrangements connected with my appointment are not yet working quite smoothly and so far I have not received a farthing from Kinsky — I fear, and indeed I almost hope, that I shall have to go abroad, perhaps too for the sake of my health. It will probably be a long time before I am in a better state of health that I am now. But in any case I shall never recover the good health I used to enjoy — '. In June he again comments on the increasing cost of living and the fact 'that the amount of money one needs is terrifying. Hence from this point of view, as indeed in

1809-1810	Overture and incidental music to *Egmont*
1810	String Quartet in F minor, Op 95, dedicated to Nikolaus Zmeskall von Domanovecz
1811	Piano Trio in B flat major, Op 97, dedicated to Archduke Rudolph
1811-1812	Symphony No 7 in A major, dedicated to Count Moritz von Fries
	Symphony No 8 in F major
1812	Violin Sonata, Op 96, dedicated to Archduke Rudolph
1814	*Fidelio*, third revision and new overture
	Piano Sonata in E minor, Op 90, dedicated to Count Moritz Lichnowsky
1815	Overture, *Zur Namensfeier*, dedicated to Prince Anton Radziwill
	Two Cello Sonatas, Op 102, dedicated to Countess Marie Erdödy
1815-1816	Piano Sonata in A major, Op 101, dedicated to Dorothea Ertmann
1816	Song-cycle, *An die ferne Geliebte*, dedicated to Prince Franz Joseph von Lobkowitz
1817-1818	Piano Sonata in B flat, Op 106, dedicated to Archduke Rudolph

every respect, my fee now is certainly not too high. My 4,000 gulden, on which I can no longer live . . . are not worth even a thousand gulden in assimilated coinage'. There were other depressing factors as well: unlucky yet again in love, Therese Malfatti rejected his proposal of marriage in the late spring. Then the summer was mostly spent in Vienna with only a few weeks in Baden.

Musically, however, three events stand out: the completion of the overture and incidental music to Goethe's *Egmont* in June; the completion of the F minor String Quartet in October; and the well-received first performance of the Fifth Piano Concerto at a Leipzig Gewandhaus concert on 28 November, with Friedrich Schneider as soloist.

Beethoven began work on the *Egmont* music in October 1809 in response to a commission from the Director of the Imperial Theatre, Joseph Hartl Edler von Luchsenstein. Though intended for the first Viennese performance of Goethe's drama on 24 May 1810, it was not in fact ready until 15 June.

Fresco by Moritz von Schwind in the Vienna Opera showing Egmont in prison (centre panel) and scenes from *Fidelio*, *c.* 1868

In a letter to Härtel (21 August 1810) Beethoven says

I composed it purely out of love for the poet; and, in order to prove this, I accepted nothing for it from the Theatrical Directors. They agreed to this arrangement and, as a reward, they treated my music, as they usually do and as they have always done, *very carelessly.* There are no people *more small-minded than our great ones*. But I must make an exception in the case of Archdukes . . .

Beethoven wrote to Goethe on 12 April 1811:

The pressing opportunity afforded me by a friend of mine and a great admirer of yours (as I am also) who is leaving Vienna very soon [Franz Oliva, who delivered Beethoven's letter to Goethe on 2 May], allows me only a moment in which to thank you for the long time I have known you (for that I have done since my childhood) — That is little for so much — Bettina Brentano has assured me that you would receive me kindly, or, I should say, as a friend [Beethoven and Goethe did not meet until July 1812, in Teplitz]. But how could I think of such a welcome, seeing that I can approach you only with the greatest reverence and with an inexpressivly profound feeling of admiration for your glorious creations! —

As with his *Faust*, Goethe's five-act *Egmont*, written in 1775-87 was based on historical fact: in this case the life and martyrdom of Lamoral, Count of Egmont (1522-68), a Flemish general and statesman who came from one of the noblest lines in 16th century Holland. Goethe chose to project the dramatic action through three principal characters: Egmont, the Duke of Alba, and William of Orange, together with Klärchen, whose love for Egmont is a deeper revelation of the man's emotions. Historical fact, however, was freely changed and distorted (as Schiller had noted in an early review) and no where more seriously perhaps than in the final scene where Egmont, in prison, hearing the distant drums of war, exclaims:

How oft this sound has summoned me to march freely on the field of battle and of victory! How gaily did my comrades step out on the dangerous path of glory! And I too step out from this prison to an honourable death; I die for liberty, for which I have lived and fought, and for which I now sacrifice myself in suffering.

Such melodrama was in fact no more than a misrepresentation of the truth, a rhetorical flourish directed at the audience. As Ronald Gray has written:

Egmont has not lived and fought for liberty, and Beethoven's inspiring music in the *Egmont* overture should not persuade us that he has. Fighting in the cause of liberty is precisely what Egmont has refused to do . . . All his final speech is in contradiction to what he has stood for throughout the action of the play, both in that he is now prepared to shed blood after all, and in that he acts in order to achieve a future object, or sees his suffering as part of a pattern of events which will lead to eventual success — yet not a word of realisation crosses his lips . . .*

Beethoven's 'intense' reaction on reading *Egmont* probably stemmed from two very basic issues: (i) the final, contradictory, scene where Egmont himself proclaims his 'sacrifice . . . in suffering' for the cause of liberty; and (ii) the presence of Klärchen, who must have symbolised for him a facet of that perfect woman of his idolisation which had found its fullest expression in Leonore. Links with *Fidelio* in fact continuously spring to mind: the way, for instance, the appearence of Klärchen (as an allegorical figure of Freedom) in Egmont's dream as he lies in prison parallels the appearance of Leonore to Florestan as he lies in the dungeon awaiting execution. It is not difficult, too, to see Alba as the Pizzarro of Goethe's tragedy, and in both *Fidelio* and *Egmont* it is the treatment of politically undesirable individuals through the tyrannous methods of 16th century Spanish overlords which forms the setting for the enactment of the two stories.

Beethoven spent 1811 correcting forthcoming publications of new works, in the process getting more and more frustrated with Breitkopf & Härtel's carelessness and inaccuracies of printing: 'Mistakes — mistakes — you yourself are a unique mistake . . . the tribunal of music at Leipzig can't produce one single efficient proof reader' (6 May). In general, however, a mood of greater relaxation

* Goethe: a Critical Introduction (London 1967)

Ihro Kaiserliche Hoheit!

Morgen in der Frühesten Früh wird der
Copist an dem letzten Stück anfangen
können, da ich selbst unterdessen noch an
mehreren andern Werken schreibe, so habe ich um
der bloßen Pünktlichkeit willen mich nicht
so sehr mit dem letzten Stücke beeilt, um
so mehr, da ich dieses mit mehr Überlegung in
Hinsicht des Spiels von Rode schreiben mußte,
wir haben in unsern Finales gern rauschende
Passagen, doch sagt dies R. nicht zu,

16.

Beethoven letter to Archduke Rudolph, December 1812

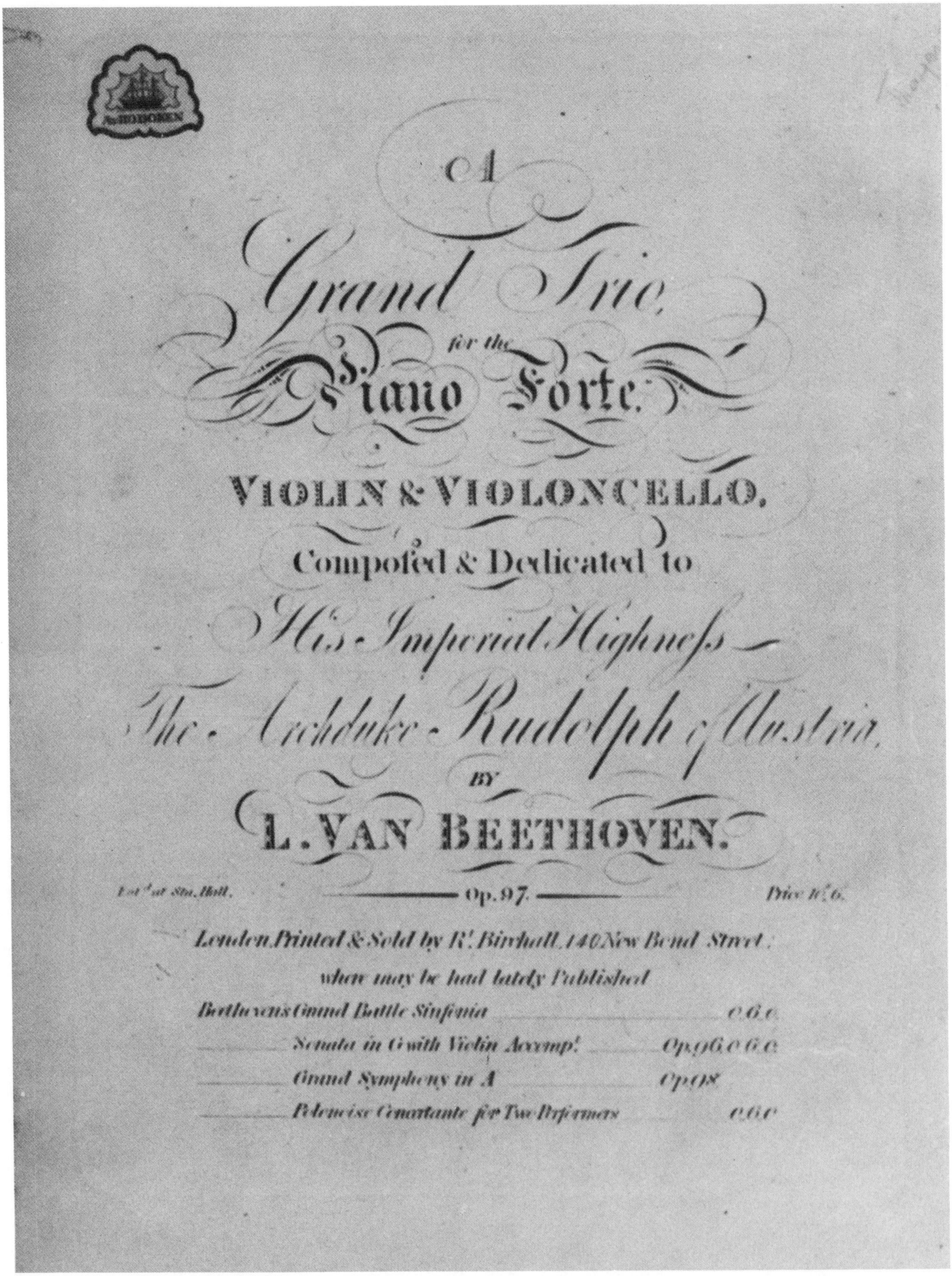

A

Grand Trio,

for the

Piano Forte,

VIOLIN & VIOLONCELLO,

Composed & Dedicated to

His Imperial Highness

The Archduke Rudolph of Austria,

BY

L. VAN BEETHOVEN.

Ent.d at Sta. Hall. —— Op. 97. —— Price 10/6.

London Printed & Sold by R.t Birchall, 140 New Bond Street;

where may be had lately Published

Beethoven's Grand Battle Sinfonia 0.6.0

———— Sonata in G with Violin Accomp.t .... Op. 96. 0.6.0

———— Grand Symphony in A .... Op. 98

———— Polonoise Concertante for Two Performers 0.6.0

Title page of English edition (1816) for the "Archduke" piano trio

Beethoven, a copy of a plaster bust commissioned from F. Klein by the piano maker Streicher, 1812: 'I love most the realm of mind which, to me, is the highest of all spiritual and temporal monarchies'

and tranquillity was the distinguishing mark of the year. In March, in the space of three weeks, he wrote out his celebrated *Archduke* Piano Trio, Op 97. Then, during the summer months at Teplitz, he worked on some incidental music for two plays by Aubust von Kotzebue — *King Stephen* and *The Ruins of Athens*, a Prologue and Epilogue respectively, commissioned for the new Theatre in Pesth, a building complete 'with Ridotto room, casino, restaurant, and coffee house', formally opened in February 1812, after a postponement of several months. Beethoven received the librettos at the end of July 1811 — 'just as I was getting into my carriage to drive to Teplitz.' The music for both was finished by 13 September, and Beethoven seems to have genuinely enjoyed the task, in spite of the fact that the dramatic content of the two plays suffered from both contrivance and paucity of invention.

Back in Vienna from Teplitz, invigorated, having enjoyed a performance of the Mass in C at Prince Lichnowsky's Grätz estate, and with much-needed overdue monies from Prince Kinsky now at last in his pocket, Beethoven set to work sketching two new symphonies: No 7 in A, and No 8 in F.

1812 saw the completion of both these works as well as the serene Op 96 Violin Sonata. It also witnessed the Viennese premiere of the Fifth Piano Concerto on 11 February, with Czerny as soloist. The occasion was in aid of the Society of Noble Ladies for Charity, and combined an exhibition of painting with a concert. Such circumstances did not lend themselves ideally to the understanding of Beethoven's music and its reception was poor, as Castelli's *Thalia* confirms:

> If this composition . . . failed to receive the applause which it deserved, the reason is to be sought partly in the subjective character of the work, partly in the objective nature of the listeners. Beethoven, full of proud confidence in himself, never writes for the multitude; he demands understanding and feeling, and because of the intentional difficulties, he can receive these only at the hands of the knowing, a majority of whom is not to be found on such occasions.

Following the enforcement on 15 March 1811 of the Austrian *Finanz-patent*, concert life in Vienna went through a period of slump and depression. The disaster of the *Finanz-patent* was graphically confirmed by Therese Brunsvik in her *Memoirs:*

> The man who went to bed in March 1811 with the comfortable feeling of being a capitalist, having provided for his wife and children, got up in the morning as a beggar. The incredible happened during the night: The Austro-Hungarian currency lost four out of five parts of its value and the fifth part was devalued soon after, in an effort to pay for war's cost and prevent government bankruptcy.

As a result, Beethoven's 4000 gulden a year was effectively devalued to a point when it had a purchasing power of little more than 1600. By 1812, however, the pace of life had adjusted somewhat and the activity of earlier years was re-kindled.

The Seventh Symphony, that orgasmic hymn of rhythm and life, was completed on 13 May, the Eighth in October, during a visit to Linz. In between Beethoven spent the summer trying to recoup his health in the Bohemian spas at Teplitz, Carlsbad and Franzensbrunn. In July at Teplitz he met Goethe, for the first time. To Carl Friedrich Zelter, director of the Berlin Singakademie since 1800, Goethe wrote:

I made Beethoven's acquaintance in Teplitz. His talent amazed me; unfortunately he is an utterly untamed personality, who is not altogether in the wrong in holding the world to be detestable but surely does not make it any the more enjoyable either for himself or others by his attitude. He is easily excused, on the other hand, and much to be pitied, as his hearing is leaving him, which, perhaps, mars the musical part of his nature less than the social. He is of a laconic nature and will become doubly so because of this lack.

Following a hastily mounted charity concert in aid of the victims of the Baden fire on 26 July when 117 houses, including the palaces of the Archduke Anton and Prince Carl Esterházy, were gutted, Beethoven continued to take the waters, walk in the woods at dawn, and intensify his love both for nature and for one Amalie Sebald. He eventually made his way to Linz, arriving on 5 October, heralded as 'the Orpheus and great musical poet of our time'. He stayed with Johann in his house by the Danube waterfront. The visit, it appears, was not altogether happy. Johann intended to marry his housekeeper, Therese Obermeyer. Beethoven objected violently, and Johann refused to be broken. Thayer chronicled the situation well:

Excited by opposition, Ludwig resorted to any and every means to accomplish his purpose. He saw the Bishop about it. He applied to the civil authorities. He pushed the affair so earnestly, as at last to obtain an order to the police to remove the girl to Vienna if, on a certain day, she should be still found in Linz. The disgrace to the poor girl; the strong liking which Johann had for her; his natural mortification at not being allowed to be master in his own house; these and other similar causes wrought him up almost to desperation. Beethoven, having carried his point, might certainly have borne his brother's anger with equanimity; might have felt pity for him and sought to soothe him in his trouble. But no; when Johann entered his room with reproaches and upbradings, he, too, became angry and a scene ensued on which — let the curtain be drawn.

The outcome was that Beethoven failed in his excitable, irrational plans: Johann married Therese on 8 November.

1813 was for Beethoven a year of increasing financial strain and domestic difficulties. Relations with his other brother, Carl, a sick man, were far from ideal, he hated Carl's wife as much as Carl now mistrusted her, and in October he had to persuade the publisher Steiner to lend the family money, such loan to be either settled in kind or to be set against the publication of future compositions by Beethoven. To complicate the situation further, Beethoven's previously agreeable arrangement with Breitkopf & Härtel came to a sudden end, and the non-appearance of monies due under the annuity contract from the Kinsky estate (the Prince had been killed in a riding accident in November 1812) and Prince Lobkowitz (who had already suspended payment in September 1811, and whom Beethoven saw fit to sue) imposed severe pressure on his already limited resources.

Plans to give some concerts, as well as to go to England, failed to materialise. The summer was once more spent in Baden, but by September Beethoven was again back in Vienna. During the autumn he worked on a *pièce d'occasion*, the so-called *Battle* Symphony or *The Battle of Vittoria*. The epic confrontation between Napoleon and Wellington at Vittoria had taken place on 21 June, and Napoleon's army had been routed. By then Beethoven had become friendly with Johann Nepomuk Mälzel, an inventor (his musical chronometer had been the famous inspiration of the

The first edition of the *Battle* Symphony in the arrangement for solo piano made by Beethoven himself

Ignaz Moscheles (1794-1870). Steel engraving by C. Mayer

second movement of the Eighth Symphony, while his metronome was patented in 1815) and entrepreneur, whose workshops were a source of constant fascination to Beethoven. Mälzel and his brother responded well to the composer and actually made him four ear trumpets at different periods. One of the more bizarre of Mälzel's inventions at this time was the panharmonicon, an instrument, based on revolving cylinders, that could imitate the orchestra and which had vast commercial potential as an entertainment gimmick. Mälzel saw Wellington's victory as an exploitable event, and since there was a vogue for musical celebrations of such things, he wasted no time in asking Beethoven to consider the task. Beethoven agreed and Mälzel helped him, as Moscheles remembered:

I witnessed the origin and progress of this work, and remember that not only did Mälzel decidedly induce Beethoven to write it, but even laid before him the whole design of it; himself wrote all the drum-marches and the trumpet flourishes of the French and English armies; gave the composer some hints, how he should introduce *Malbrook* in a dismal strain; how he should depict the horrors of the battle and arrange *God save the King* with effects representing the hurrahs of a multitude.

In its original version, then, the *Battle* Symphony was written for the panharmonicon. Mälzel, however, needed funds to go to England, and he knew that Beethoven wanted both money and a concert: he had not after all given a benefit *Akademie* for himself since 1808. Accordingly he suggested that a charity concert be held for soldiers wounded at the Battle of Hanau. Its anticipated success, he argued, would then lead to further concerts, the resulting proceeds to be divided between himself and Beethoven. In order to tempt Beethoven further, Mälzel, a good psychologist, agreed to return the score of the *Battle* Symphony so that it could be re-written and arranged for orchestra, and suggested that the as yet unheard Seventh Symphony be included in the programme as well. In between would come just two marches by Dussek and Pleyel, played on another of Mälzel's inventions, the mechanical trumpeter. Beethoven thought this an excellent plan, and the concert was fixed for Wednesday 8 December 1813 in the Great Hall of the University.

If the *Akademie* of five years earlier had been one of the most historically noteworthy events in Beethoven's life, this 1813 one at last brought Beethoven popular fame: as Schindler said, 'all the hitherto divergent voices . . . united in proclaiming him worthy of the laurel'. Mälzel, a popular and energetic figure with a charitable cause to promote, succeeded in making the evening a much publicised, much anticipated celebrity event. Schuppanzigh led the violins, Spohr — the newly appointed leader of the Theater an der

Ludwig Spohr (1784-1859. Pastel self-portrait, 1807 (Landesmuseum, Brunswick)

Wien orchestra — sat next to him, Dragonetti led the double-basses, Romberg led the bassoons, Salieri, still the imperial *Kapellmeister*, directed the battle percussion, Meyerbeer and Hummel played the drums, and Moscheles took the cymbals. Beethoven conducted. Spohr's illuminating reminiscences of the occasion, though often quoted, still bear repetition:

Beethoven had accustomed himself to indicate expression to the orchestra by all manner of singular bodily movements. So often as a *sforzando* occurred, he tore his arms, which he had previously crossed upon his breast, with great vehemence asunder. At *piano* he crouched down lower and lower as he desired the degree of softness. If a *crescendo* then entered he gradually rose again and at the entrance of the *forte* jumped into the air. Sometimes, too, he unconsciously shouted to strength the *forte* . . .

Franz Wild, a famous tenor, whose autobiography was published in 1860, supported Spohr in his own memories of the evening, but had this to say about the *Battle* Symphony*.

his arms and hands would be in motion as if with the music a thousand lives had taken possession of his every limb. At the beginning this did not endanger the effect of the work, for at first the crouching and stretching of his body corresponded respectively to the decrease and the increase of the sound. But suddenly the genius found himself ahead of the orchestra. He became invisible at the *forte* passages and reappeared at the *piano* passages. Danger now threatened, and at the decisive moment, *Kapellmeister* Umlauf took command, making it clear to the orchestra that they should follow him. For a long time Beethoven did not notice anything. When at last he became aware of it, there came to his lips a smile which, if ever it had been my good fortune to see one, deserves the appellation 'heavenly'.

Public response was immediate. The *allegretto* of the Seventh Symphony had to be repeated, 'applause rose to the point of ecstasy', and the press reacted with unequivocable praise. The entire programme had to be repeated before the week was out, on Sunday the 12th at noon, and as a result the total receipts were boosted to over 4,000 florins, all of which, according to the *Wiener Zeitung* for 20 December, was 'reverently turned over to the "hohen Kriegs-Präsidio" for the purposes announced'. It provided an unexpectedly splendid finish to a dark year.

* Thayer attributed Wild's remarks to a later concert: however the account began with a specific reference 'the first performance' of the *Battle* Symphony.

Chapter 12

The Congress of Vienna

'O man, help yourself' — Beethoven

The triumph of that 1813 concert was to prove a very real turning point in Beethoven's position in Vienna. From now on he began to enjoy a public fame and reputation and a financial reward of a kind that he had not previously experienced. Even so he remained a bitter, suspicious, often irrationally angry man. On 18 December, so soon after his success, he could write: 'In everything I undertake in Vienna I am still surrounded by innumerable enemies. I am on the verge of despair — My brother [Carl?] whom I have loaded with benefits, and owing partly to whose deliberate action I myself am financially embarrassed, is — my greatest enemy!'.

In his sour, often cantankerous mood, he frequently ran the risk of losing all but his closest friends and admirers. Karl Lichnowsky, however, never forsook him, and several anecdotes of this period have survived, testifying to the remarkably understanding relationship that existed between the two men. At the time Beethoven lived on the fourth floor of the Pasqualati house on the Mölker Bastei, his rooms offering a commanding view across the Glacis. It was to here that Lichnowsky would come and visit him. Thayer reported one such meeting on the authority of Röckel, the 1806 Florestan:

> When he [Beethoven] invited Röckel to visit him, he added that he would give his servant special instructions to admit him at any time, even in the mornings when he was working. It was agreed that if Röckel were admitted and found that Beethoven was very busy, he would go through his room to the adjoining bedroom. There he would wait a certain length of time. If the composer did not appear, Röckel was to leave again quietly. One morning, on his first visit, it so happened that at the front door Röckel saw a carriage in which a lady was sitting. When he arrived at the fourth floor, there was Prince Lichnowsky arguing with the servant. He wished to be admitted, but the servant declared he could admit no one because his master was busy and had left strict orders to admit no one at all. Röckel, however, who did have permission, told Beethoven that Lichnowsky was outside. Though in bad humour, he [Beethoven] could not go on refusing to admit the Prince. Lichnowsky and his wife had come to invite

'L'art unit tout le monde': the famous Höfel engraving of Beethoven after the pencil drawing by L. Letronne, 1814. According to contemporary opinion this was a particularly faithful likeness and it was widely available during the Congress

Beethoven for a drive, and in the end Beethoven consented; yet even as he entered the carriage, Röckel observed, his face bore a dour expression.

Others, however, were less tolerant and quarrels came about, the wounds of which only rarely healed. Soon after the December concert, Mälzel, for example, fell foul of the master and Beethoven went out of his way to ensure that any profits from forthcoming benefit concerts featuring the *Battle* Symphony would remain his alone, and would not be shared with Mälzel as originally agreed. The first demonstration of this was on 2 January 1814, when the *Battle* Symphony and the Seventh were repeated, this time in the larger hall of the Redoutensaal. Mälzel's mechanical trumpet was dispensed with to be replaced by some music from *The Ruins of Athens*. As Thayer says, 'What [Mälzel's] feelings were now, to find himself deprived of all share in the benefit resulting from [his original services], and therefore left without compensation, may readily be conceived'. The *Battle* symphony rapidly gained in popularity, but Mälzel got nothing. He tried to obtain the right of first performance in England, but Beethoven repeatedly raised objections. In the end Mälzel resorted to deceit: he managed, by devious means, to obtain performing parts and reconstruct the work for his own guidance (the music itself was not published until February 1816). He then included it in two of his own concerts in Munich in March 1814. Beethoven's wrath knew no limits. Increasingly prone to using solicitors, he proceeded to sue Mälzel, a pointless exercise, since Mälzel was by then heading for England and was in consequence out of the jurisdiction of Austrian law. He also sent a copy of the work to the Prince Regent, and on 25 July 1814, lodged an 'Explanation and Appeal to the Musicians of London' in which he claimed that if Mälzel was to play the *Battle* Symphony he would be committing 'a fraud on the public'. In a Deposition prepared for his lawyer, Beethoven concluded excitably that Mälzel was a 'coarse fellow, entirely without education or culture', and he spoke of his 'bad patriotic character'. So much energy to so little avail. The suit dragged on until finally in 1817 Mälzel returned to Vienna, patched up his differences with Beethoven, split the costs of the case, and once again shared a meal in friendship. Beethoven for his part publicly praised Mälzel's newly developed metronome, and in the Leipzig *Allgemeine Musikalische Zeitung* for 17 December 1817 published a list of suggested metronome markings for the first eight Symphonies. Mälzel went on his way and died in July 1838 on an American brig sailing between Philadelphia and the West Indies, the richer, apparently, by half a million dollars.

Such petty irritations apart, and in spite of the continuing legal entanglement with the Kinsky estate, 1814 was a year of glory for

The Kinsky Palace in Vienna

Beethoven: 'My kingdom is in the air', he wrote to Count Franz Brunsvik on 13 February: 'As the wind often does, so do harmonies whirl around me, and so do things often whirl about too in my soul'. Sunday 27 February saw another *Akademie*, including once more the Seventh Symphony (with the *allegretto* again encored), the *Battle* Symphony, and the first performance of the Eighth. The *Allgemeine Musikalische Zeitung* wrote of the latter:

The greatest interest of the listeners seemed centred on this, the *newest* product of B's muse, and expectation was tense, but this was not sufficiently gratified after the *single* hearing, and the applause which it received was not accompanied by that enthusiasm which distinguishes a work which gives universal delight; in short — as the Italians say — it did not create a furore. This reviewer is of the opinion that the reason does not lie by any means in weaker or less artistic workmanship (for here, as in all of B's works of this class, there breathes that peculiar spirit by which his originality always asserts itself); but partly in the faulty judgment which permitted this symphony to follow that in A major, partly in the surfeit of beauty and excellence which must necessarily be followed by a reaction. If this symphony should be performed *alone* hereafter, we have no doubt of its success.

Schindler, a pupil of Schuppanzigh, reported an audience of 5,000, and Beethoven further had the pleasure of one of the largest orchestras he had yet conducted. 18 first and 18 second violins, 14 violas, 12 cellos, 7 double-basses and 2 contra-bassoons are specifically mentioned in one of his notes — exceptional forces for the day, when one considers that the Leipzig Gewandhaus Orchestra in 1831 still only had a string force of 8 - 8 - 4 - 3 - 3, while the Vienna

Court Opera as late as 1842 could only muster a string complement of 9 - 9 - 4 - 5 - 5. More of Beethoven's music turned up in other programmes and at the Annual Spring *Akademie* at the Kärnthnerthortheater on 25 March he conducted the *Battle* Symphony again: it had rapidly become the Viennese craze of the year. Then on 11 April in the hall of the Hotel zum Römischen Kaiser, a few days before the much-lamented death of Karl Lichnowsky on the 15th, Beethoven consented to play the piano once more, this time with Schuppanzigh and Linke in the first performance of his last Piano Trio, the *Archduke* in B flat. Spohr recalled one of the rehearsals in Beethoven's rooms:

It was not a treat, for, in the first place, the piano was badly out of tune, which Beethoven minded little, since he did not hear it; and secondly, on account of his deafness there was scarcely anything left of the virtuosity of the artist which had formerly been so greatly admired. In *forte* passages the poor deaf man pounded on the keys till the strings jangled, and in *piano* he played so softly that whole groups of tones were omitted, so that the music was unintelligible unless one could look into the pianoforte part. I was deeply saddened at so hard a fate. If it is a great misfortune for any one to be deaf, how shall a musician endure it without giving way to despair? Beethoven's continual melancholy was no longer a riddle to me.

Beethoven played it again shortly afterwards at one of Schuppanzigh's morning concerts in the Prater; after that he was not to touch the piano again in public, save as an accompanist.

The first real proof of Beethoven's new-found fame and popularity came less in these concerts, however, than in the request of three singers — Saal, Vogl and Weinmüller — to mount a revival of *Fidelio*, that sickly, forgotten child of nearly a decade earlier, for the purpose of a forthcoming joint benefit concert. The directors of the Kärnertortheater decided in favour of the idea, and Beethoven, gratified, agreed, on condition however that the work be revised yet again. The task of reworking Sonnleithner's libretto was entrusted to Georg Friedrich Treitschke. The action was tightened, 'the scene of the entire first act was laid in an open court', and the finale to the same was given 'more occasion'. Writing of the second act, Treitschke had this to say:

A scene from the 1814 production of *Fidelio* as illustrated in the *Wiener Hoftheater Almanach*

Beethoven at first wanted to distinguish poor Florestan with an aria, but I offered the objection that it would not be possible to allow a man nearly dead of hunger to sing *bravura* . . . Beethoven came to me about seven o'clock in the evening. After we had discussed other things, he asked how matters stood with the aria? It was just finished, I handed it to him. He read it, ran up and down the room, muttered, growled, as was his habit instead of singing — and tore open the pianoforte. My wife had often vainly begged him to play; to-day he placed the text in front of him and began to improvise marvellously — music which no magic could hold fast. Out of it he seemed to conjure the motive of the aria. The hours went by, but Beethoven improvised on. Supper, which he had purposed to eat with us, was served, but — he would not permit himself to be disturbed. It was late when he embraced me, and declining the meal, he hurried home.

At the very end Treitschke introduced a further change in scenery so that the great conclusion of liberation would be 'in full daylight upon a bright green courtyard of the palace'. By March 1814 Beethoven was able to write to Treitschke: 'I have received with great pleasure your corrections for the opera. And now I feel more firmly resolved to rebuild the desolate ruins of an old castle'. In spite of extensive re-writing and re-casting Beethoven was still not entirely happy with the result. 'This opera', he swore, 'will win for me a martyr's crown', and in a letter to Treitschke dating from about 14 May (and now in the Library of Congress) we find him reflecting: '. . . this whole opera business is the most tiresome affair in the world, for I am dissatisfied with most of it — and — there is hardly a number in it which *my present dissatisfaction would not have to patch up here and there with some satisfaction* — well, that is a very different thing from being able to indulge in free meditation or inspiration'.

The first performance of this third and final version of *Fidelio* was scheduled for 23 May. Treitschke remembered that

The final rehearsal was on May 22nd, but the promised new overture was still in the pen of the creator. The orchestra was called to rehearsal on the morning of the performance. B. did not come. After waiting a long time we drove to his lodgings to bring him, but — he lay in bed, sleeping soundly, beside him stood a goblet with wine and a biscuit in it, the sheets of the overture were scattered on the bed and floor. A burnt-out candle showed that he had worked far into the night. The impossibility of completing the overture was plain; for this occasion his overture to *Prometheus* [actually *The Ruins of Athens*] was taken and the announcement that because of obstacles which had presented themselves the new overture would have to be dispensed with today, enabled the numerous audience to guess the sufficient reason.

The Lobkowitzplatz in Vienna with the late 17th Century palace of Prince Lobkowitz in the foreground. Oil painting by B. Bellotto (Kunsthistorisches Museum, Vienna)

The evening was an unquestionable triumph. Anna Milder-Hauptmann, now older and more experienced, re-created her original rôle of Leonore to memorable effect, Vogl took the part of Pizarro, and Radicci was Florestan. Unlike the 1805 and 1806 performances, the new production had been in rehearsal for some time (since mid-April, in fact), and Treitschke says that it 'was capitally prepared. Beethoven conducted, his ardour often rushed him out of time, but *Kapellmeister* Umlauf, behind his back, guided everything to success with eye and hand. The applause was great, and increased with every representation'. The Viennese press of the day confirmed the success of the evening. Another performance followed on the 26th, this time with the newly-composed *Fidelio* overture itself. Once more the reception was 'tempestuous'. The opera was to be staged again and again throughout 1814: including the first night, some 20 performances in all took place that year. Of these, that on 18 July was for Beethoven's own benefit: complimentary tickets were cancelled and 'the house was very full; the applause extraordinary; the enthusiasm for the composer, who has now become a favourite of the public, manifested itself in calls before the curtain after every act' (*Wiener Zeitung*).

Although this final version of *Fidelio* was to remain unpublished in score until a French edition (in *three* acts) appeared in 1826, Artaria in Vienna wasted no time in issuing a vocal score in August, arranged by Moscheles, then just twenty.

Coincidentally, it was on July 18th, the day of Beethoven's benefit, that Metternich returned to announce the impending Congress of Vienna that was eventually to restore, for better or worse, some semblance of sanity and reason to a Europe that for a quarter of a century had been ravaged by strife and war. Political historians have summed-up the Congress as 'one of the most important international conferences of European history'. The people who were actually there remembered it rather differently. For them, it was the 'dancing Congress', and Vienna was a carnival city which offered plenty of excuses for pleasurable diversion, for entertainment, for half-hearted duels, for passionate affairs of the heart, clandestine and public. By the time of the Final Act of the Congress, nearly nine months later, much ground had been covered, but in so haphazard a fashion and with so little sense of organisation that the surprise of it is that it happened at all. Talleyrand, the French representative, wrote home to Louis XVIII that 'The Tsar of Russia, loves, the King of Denmark drinks, the King of Württemberg eats, the King of Prussia thinks, the King of Bavaria talks — and the Emperor of Austria pays'. And how he paid! Banquets, balls in the Redoutensaal, concerts, exhibitions, hunting trips, sleigh parties, firework displays, balloon ascents (by Kraskowitz, a celebrated figure), were but a sample of what the specially appointed Festival Committee were able to offer the countless heads of state and reinstated royal families of Europe who streamed into Vienna for the best part of a year. The cost was staggering — 500,000 gulden (£50,000) *a day* to feed the guests alone. Vienna became overrun with visitors. Over 100,000 are said to have converged on the place. Added to the royal households, as Dorothy Gies McGuigan has written, were 'ministers, statesmen, diplomats, aides, and secretaries by the hundred. Besides these there were the lobbyists, place-seekers, artists, writers, inventors, philosophers, actors and actresses, dancers, acrobats, prostitutes, pickpockets, swindlers, reformers burning with a cause, political dreamers with magnificent constitutions in their pockets — all congregating on Vienna to see and be seen, to bribe or make money, to get back an old kingdom or acquire a new one; everybody, in short, who hoped to snatch some plum out of the rich pie of Europe. . .'*

The musical life of the city was no less geared to the Congress and its requirements. *Fidelio* was given a royal performance on 26 September and Handel's *Samson* followed on 10 October. Then a Grand Gala Concert of Beethoven's music was announced at the Redoutensaal for 20 November. It had to be postponed, however, to the 22nd and then the 27th, a Sunday. At this point a problem arose of a kind nobody had envisaged: 'The English,' a report prepared for the Viennese Secret Police, a particularly censorial body, explained, 'are so religious that they do not listen to music on Sundays'. The *Akademie* in consequence had to be delayed again, this time to Tuesday the 29th at noon. The same police report suggests that in the end it was perhaps less than wholly successful: 'Yesterday's musical Academy did not in any way increase esteem for the talent of H. Beethoven. There are factions *pro* and *contra*

* Dorothy McGuigan's estimate in *The Habsburgs*. Harold Nicolson, *The Congress of Vienna*, suggested a *total* cost of 'no less than thirty million florins' (say, 150 million Austrian gulden) for the duration of the Congress. Talleyrand quoted a figure of 220,000 gulden per day, a figure scarcely less astronomical.

The Congress of Vienna gathers. Painting by Isabey

Beethoven. In contrast to Rasumowsky, Apponyi, Kraft, who deify Beethoven, there exists a substantial majority of knowledgeable people who want to hear no music whatsoever by Herr Beethoven'. Tomášek was present beforehand and reported similarly on the programme, which comprised the Seventh and the *Battle* symphonies, and a new cantata, *Der glorreiche Augenblick. Augenblick* was a deliberately topical piece, to words by Alois Weissenbach, who, Thayer believed, 'must have profoundly studied and heartily adopted the principles of composition as set forth by Martinus Scriblerus in his "Treatise of Bathos, or the Art of Sinking in Poetry": for anything more stilted in style, yet more absurdly prosaic, with nowhere a spark of poetic fire to illuminate its dreary pages, is hardly conceivable'. Tomášek wrote in his *Memoirs* (1845):

The concert concluded with *The Battle of Vittoria*, which carried away the major portion of the audience with enthusiasm. I myself, on the contrary, was very painfully affected on finding Beethoven, whom Providence has perhaps endowed with the loftiest throne in the realm of tone, among the crassest of materialists. They do tell me that he himself has called the work a stupid thing, and that he likes it only because it was a success that took away the breath of the Viennese. I myself believe that it was not the *Battle*, but his other magnificent works with which, little by little, Beethoven gained Vienna's favour. When the orchestra was almost entirely submerged by the godless din of drums, the rattling and slambanging, and I expressed my disapproval of the thundering applause to Mr. von Sonnleithner, the latter mockingly replied that the crowd would have enjoyed it even more if their own empty heads had been thumped in the same way. The concert was held with Umlauf conducting, Beethoven

Biedermeier Vienna dances (Theatermuseum, Munich).
'For the nobility, the chief thing at the theatre is the ballet . . . they have sense only for horses and dancers' — Beethoven, 1825

standing beside him and beating time, though usually his beat was wrong because of his deafness. This, however, caused no confusion, since the orchestra followed only Umlauf's beat. Quite deafened by the cataract of noise I was glad to get out into the open again.

Others, however, took a very different view of the occasion. The *Diary* of Carl Betruch, a Weimar publisher whose effort in 1815 to secure a law against the piracy of copyright was an especially noteworthy endeavour, liked the concert and reported that the royal guests included the Tsar (Alexander I) and his Empress — Elisabeth Alexiewna — the King of Prussia and the Royal Prince of Sicily: 'The hall was very full'. The *Wiener Zeitung* for 30 November spoke of 'ecstatic pleasure', and commented on the fact that 'seated in the orchestra were to be seen the foremost virtuosi, who were in the habit of showing their respect for [Beethoven] and art by taking part in [his] Academies'. A repeat performance on Friday December 2 for Beethoven's benefit encountered a half-empty hall, but another on December 25, for the benefit of St. Mark's Hospital, was received once again with enthusiasm and praise.

The Congress brought other accolades. Beethoven, possibly through the efforts of Count Rasumowsky (who was to remember the year tragically for the destruction of his palace by fire on the night of 30/31 December following a banquet for 700 guests) was presented to the Empress of Russia. She, in turn, accepted the dedication of a Polonaise for piano (Op 89) as well as that of Czerny's two-piano arrangement of the Seventh Symphony—according to Beethoven, 'one of the happiest products of my poor talents'. Then, at a court function on 25 January 1815 to celebrate the birthday of the Empress, Beethoven offered to play the piano once more, this time accompanying Franz Wild in his early *Adelaide.*

The Congress of Vienna came to an official close with the ratification of the Final Act on 9 June 1815, just days before the Battle of Waterloo. For Beethoven, in his mid-forties, it had been a period of deserved fame, of prolonged applause, of popular acceptance. As Thayer put it, he 'might well have adopted Kotzebue's title, "The Most Remarkable Year of my Life", and written his own history for 1814, in glowing and triumphant language.'

Chapter 13

'The most celebrated of living composers'

'It has sometimes been said abroad that Beethoven was neglected and oppressed in Vienna. The truth is that he enjoyed, even as a young man, all possible support and an encouragement and respect on the part of our nobility' — Czerny

Creatively the final decade or so of Beethoven's life marked the period of the last five great sonatas 'für das Hammerklavier' (1816-22), the monumental 33 Variations on a Waltz of Diabelli for piano (1819-23), the gigantic affirmation of the *Missa Solemnis* for soloists, choir, organ and orchestra (1819-23), the no less galactic might of the Ninth Symphony (1822-24) and the pioneering inward-searching world of the last five string quartets (1822-26). Alongside these masterpieces of history, were countless unfulfilled plans for other works. The sketchbooks, letters, and, later, the conversation-books for the years 1815-1827, show a mind teeming with ideas. Plans for a Tenth Symphony in C minor (1825-26), a 'musical leviathan' possibly intended for the Philharmonic Society of London, are well known, but the period saw, too, aspirations in many other directions: an overture on B-A-C-H, the notes B flat-A-C-B natural in German nomenclature (1822-24), a 'Characteristic Overture' in E flat (*c.* 1824-25), a Sixth Piano Concerto in D and a Horn Concerto in G (both 1815), various chamber works (including a Flute Quintet in 1824), and a pair of piano-duet sonatas (1824). As for the operatic stage, Beethoven was in love with it to the very end. Out of a total of forty projected operas between 1801 and 1826, over half date from 1816 onwards: they included such themes as *Bacchus, Romulus and Remus, Antigone, Orest, Melusine, Romeo and Juliet, Kenilworth* (after Scott) and *Claudine von Villa Bella* (after Goethe). Schiller, Schlegel and Voltaire were other sources of inspiration, and both Rellstab and Grillparzer kept Beethoven tempted with ideas.

Beethoven's last piano, a Graf (Fischer & Kock)

An increasing admiration for baroque and pre-classical masters produced its share of projects as well. Handel, in particular, was a

revered model. From the early Vienna days, when he had heard his music in van Swieten's rooms, Beethoven worshipped the ideal that he felt Handel embodied. 'To him I bow the knee', he remarked in 1824; two years later he expressed the piano to be an inadequate instrument: 'In the future I shall write in the manner of my grand-master, Handel. . .'. In the last months of his life, in December 1826 in fact, the event that most cheered him was the receipt from London of Dr. Arnold's edition of Handel's work, in 40 calf-bound volumes: 'I have long wanted them', Beethoven said, 'for Handel is the greatest, the ablest composer that ever lived. I can still learn from him'. Bach, as early as 1801 had been 'the immortal god of harmony', and he remained similarly revered in the last years. As a writer of pure church music, Palestrina was held to be sacrosanct. The outcome of such influences, distinctly unfashionable for their time, not only became overtly manifest, of course, in things like the *Missa Solemnis* or the Ninth's choral finale (particularly at the words 'seid umschlungen Millionen! Diesen Kuss der gunzen Welt!' — 'I embrace you all ye millions, with one kiss greet all the world' — but also in the admirably controlled archaisms of the substantial overture to *The Consecration of the House* (1822). The sketchbooks for the period show Beethoven deliberately copying out, intentionally absorbing, passages from Handel's *Messiah*, from Bach's *Art of Fugue*. They also reveal plans for a Requiem Mass (1818-26), another ordinary Mass (1824, in C sharp minor) and a setting of *Veni Creator Spiritus* (1825-26). Then there are ideas for consciously Handelian oratorios and cantatas: *The Passions* (1818), *Judah*, (1819-22), *The Four Elements* and *Saul and David* (both 1826), and so on. Other oratorios were contemplated at different times for the Vienna Synagogue and the newly-founded Gesellschaft der Musikfreunde. Beethoven's enthusiasms new no bounds: in spite of tribulations, and deteriorating health and domestic strife, his intellectual energy, it is clear, remained undiminished, his mind as receptive as it had always been.

Sketches for the unfinished Tenth Symphony, according to Schindler the last music that Beethoven wrote (Staatsbibliothek, Preussisches Kulturbesitz, Berlin)

In these last years he remained, too, as alive as ever to the continuing need of getting his music, old and new, both published and performed. Since earlier differences with Breitkopf & Härtel in Leipzig had effectively cut off that source of publication (not to be resumed again until February 1822 — the publication of the *Fidelio* overture in parts — and 1826, the issue of the Fifth and Sixth symphonies in full score) he now turned increasingly to Steiner in Vienna, and then to Simrock in Bonn, to the Schlesingers in Berlin and Paris, and to Schott in Mainz.

Sigmund Anton Steiner (1773-1838) had set himself up in business in the first years of the 19th century (he acquired

George Frederick Handel (1685-1759)

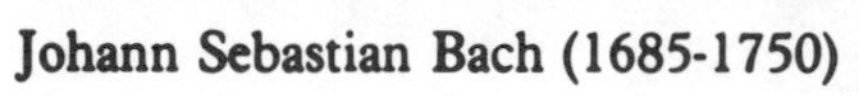

Johann Sebastian Bach (1685-1750)

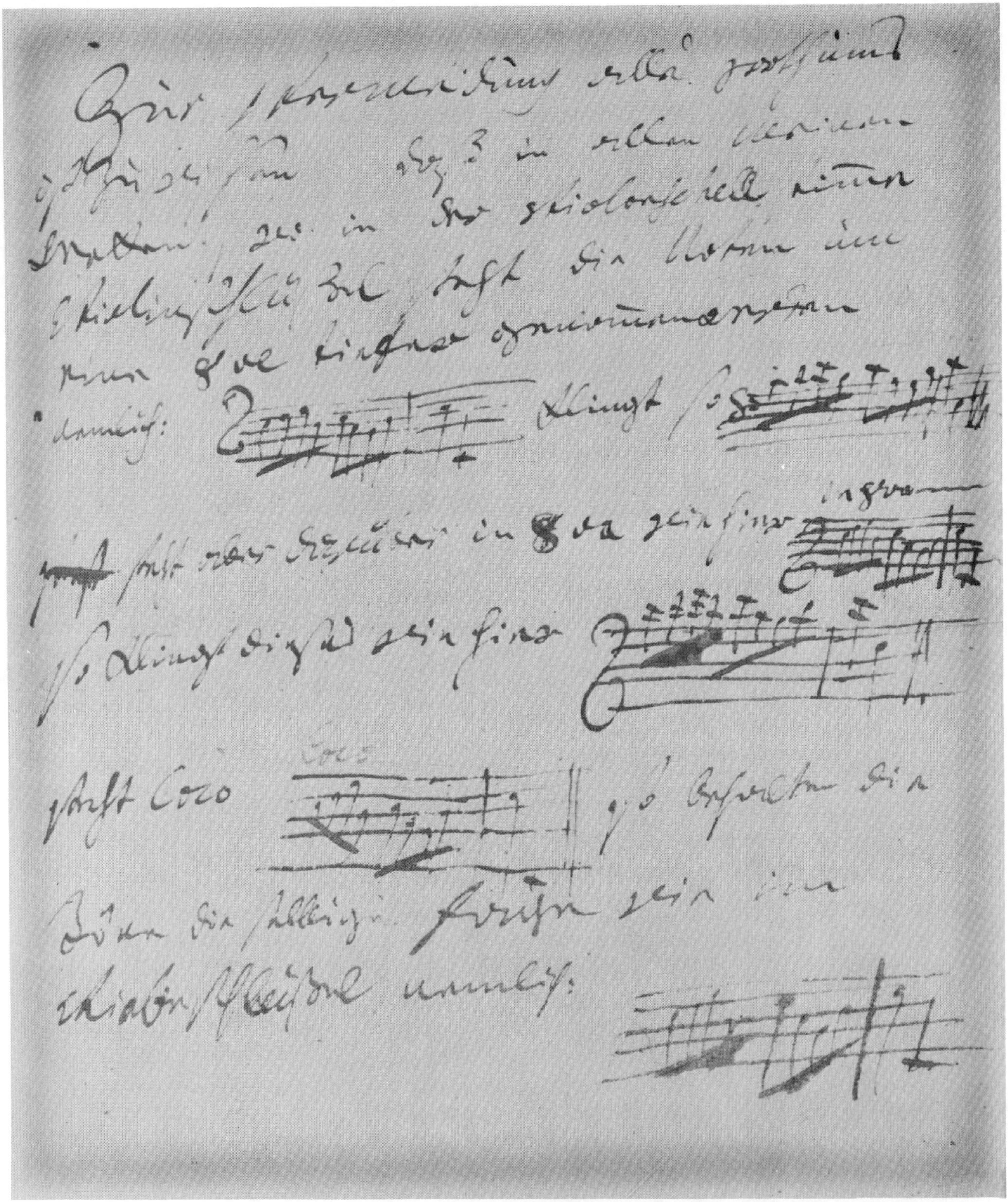

Beethoven letter to Steiner, September 1816

'I shall seize Fate by the throat: it shall certainly not bend and crush me'. Oil painting of Beethoven by W.J. Mähler, 1815 (Karajan Collection, Salzburg)

Senefelder's lithographic printing works in 1804, and by 1823 had taken over the Bureau des Arts et d'Industrie as well). In letters and dealings of the period, Beethoven affectionately and boisterously called Steiner Lieutenant General (Beethoven himself *of course* was the Generalissimo), while Steiner's partner, Tobias Haslinger (who joined the company in 1814 and took it over after Steiner's retirement in 1826), was referred to as the Adjutant. Anton Diabelli, then copyist, proof-reader and general factotum, was variously both Diabolus or Provost Marshal. The military connotations were carried further in that Steiner's shop became headquarters, and poor work or carelessness was eagerly rewarded with a grand court martial, presided over by the Generalissimo himself. Steiner returned the cordiality, lent Beethoven money, and generally helped in whatever way he could. It was, for a time at least, to be a particularly happy, relaxed relationship. With Steiner Beethoven eventually published the Seventh and Eighth Symphonies, and the *Battle of Vittoria* in 1816-17 (both in score *and* parts, then a rare procedure for the period — usually works appeared in parts only), the Quartet, Op 95, the Violin Sonata, Op 96, the *Archduke* Trio and the *An die ferne Geliebte* song cycle in 1816, and the Piano Sonatas Opp 90 and 101 in 1815-17. Lesser works followed.

Once again not everyone, however, found Beethoven that easy to get on with. He may have had his own reasons, his own code of moral conduct, but often he gave others the impression of being an unreliable businessman with little concern for either scruples or fairness. He would craftily offer early works as new ones, he would try to command large sums for relatively insubstantial pieces (when he submitted the Op 119 Bagatelles to Carl Friedrich Peters in 1822, Peters returned them with the observation that they were not worth the money being asked — 'eight gold ducats [36 gulden] apiece' — and that Beethoven should not waste time with such trifles), and he thought nothing of the ethics of offering the same work to several publishers simultaneously. The classic example of this was the *Missa Solemnis*. Between 1820 and 1824 it was offered to *seven* different publishers (Simrock, A.M. Schlesinger [Berlin], Peters, Artaria, Diabelli, M. Schlesinger [Paris] and Probst). On the same day that Beethoven offered it to Probst (10 March 1814), he also wrote to Schott, who finally secured the publication-rights for 1000 gulden (£100). In an unpublished essay on the *Missa Solemnis*, Arthur Hutchings rightly observed some years ago on how the absence of adequately enforceable copyright laws in the early 19th century heavily loaded the commercial dice against author and composer, a situation that was in fact to continue until relatively recently. His conclusion provides an apposite summing-up of the situation that faced Beethoven:

Beethoven's rapacity and duplicity concerning the sale of his works has been called 'shamelessly dishonest' and 'inexcusable' by idolaters of Beethoven the artist. Many of us who are not idolaters and seek no excuse for Beethoven the Bargainer, feel like onlookers who rejoice when a fox, or even a human criminal, outwits his pursuers. Beethoven was the first great composer who consistently stood out for what he thought his right though it may have been more than his legal rights; to secure it he took payment and failed to deliver what he had led the payers to expect. He knew of Mozart's misery, and it is sometimes forgotten that he himself at least knew the dread of penury.

* * *

Regarding performances, Beethoven continued to enjoy much of his earlier success, though so far as personal benefits or Academies were concerned, the period 1815-27 witnessed just the one on 7 May 1824 at the Kärntnertortheater, when the first performance of the Ninth Symphony was given. Beethoven's music, however, was included in a number of other programmes, not least in those of the Gesellschaft der Musikfreunde (established in 1813 by Sonnleithner under the patronage of the Archduke Rudolph). The Op 104 String Quintet, a reworking of the early Op 1 No 3 Piano Trio, was included in one of their programmes for December 1818, and their 1820 season (February, April and November) honoured Beethoven with performances of the Third, Fifth and Eighth Symphonies. Subsequently, on 29th November 1825, the Society elected Beethoven as an honorary member, together with Cherubini, Spontini and Spohr. Yet another distinction to add to all those others of a decade which had begun in December 1815 with a 'solemn' confirmation of Beethoven as an honorary citizen of Vienna.

Ignaz Schuppanzigh, 'My lord Falstaff' as Beethoven called him (1776-1830). Caricature, 1810

Franz Xaver Gebauer's *Concerts spirituels*, held in the Landständischer Saal, also featured a good deal of Beethoven's work. The first four symphonies and the *Pastoral* were given in 1819-20, as well as the Mass in C. The remaining symphonies (Nos 5, 7, 8) appeared in the 1820-21 season, together with the *Christus* oratorio. Then there were Widows and Orphans and St. Mark's Hospital Fund concerts, as well as other benefits. Works like the Seventh and Eighth Symphonies seem to have been recurrent favourites.

Following the destruction of Rasumowsky's palace, Schuppanzigh left for a tour of Germany, Poland and Russia, not returning to Vienna again until 1823. Before he left he gave a farewell concert at Count Deym's palace on 11 February 1816. The programme comprised the Op 59, No 3 Quartet, the Septet, and the

Quintet for piano and wind Op 16 (presumably in the piano and string trio alternative arrangement) in which Czerny took part. With the temporary abandonment of the Schuppanzigh Quartet, the cellist Linke also left to become chamber virtuoso to the Countess Erdödy, and in turn gave a farewell concert at the Hotel zum Römischen Kaiser on 18 February 1816. With Czerny he played the big Op 69 Cello Sonata, and Stainer von Felsburg offered one of the piano sonatas, probably Op 90 in E minor, one of the few known *public* performances of Beethoven's piano sonatas in Vienna in his lifetime and the more exceptional for that fact.

When Schuppanzigh returned to Vienna in 1823, he and Linke, now first cellist at the Theater an der Wien, resumed their former collaboration with Joseph Mayseder and the viola player, Franz Weiss. Between them they again established that virtually unparallelled level of chamber music-making in Vienna for which they had been famous since 1808. Again, too, the quartets of Beethoven became the staple fare of their repertoire. The Op 95 Quartet and the evergreen Septet were played on 1 February 1824, both works to be repeated on 23 January of the following year. 1825 was a year rich in Beethoven quartet performances: six of the new E flat, Op 127, alone, including the première on 6 March, and five of the A minor, Op 132, first heard on 9 September (in public on 6 November). The year witnessed, too, several piano trio performances with Czerny and Anton Halm, as well as the Mass in C at the Karlskirche (18 September) and the *Eroica* (27 November). On 21 March 1826, Halm played the *Archduke* Trio at a concert which also included the Schuppanzigh Quartet in the first performance of the original version of the B flat Quartet, Op 130, complete with the massive, uncompromising Grosse Fuge finale.

Equally important in assessing Beethoven's reputation in Vienna, contrary to whatever he might have thought or imagined, were the revivals of *Fidelio*. Among these the 1822 production at the Kärtnertortheater in November and December was especially notable for introducing Wilhelmine Schröder from Hamburg in the rôle of Leonore. Schröder, one of the greatest Leonores of all time (she recreated the part when *Fidelio* was first staged in London, at His Majesty's Theatre, 18 May 1832), was then still only eighteen, yet with already a considerable reputation created through appearing as Pamina in Mozart's *Die Zauberflöte* and Agathe in Weber's *Der Freischütz* which she had sung in Vienna earlier that year under the composer's direction. Beethoven was moved and overwhelmed, the more so since his attempt to conduct the revival had yet again failed dismally on account of his inability to hear. Less than two years later he was still desperately trying to conduct in public but, as we have noted elsewhere, years

Wilhelmine Schröder (1804-60). Steel engraving by K. Mauer, *c.* 1825

of experience had by now taught orchestras to ignore his beat and to follow instead that of Michael Umlauf, the *Kapellmeister* of the two court theatres, who would stand either beside or behind Beethoven. If matters in this respect had already been less than ideal in 1813-14, there is no doubt that they had badly disintegrated by 1819, when Beethoven again ventured into public with the Seventh Symphony, while the first performance of the *Consecration of the House* Overture and incidental music at the opening of the new Josephstadttheater, 3-6 October 1822, had been an even more sorry affair, not helped by Beethoven reverting to the practice of actually directing from the piano. Schröder, in a reminiscent published in 1846, remembered Beethoven's breakdown as he sat before the orchestra at a rehearsal for *Fidelio*:

With a bewildered face and unearthly inspired eyes, waving his baton back and forth with violent motions, he stood in the midst of the performing musicians and didn't hear a note! If he thought it should be *piano* he crouched down almost under the conductor's desk and if he wanted *forte* he jumped up with the strangest gestures, uttering the weirdest sounds. With each piece our courage dwindled further and I felt as though I were watching one of Hoffmann's fantastic figures appear before me. The inevitable happened: the deaf master threw the singers and orchestra completely off the beat and into the greatest confusion, and no one knew any longer were they were.

Schindler's account makes a poignantly sad finish to the story:

The impossibility of going ahead with the author of the work was evident. But how, in what manner inform him of the fact? Neither Duport, the director, nor Umlauf was willing to speak the saddening words: 'It will not do; go away, you unhappy man!' Beethoven, already uneasy in his seat, turned now to the right now to the left, scrutinizing the faces to learn the cause of the interruption. Everywhere a heavy silence. Then he summoned me. I had approached near him in the orchestra. He handed me his notebook with an indicatation that I write what the trouble was. Hastily I wrote in effect: 'Please do not go on; more at home.' With a bound he was in the parterre and said merely: 'Out, quick!' Without stopping he ran towards his lodgings. Inside he threw himself on the sofa, covered his face with his hands and remained in this attitude till we sat down to eat. During the meal not a word came from his lips; he was a picture of profound melancholy and depression. When I tried to go away after the meal he begged me not to leave him until it was time to go to the theatre.

Wilhelmine Schröder, was, of course, but one of that new generation who had grown up from the beginning in an atmosphere steeped in the sound of Beethoven's music and dominated by the elemental power of his charisma. The roguish young Franz

Full score for the beginning of Agathe's aria from *Der Freischutz*

VARIATIONEN
uber ein französisches Lied für das
Piano-Forte auf vier Hände
VERFASST UND DEM
Hn. Ludwig van Beethoven
Zugeeignet von seinem Verehrer und Bewunderer
Franz Schubert.
No. 996 10tes Werk
Eigenthum der Verleger.
Wien bey Cappi und Diabelli, Graben No. 1133.

Title page of a Schubert work dedicated to Beethoven and published in 1822

Franz Liszt in 1824

Schubert was another. With Louis Schlösser, a violinist in the orchestra at Darmstadt, he went to the 1822 revival of *Fidelio*. Schlösser wrote:

Together with us, three gentlemen, to whom I paid no further attention because their backs were turned to me, stepped out of a lower corridor; yet I was not a little surprised to see all those who were streaming by toward the lobby crowding to one side, in order to give the three plenty of room. Then Schubert very softly plucked my sleeve, pointing with his finger to the gentleman in the middle, who turned his head at that moment so that the bright light of the lamps fell on it and — I saw, familiar to me from engravings and paintings, the features of the creator of the opera I had just heard, Beethoven himself. My heart beat twice as loudly at that moment; all the things I may have said to Schubert I now no longer recall; but I well remember that I followed the Desired One and his companions (Schindler and Breuning, as I later discovered) like a shadow through crooked alleys and past high, gable-roofed houses, followed him until the darkness hid him from sight.

There were other disciples and admirers too. For example, in February 1818, Beethoven received a handsome present of a six-octave grand piano from John Broadwood in London, an instrument that was to subsequently pass on to Liszt. Then on 3 April 1820 the amazing Leopoldine Blahetka, a mere eight-year old, played the B flat piano Concerto. The Irishman, John Field, offered the Third Concerto in 1823. At the Royal Opera House in Dresden, Weber conducted the final version of *Fidelio* on 29 April 1823, with Wilhelmine Schröder, fresh from her Vienna triumph.* Then on 26 March 1824, Prince Nikolas Galitzin, who commissioned three of the late quartets (Opp 127, 130, 132), was largely responsible for the first complete performance of the *Missa Solemnis*, in St Petersburg. The following year, on 23 May at the seventh Lower Rhenish Musical Festival held at Aix-la-Chapelle, Ferdinand Ries conducted the *Christus* oratorio as well as the Ninth Symphony. Even the Americans were interested: according to one of the conversation books, the Boston Music Society approached Beethoven in the autumn of 1822 with a view to his writing an oratorio.

Countless visitors came to pay homage. Some were to become celebrated. The eleven-year-old Franz Liszt, for example, visited Beethoven in April 1823. He was then studying with Czerny, increasingly a teacher and pianist in demand. Ludwig Rellstab, who in later years was responsible for likening the C sharp minor Sonata from Op 27 to a vision of Lake Lucerne seen from a boat by

Ferdinand Ries (1784-1838). He settled in London between 1813 and 1824, renewing his old friendship with Salomon, and gaining a reputation 'as one of the finest pianoforte performers of the day' (*The Harmonicon*). He was among Beethoven's most gifted early pupils. Anonymous portrait in oils, *c.* 1814 (Beethoven-Haus, Bonn)

*Dresden had already heard the *1805* version in April 1815.

The Argyll Rooms, Regent Street, scene of the first English performance of the Ninth Symphony. In the distance is All Souls, Langham Place. Drawing by W. Westall, 1825 (British Museum, Crace Collection)

moonlight, came in 1825. That same year Sir George Smart (1776-1867) one of the original members of the Philharmonic Society of London, one of its conductors from 1821 onwards, and one of the organists at the Chapel Royal, also paid Beethoven a visit and in his *Journal* left a memorable account of the occasion. Another English visitor was Cipriani Potter (1792-1871), later to become Principal of the Royal Academy of Music (in 1832). As a noted pianist it was he who introduced for the first time several of the Beethoven piano concertos to England at concerts of the Philharmonic Society given in the Argyll Rooms, Regent Street in 1824 and 1825. He met Beethoven in 1817: the master felt he had a 'talent for composition'.

* * *

Support for Beethoven had, of course, always been strong in England. The Philharmonic Society, whose members and associates included a number of confirmed Beethoven devotees, not to say friends — J.B. Cramer, Clementi, William Ayrton, Salomon, Smart, Bridgetower, Ferdinand Ries and Potter, to name a few — was one particularly outstanding indication of what the broad mass of English musicians and 'music connoisseurs' felt about Beethoven in the years up to his death. From the outset they included his works in their programmes: all the eight concerts of the first season in 1813 under the immediate patronage of the Prince Regent offered music by Beethoven, including three unspecified symphonies, the *Prometheus* Overture, the Septet and various unidentified chamber works. Successive years showed a similarly heavy bias. The *Eroica* was conducted by Cramer on 28

February 1814, and that same season ended in May with selections from *Christus* which Sir George Smart had already conducted at the Theatre Royal, Drury Lane a few months earlier on 25 February. The following year the Society was in touch with Beethoven through the intermediacy of one of their members, Charles Neate, who was then in Vienna. They offered him 75 guineas for the purchase of three new overtures. They got *The Ruins of Athens, King Stephen*, and *Namensfeier*, none, however, a sample of Beethoven at his most inspired and none exactly new or 'composed for the Society' as had been expected. A letter from Beethoven to Neate, 18 December 1816, takes a defensive, accusatory stand: 'I was very sorry to hear that the three Overtures were not liked in London. I by no means reckon them amongst my best works . . . but still they were not disliked here and in Pest, where people are not easily satisfied. Were there no faults in the execution? Was there no party spirit?' Notwithstanding this the Society were still well-disposed. The Fifth Symphony had already been introduced to England for the first time on 15 April 1816, and the English première of the *Fidelio* Overture followed in 1817, in which season the Sixth and Seventh Symphonies were also played. Still interested in consolidating their association with Beethoven, the Philharmonic Society that same summer offered him (through Ferdinand Ries) 300 guineas for 'writing two New Symphonies to remain the property of the Society' and invited him to come to London. Beethoven replied to Ries in typical mood on 9 July 1817:

[1] I shall be in London during the first half of January, 1818, at latest.
[2] The two grand symphonies, which are entirely new, will then be ready and they will become and remain the sole property of the Society.
[3] For these symphonies the Society will pay me 300 guineas and 100 guineas for my travelling expenses, which, however, will far exceed that sum, since it is essential for me to have a travelling companion.
[4] As I am beginning at once the task of composing these symphonies, the Society (after accepting my statement) will remit to me in Vienna the sum of 150 guineas, so that I may provide myself without delay with a carriage and make other arrangements for the journey.
[5] I accept the conditions about not appearing with another orchestra or in public, about not conducting and about the preference to be given to the Society in similar conditions; and in view of my love of honour this was a foregone conclusion.
[6] I am to count on the support of the Society in organizing and promoting one or, if circumstances permit, several concerts for my benefit. Both the particular friendship of some Directors of your estimable assembly and, in general, the kind interest of all artists, in my work guarantee the success of such an undertaking. And this makes me all the more eager to fulfil their expectations.

But the Society remained firm in their resolve to offer no more than 300 guineas. Beethoven likewise would not relent, and the proposition came to nothing. Five years later, however, we find him asking Ries (6 July 1822): 'Have you any idea what fee the *Harmony Society* would offer me for a grand symphony?'. On 10 November a directors' meeting agreed that 'an offer of £50 be made to Beethoven for a M.S. Sym^{y}. He having permission to dispose of it at the expiration of Eighteen Months after the receipt of it. It being a proviso that it shall arrive during the Month of March next'. By comparison with the offer of 1817, and the subsequent payment in January 1823 of £25 for the *Consecration of the House* Overture, a mere £50 for a new symphony was slight payment indeed.

Beethoven nevertheless accepted. The new symphony, the Ninth in fact, did not materialise however, until the spring of 1824, over a year late. The Society grew impatient but still waited. When the autographed copy finally arrived it was expressly marked 'written for the Philharmonic Society in London'. Although they must have in consequence expected the right of first performance, they were in the end deprived of the privilege. By the time Sir George Smart conducted the Symphony on 21 March 1825, in a performance that was monumental in the annals of the Society though less successful in terms of public approval or critical reception, it had already been played twice in Vienna. When the score was finally published by Schott in August 1826, the Soceity were still denied their rightful share in its glory — the dedication read to King Friedrich Wilhelm III of Prussia.

In spite of all this neither Beethoven nor the Philharmonic Society forgot each other. Barely five weeks before his death, and in a weakened state, he wrote a pitiful letter to Moscheles in London:

A few years ago the Philharmonic Society in London made me the handsome offer to organise a concert for my benefit. At that time I was not, thank God, in such circumstances as to have to avail myself of this noble proposal. But now I am in a very different position, since for almost three months I have been confined to bed with an extremely trying illness. It is dropsy — Schindler will tell you more about it in a letter which he is enclosing. You have known for a long time all about the kind of life I lead; and you are aware too how and on what I live. For a considerable time now composing has been out of the question for me, and unfortunately I may find myself faced with the prospect of being in want — You have not only extensive acquaintanceships in London but also considerable influence with the Philharmonic Society. So I beg you to exert your influence to the utmost so that the Philharmonic Society may now take up their noble decision again and carry it out without delay.

The Society agreed to send Beethoven £100 as an advance against the proposed concert. On Sunday 18 March, a week and a day before his death, he dictated Schindler a letter to be sent to Moscheles: 'I cannot put into words the emotion with which I read your letter of March 1st. The Philharmonic Society's generosity in almost anticipating my appeal has touched my innermost soul — I request you, therefore, dear Moscheles, to be the spokesman through whom I send to the Philharmonic Society my warmest and most heartfelt thanks for their particular sympathy and support'.

* * *

Of all the glories and triumphs that Beethoven experienced in 1815-27, three in particular have to stand out as not only uniquely remarkable examples of creative power, but also as long-since acclaimed landmarks in the heritage of European culture: the *Diabelli* Variations, the *Missa Solemnis* and the Ninth Symphony, with its choral finale setting Schiller's *An die Freude.*

It is a curious irony of fate that Beethoven as a child opened his account as a composer for the piano with some variations on a seemingly superficial march by Dressler, and then forty years later as a man, all but closed it with another set of variations, this time on an even more insignificant-sounding tune, a waltz or 'cobbler's patch' by Sigmund Steiner's sometime copyist, Diabelli. The idea for writing such a work was first suggested by Diabelli himself sometime in 1819 or 1820. He planned to issue a collection of variations by different composers entitled *Vaterländischer Künstlerverein* (Native Society of Artists), and asked Beethoven for a contribution. According to Schindler Beethoven refused but then got progressively more interested in dealing with the creative challenge that Diabelli's waltz posed. A single variation, however, was scarcely his style: he planned six or seven, then nine, then twenty-five. On 5 June 1822 he offered the work to Peters in Leipzig for 30 gold ducats (122 gulden, or just over £12). By the time the complete set of 33 'grand variations' was finished (March or April 1823) Peters had refused the offer, and Diabelli issued the set in June 1823 as Part I of his proposed collection. Part II (including variations by the Archduke Rudolph, Gelinek, Halm, Hummel, Liszt, Mayseder, Moscheles, Mozart's son, Pixis, Schubert, Sechter, the Abbé Stadler, Tomásek, Umlauf and Voríšek, appeared later, the two volumes being advertised together in the *Wiener Zeitung* for 9 June 1824. Beethoven's set was announced by Diabelli in the most gloriously respectful terms imaginable (*Wiener Zeitung*, 16 June 1823):

Original edition of the *Diabelli* Variations.

We present here to the world Variations of no ordinary type, but a great and important masterpiece worthy to be ranked with the imperishable creations of the old Classics — such a work as only Beethoven, the greatest living representative of true art — only Beethoven and no other, can produce. The most original structures and ideas, the boldest musical idioms and harmonies are here exhausted; every pianoforte effect based on a solid technique is employed and his work is the more interesting from the fact that it is elicited from a theme which no one would otherwise have supposed capable of a working-out of that character in which our exalted Master stands alone among his contemporaries. . . We are proud to have given occasion for this composition, and have, moreover, taken all possible pains with regard to the printing to combine elegance with the utmost accuracy.

For Tovey in 1900 the *Diabelli* was simply 'the greatest set of variations ever written', an opinion that needs neither justification nor elaboration so elemental a reflection is it of the massive genius, the noble mind, the humorous spirit that this extraordinary masterpiece embodies.

The Archduke Rudolph. Oil painting by J.B. Lampi the Younger (Historisches Museum, Vienna)

The *Missa Solemnis*, imposingly 'dedicated with the deepest respect to His Imperial Highness the most eminent Cardinal Rudolph, Archduke of Austria, Prince of Hungary and Bohemia, Archbishop of Olmütz', was composed during much the same period — 1819-23 — as the *Diabelli* Variations, and material for both works is found in the same sketchbooks. Like the earlier Mass in C, the *Missa Solemnis* was composed for a specific occasion, this time the resplendent enthronement of the Archduke Rudolph as Archbishop of Olmütz at Cologne Cathedral. Unfortunately for Beethoven, however, the ceremony, officially announced on 4 June 1819, took place on 19 March 1820, by which date the *Missa* was far from ready. In fact Beethoven was unable to present the Archduke with a finished manuscript until exactly three years later to the day, 19 March 1823. By then he had plans to postpone the work's actual publication in order to first sell manuscript copies to the various heads of Europe and others, and so raise some much-needed money. He even wrote to Goethe in Weimar, though to no avail. In the end he secured ten subscribers, listed in a letter to Schott, 25 November 1825. They comprised Alexander I of Russia, Friedrich Wilhelm III of Prussia, Louis XVIII of France, Frederick VI of Denmark, Frederick Augustus I the Elector of Saxony, Ludwig I the Grand Duke of Darmstadt, Ferdinand III the Grand Duke of Tuscany, Prince Galitzin, Prince Radziwill, and the Caecilia Foundation of Frankfurt. Schott eventually published the score a week or so after Beethoven's death: he thus never saw in print the work that he regarded to be the greatest single achievement of his life.

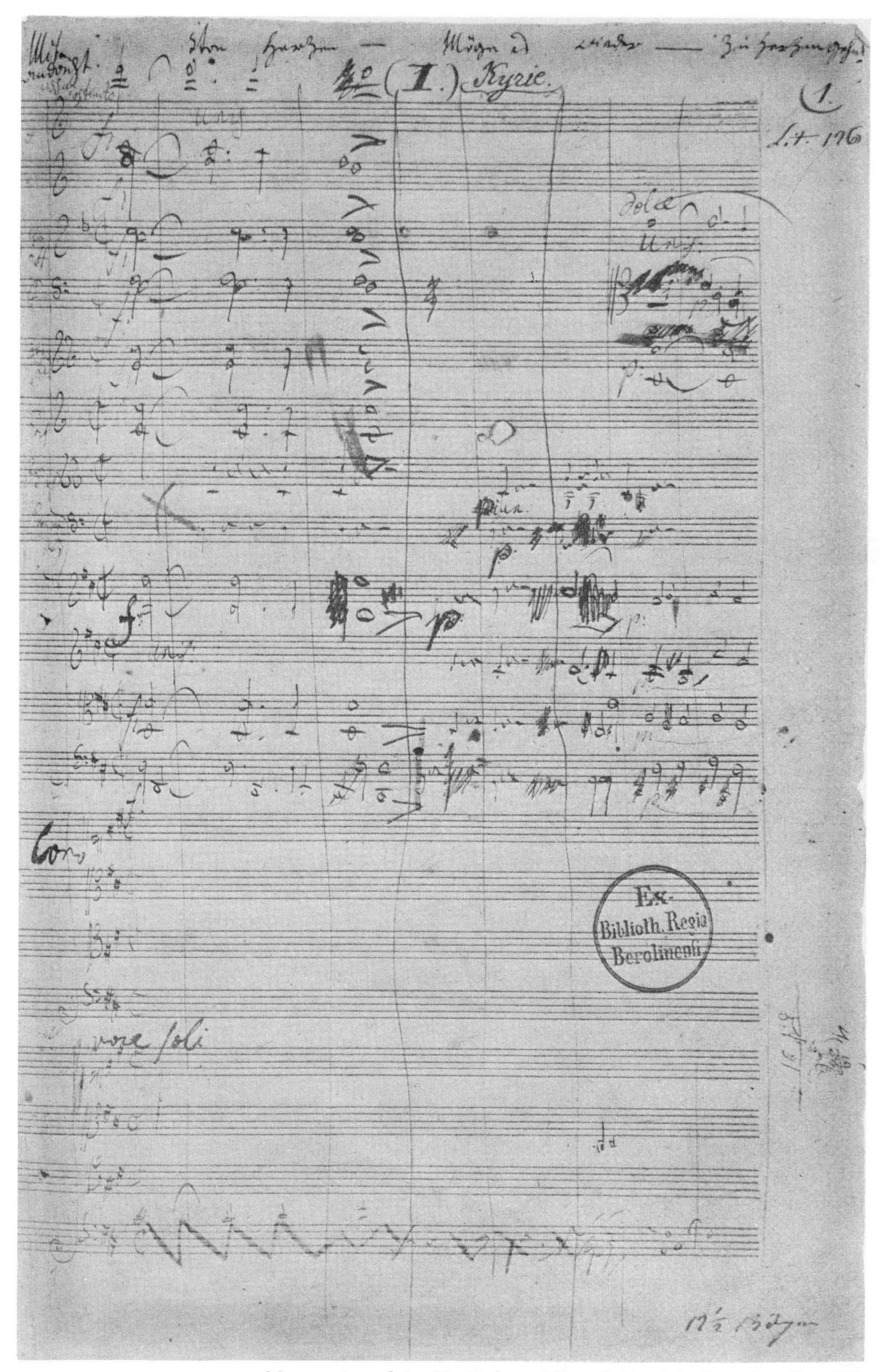

Manuscript of the Kyrie from *Missa Solemnis* in D major, Op. 123

The poet Schiller, engraving by J. P. Schweyer

Schiller's *An die Freude,* on which Beethoven based the last movement of his Ninth Symphony

Thalia.

Zweytes Heft.

1.

An die Freude.

Freude, schöner Götterfunken,
Tochter aus Elisium,
Wir betreten feuertrunken
Himmlische, dein Heiligthum.
Deine Zauber binden wieder,
was der Mode Schwerd getheilt;
Bettler werden Fürstenbrüder,
wo dein sanfter Flügel weilt.

Chor.

Seid umschlungen Millionen!
Diesen Kuß der ganzen Welt!
Brüder — überm Sternenzelt
muß ein lieber Vater wohnen.

A Wem

Original edition of the *Missa Solemnis*, published posthumously

As we have seen, the first complete performance actually took place in St. Petersburg at the instigation of Prince Galitzin who wrote to Beethoven:

For several months I have been extremely impatient to hear this music performed, the beauties of which I foresaw from score. The effect of this music on the public cannot be described and I doubt if I exaggerate when I say that for my part I have never heard anything so sublime; I don't even except the masterpieces of Mozart which with their eternal beauties have not created for me the same sensations that you have given me, Monsieur, by the 'Kyrie' and 'Gloria' of your *Mass*. The masterly harmony and the moving melody of the 'Benedictus' transport the heart to a plane that is really blissful. The whole work in fact is a treasure of beauties; it can be said that your genius has anticipated the centuries and that there are not listeners perhaps enlightened enough to experience all the beauty of this music; but it is posterity that will pay homage and will bless your memory much better than your contemporaries can.

The first Viennese performance, at the 7 May 1824 concert which included the Ninth Symphony, was incomplete (only the 'Kyrie', 'Credo' and 'Agnus dei' were given) and it appears that it was not heard in its entirety in Vienna until as late as 1845, in which year Liszt also conducted it at the Beethoven Festival in Bonn. By then it had already been performed liturgically in 1835 at the Cathedral of Pressburg (Bratislava).

Beethoven headed the manuscript with the famous words: 'From the heart — may it go to the heart'. To absorb the meaning of the Latin text he had it translated into German, he studied the old masters, he immersed himself totally in spiritual contemplation. Joseph Schmidt-Görg had written that

Here in this most mighty of his last works, he wrote from the very depths of his being; undefeated by years of suffering, he found music for sacred words of humble adoration, jubilant praise, and the wholehearted affirmation of faith. We know that on his deathbed he uttered the words 'Plaudite amici, comoedia finita est!' and in the earliest existing sketch-book for the *Missa* he wrote against the theme of the fugue 'Et vitam venturi saeculi', the words 'Applaudite amici'. These words shed a bright light on the reason why, after the tremendous closing fugue of the 'Credo' there is a hushed epilogue whose light ascending figures seem almost to melt away. Revealing remarks of this kind occur only very rarely in Beethoven's sketches. Here we are made to think of floating, blessed spirits, redeemed children of this world entering into eternal life. Life everlasting — the highest fulfilment of earthly hope. Beethoven, the sufferer, often sang of hope, and it remained with him from the *Missa* until his last breath.

So finally to the Ninth Symphony, the work that, *Fidelio*, apart, was to give Beethoven the greatest trouble in its creation. In the main Beethoven wrote it out in 1822-24, but its origins can actually be traced much further back, to as early as 1792/93 in fact, when Beethoven proposed to set Schiller's *An die Freude** with its characteristic elements of freedom and justice. The earliest mention of the Ninth *per se* seems however to be among sketches for the Seventh and Eighth Symphonies, included in the so-called Petter sketchbook now in the Beethoven-Haus, Bonn and dating from 1812. At this stage references were purely in the form of brief written notes, such as '2te Sinfonie, D moll' and 'Sinfonia in D moll 3te sinf'. In a letter to his publishers, Breitkopf & Härtel, dated about 24 May 1812, Beethoven remarked 'I am composing three new symphonies, one of which [No 7] is already finished' — thus the description of a D minor symphony as No 2 or No 3 presumably refers to its context within these 'three new symphonies'.

More concrete evidence for a new symphony emerges among sketches dating from 1815, the most significant of which indicates that Beethoven was thinking in terms of vocal participation in the symphony: 'Sinfonie at the beginning only 4 voices, 2 viol, viola, basso among them *forte* with other voices and if possible bring in all the other instruments one by one and gradually'. Thayer considered that this could not be associated specifically with the Ninth, but the remark does go some way to show that Beethoven was at least contemplating a symphony in which vocal participation was an intended part. The idea of a symphonic work with voices was not an entirely new concept; only the year before, in 1814, Peter von Winter had produced a *Battle* Symphony with voices, and Beethoven himself had similarly experimented in the Choral Fantasia of 1808-09, while early drafts for the orchestral *Namensfeier* Overture, Op 115, show an overture *with chorus*, the text taken, significantly, from *An die Freude*.

1815 saw the emergence of the earliest recognisable thematic sketch for the Ninth — an idea in D minor that was finally to form the basis of the scherzo. Two to three years later the first beginnings of serious drafts for a symphony in D minor are traceable. Nevertheless in the period up to 1822 Beethoven's notebooks show considerable confusion in reaching any definite scheme or basic plan of movements. This is unusual, for while sketches for the previous symphonies show varying degrees of uncertainty, the overall plans were all more or less established at an early stage, and while material was discarded in the process of evolving the music the vast majority of individual ideas remained throughout peculiar

* Originally *An die Freiheit*, (To Freedom) a title that was politically censored.

The Ninth Symphony, sketches for the finale. At one stage Beethoven contemplated a purely instrumental concluding movement (Gesellschaft der Musikfreunde, Vienna)

to their respective context of movements. With the exception of the opening idea of the first movement, the same cannot be said of the Ninth, and from the beginning of the first melodic sketches one senses Beethoven groping for a ground-plan. At least four symphonic structures were attempted and discarded, quite apart from written notes in the sketches suggesting alternative schemes. Of the various projected outlines only two can be positively given as Beethoven's intended plans for the symphony which was to become the *Choral*, namely the first (1817-18) and the last before work began on the symphony proper in 1822. This last comprises a thematic list, in which the *Adagio* of a proposed five-movement symphony is left blank (sketches for the actual slow movement of the Ninth belong to 1823, at a somewhat later date than the rest of the symphony). In between came a whole lot of other ideas and ground plans.

First in 1818, 'A symphony in the ancient modes'. A memorandum in the sketchbook reads '*Adagio Cantique*, Pious song in a symphony in the ancient modes — praise to God — allelujah — either alone or as introduction to a fugue. The whole 2nd sinfonie might be characterised in this manner in which case the vocal parts would enter in the last movement or already in the *Adagio*. The violins, etc., of the orchestra to be increased tenfold in the last movement, in which case the vocal parts would enter gradually — in the text of the *Adagio*'s Greek myth, *Cantique Ecclésiastique* in the *Allegro*, feast of Bachus [*sic*]'. In the summer of

1822 Beethoven told Rochlitz that he was thinking of two symphonies which would be different from each other and the remarks in the above memorandum suggest that he was already thinking along such lines in 1818. Furthermore while the 1817-18 drafts show a purely instrumental symphony, vocal participation in the '2nd sinfonie' was intended from the beginning, with a text related to Greek antiquity.

Later came a Sinfonia in D minor/major (1822) relating back, interestingly, to the Second Symphony and forward to the first distinguishable outline of the famous *An die Freude* tune in the finale of the Ninth. The sketches for 1822 also witness a *Sinfonie allemand*, primarily associated with Schiller's lines, and concluding with the words, 'End of the sinfonie with Turkish music and vocal chorus', an idea more than retained when Beethoven came to writing the Ninth. By the end of that year, as we have seen, the Philharmonic Society had commissioned him to compose a new symphony, a gesture that was enough to at long last stimulate and channel his creative energy towards a definable goal.

The first performance of the Ninth, following weeks of indecision and aggravation and just two rehearsals, was seemingly less than

Vienna, the Imperial Court Theatre by the Kärtntnertor. Anonymous coloured engraving

entirely successful. According to Joseph Carl Rosenbaum the Kärntnertortheater was 'not very full . . . Many boxes empty, no one from the Court. For all the large forces, little effect. B's disciples clamoured, most of the audience stayed quiet, many did not wait for the end.' Sonnleithner confirms that 'Beethoven himself stood at the head of the forces, but the actual conducting of the orchestra was looked after by Umlauf, who beat time, and Schuppanzigh as first violin'. Even so, the orchestra was not all that confident: 'the double-bass players had not the faintest idea what they were supposed to do with the recitatives', says Sonnleithner. Schindler, the conversation books, and the reactions of the press suggest, however, that the evening still had its moments, not to say its valedictory sadness, as well. Schindler wrote:

As for the musical success of this memorable evening, it could be favourably compared to any event ever presented in that venerable theatre. Alas! the man to whom all this honour was addressed could hear none of it, for when at the end of the performance the audience broke into enthusiastic applause, he remained standing with his back to them. Then it was that Caroline Unger [the contralto soloist] had the presence of mind to turn the master towards the proscenium and show him the cheering throng throwing their hats into the air and waving their handkerchiefs. He acknowledged his gratitude with a bow. This set off an almost unprecedented volly of jubilant applause that went on and on as the joyful listeners sought to express their thanks for the pleasure they had just been granted.

In spite of everything the financial returns of the evening (as well as those from a later repeat performance on 23 May) were disappointing. Only 420 florins (£42) remained after all costs had been settled. Beethoven, at first dejected, then became suspicious, and a scene was enacted reminiscent of what had happened in 1806 over the receipts of *Fidelio*. Schindler takes up the narrative:

Beethoven felt under obligation to Umlauf, Schuppanzigh, and me for the trouble we had taken. To express his thanks, he proposed a dinner at the tavern 'Zum wilden Mann' in the Prater . . . He appeared with stormy countenance, accompanied by his nephew. He was the reverse of cordial; everything he said was biting and critical. We all expected some sort of outburst. As soon as we had sat down he launched into a discourse on the financial outcome of the first concert, accusing the manager, Duport, and me point-blank of conspiring to cheat him. Umlauf and Schuppanzigh attempted to prove to him the impossibility of any fraud, reminding him that every coin had passed through the hands of both theatre cashiers, that the reports agreed exactly, and that his nephew had, at the insistence of the apothecary-brother and contrary to all custom, stayed with the cashiers as a sort of inspector. Beethoven, however, stuck to his accusations adding that he had been informed by the fraud by reliable sources [possibly his own brother, Johann, a man particularly resentful to Schindler]. I waited to hear no more. As quickly as possible Umlauf and I departed, and Schuppanzigh, after having received a few volleys on his ample person, soon followed. We repaired to the tavern 'Zum goldenen Lamm' in Leopoldstadt to resume in peace our interrupted meal. The furious master was left to vent his spleen on the waiters and the ceiling beams and to eat the elaborate meal alone in the company of his nephew.

Beethoven then felt compelled to write Schindler a caustic letter, the sentiments of which were patently clear:

I do not accuse you of having done anything wicked in connection with the concert. But stupidity and arbitrary behaviour have ruined many an undertaking. Moreover I have on whole a certain fear of you, a fear lest some day through your action a great misfortune may befall me. Stopped-up sluices overflow quite suddenly; and that day in the Prater I was convinced that in many ways you had hurt me very deeply — In any case I would much rather try to repay frequently with a small gift the services you render me, than *have you at my table*. For I confess that your presence irritates me in so many ways. If you see me looking not very cheerful, you say 'Nasty day again, isn't it?' For owing to your vulgar outlook how could you appreciate anything that is not vulgar?! In short I love my freedom far too dearly. I will certainly invite you occasionally. But it is impossible to have you beside me permanently, because such an arrangement would upset my whole existence . . . In no circumstances would I care to entrust my welfare to you, because you never reflect but act quite arbitrarily. I have found you out once already in a way that was unfavourable to you; and so have *other people* too — I must declare that the purity of my character does not permit me to reward your kindnesses to me with friendship alone, although of course I am willing to serve you in any matter connected with your welfare —

Such accusations, such explosion of temper, such hastiness . . . The inevitable breach was not be be patched over until the end of 1826. By then it was too late.

Chapter 14

Apotheosis

'It is a lovely thing to live with courage, and to die leaving everlasting fame' — Alexander the Great

With the Congress of Vienna it was ironically not only Napoleonic Europe that was laid to rest, it was virtually the whole world that Beethoven had known as well. From then on, to have genius, to gain public fame and universal celebration, was one thing, to actually survive within material surroundings in which the familiar old order had gone, quite another. In 1815, most of Beethoven's patrons were no more: only the Archduke Rudolph remained, always faithful, yet increasingly preoccupied in politics and administration. New patrons, like Prince Galitzin or Friedrich Wilhelm III were far away. If Beethoven wanted to talk he could only turn to his casual visitor or to Schindler, an officious young man whom Heine described in 1841 as 'a long black beanpole with a horrible white necktie and the expression of a funeral director . . . How could the great artist bear such an unpleasant, intellectually poverty-stricken friend?'. With his health and his hearing under that malignant sentence of death that had cursed his life since youth, Beethoven increasingly became more embittered, more introverted. The image he presented often seems to have been demented, wild, untamed. He gained a reputation of being 'savage and unsociable'. The poet Carpani observed that he was 'a misanthrope' and a crank. A page in one of his notebooks reads:

Beethoven. Oil painting by F. Schiman, 1818-19. The curious slant of the eyes has been attributed to an excess of coffee (Beethoven-Haus, Bonn)

My decree is to remain in the country; how easy it is to do that in whatever corner. My unfortunate hearing does not plague me there. It is as if every tree spoke to me in the country, holy! holy! Ecstasy in the woods! Who can describe it? If all comes to nought the country itself remains, Baden, Untere Brühl etc. In the winter it would be easy to rent a lodging from a peasant; around this time it is surely not expensive. Sweet stillness of the woods! The wind which blows already on the second nice day cannot retain me in Vienna, because it is my enemy.

Sir John Russell, an Englishman who visited Vienna in the early 1820s, confirmed the impression:

Beethoven is the most celebrated of the living composers in Vienna, and, in certain departments, the foremost of his day. Though not an old man, he is lost to society in consequence of his extreme deafness, which has rendered him almost unsocial. The neglect of his person which he exhibits gives him a somewhat wild appearance. His features are strong and prominent; his eye is full of rude energy; his hair, which neither comb nor scissors seem to have visited for years, overshadows his broad brow in a quantity and confusion to which only the snakes round a Gorgon's head offer a parallel. His general behaviour does not ill accord with the unpromising exterior. Except when he is among his chosen friends, kindliness or affability are not his characteristics. The total loss of hearing has deprived him of all the pleasure which society can give and perhaps soured his temper. He used to frequent a paricular cellar, where he spent the evening in a corner, beyond the reach of all the chattering and disputation of a public room, drinking wine and beer, eating cheese and red herrings, and studying the newspapers. One evening a person took a seat near him whose countenance did not please him. He looked hard at the stranger, and spat on the floor as if he had seen a toad, then glanced at the newspaper, then again at the intruder, and spat again, his hair bristling gradually into more shaggy ferocity, till he closed the alternation of spitting and staring, by fairly exclaiming, 'What a scoundrelly phiz!', and rushing out of the room. Even among his oldest friends he must be humoured like a wayward child.

The *Diary* of Carl von Bursy, a doctor, reported a previous encounter on 1 June 1816:

He misunderstood me very often, and had to use the utmost concentration when I was speaking, to get my meaning. That, of course, embarrassed and disturbed me very much. It disturbed him, too, and this led him to speak more himself and very loudly. He told me a lot about his life and about Vienna. He was venemous and embittered. He raged about everything, and is dissatisfied with everything, and he curses Austria and Vienna in particular. He speaks quickly and with great vivacity. He often banged his fist on the piano and made such a noise that it echoed around the room. He is not exactly reserved; for he told me about his personal affairs and related much about himself and his family. That is precisely the *signum diagnosticum* of hypochondria. I was rather pleased with this hypochondria, because I learned so much about his life from his very lips. He complains about the present age, and for many reasons. Art no longer occupies a position high above the commonplace, art is no longer held in such high esteem and particularly not as regards recompense. Beethoven complains of bad times in a pecuniary sense. Can one believe that a Beethoven has grounds for such complaints?

'Why do you stay in Vienna when every foreign potentate would be glad to give you a place at his court or next to his throne?' 'Certain conditions keep me here', said he, 'but everything here is mean and dirty. Things could not be worse. From top to bottom everything is shabby. You can't

Drawing of Beethoven

Engraving of Beethoven, for comparison with Stieler's painting

trust anyone. What is not written down in black and white, no one will honour. They want your work and then pay you a beggar's pittance, not even what they agreed to pay...'

This prevalent eccentricity of Beethoven's manner did nothing, of course, for his relationships with landlords or servants. Rossini, who tried to collect funds to buy him a house, encountered the generalised reaction that 'On the day after [Beethoven] finds himself the owner of a house, he will sell it. He will never know how to adjust himself to a permanent home; he feels the need of changing his lodgings every six months, and his servants every six weeks. . .' The period 1815-27 shows, in fact, no less than 31 changes of winter and summer abode, and a good deal of aggravation and swearing on all sides, while the *Diaries* for 1819-20 reveal housekeepers, and kitchen and chamber maids, eagerly arriving and hurriedly departing with monotonous regularity.

Beethoven working on his *Missa Solemnis*. Oil painting by J. Stieler, 1819-20. Schindler spoke at one stage of 'singing, howling, stamping. . . Beethoven stood before us with distorted features, calculated to excite fear. He looked as if he had been in mortal combat with the whole host of contrapuntists, his everlasting enemies'

There was nevertheless, another side to Beethoven's personality. There were times when the angry, wounded lion would soften into something more yielding and vulnerable. Rossini visited him in 1822, and years later remarked to Wagner on 'the indefinable sadness spread over his features. . . the [bass] voice. . . soft and slightly veiled'. That same year Rochlitz wrote to his wife:

I was about to go to dinner when I met the young composer Franz Schubert, an enthusiastic admirer of Beethoven. The latter had spoken to Schubert concerning me. 'If you wish to see him in a more natural and jovial mood', said Schubert, 'then go and eat your dinner this very minute at the inn where he has just gone for the same purpose'. He took me with him. Most of the places were taken. Beethoven sat among several acquaintances who were strangers to me. He really seemed to be in good spirits. . . He impressed me as being a man with a rich, aggressive intellect, an unlimited, never resting imagination. I saw him as one who, had he been cast away on a desert isle when no more than a growing, capable boy, would have taken all he had lived and learned, all that had stuck to him in the way of knowledge, and there have meditated and brooded over his material until his fragments had become a whole, his imaginings turned to convictions which he would have shouted out into the world in all security and confidence...

. . .Our third meeting was the merriest of all. He came here, to Baden, this time looking quite neat and clean, and even elegant. Yet this did not prevent him — it was a warm day — from taking a walk in the Helenental. This means on the road all, even the Emperor and the imperial family, travel and where everyone crowds past everyone else on the usually narrow path; and there he took off his fine black frockcoat, slung it across his shoulder from a stick, and wandered along in his shirt-sleeves.

Just as our idea of the Beethoven manner in the last years has to some extent been distorted by his biographers and even by the reminiscences of his friends and contemporaries, so, too, has the concept of Beethoven's physical image. He is often portrayed, for instance, as having been dirty and unkempt, deprived of adequate clothing and indescribably poor. True, he himself was sometimes responsible for the latter statement in his letters, and there is plenty of evidence to show that he owed money and was often in debt, but an examination of his estate nevertheless reveals a rather different situation. He had, for instance, sufficient bank shares from the National Bank of Austria, to yield 7441 florins at the time of his death, while payments from the Archduke Rudolph, as well as the Lobkowitz and Kinsky treasuries, are also apparent. He had, too, a quantity of furniture and an assortment of kitchen and table ware (14 china plates, 1 tin cup, glasses, bottles, bowls, 4 brass candleholders, a rotisserie, some silver, and so on). His personal wardrobe, interestingly, was extensive and scarcely the possession of an impecunious man who cared nothing for his appearance; two cloth swallow-tailed coats, two spencers, two Prince Alberts, one blue cloth overcoat, 16 assorted knee stockings, eight pair of trousers, two hats, six pair of boots, three pair of suspenders, one dressing gown, 14 shirts, 20 undershirts, 20 ascots and handkerchiefs, 18 pair of socks, eight night shirts, 14 pair of underpants six nightcaps, six razors, two small pistols and a cane. According to Schindler, Beethoven 'knew how to dress decently for the street as well as for the drawing room. In this regard it must be said of the master that, until the last days of his life, conditions permitting, he was fond of dressing painstakingly and that there was always harmony in his apparel. A frock-coat of fine blue cloth with metal [brass] buttons (blue was his favourite colour at that time) suited him excellently. Such a frock-coat, with another of dark green cloth, was never missing from his wardrobe. During the summer one always saw him in fair weather in white trousers, shoes and white stockings (then the fashion). His waistcoat and necktie were white at every season and were conspicuous for their exemplary cleanliness even on weekdays.'

Elsewhere, Schindler says:

Washing and bathing were among the most indispensible necessities of existence for Beethoven. In this respect he was a thorough Oriental. Mohammed has by no means prescribed too many ablutions to suit him. If, while he was working, he did not go out during the forenoon, in order to compose himself, he would stand at the wash-basin, often in extremest *negligée* and pour great pitchersful of water over his hands, at the same time

Anton Schindler
(1795-1864)
Undated photograph

howling, or for a change, growling out the whole gamut of the scale, ascending and descending; then, before long, he would pace the room, his eyes rolling or fixed in a stare, jot down a few notes and again return to his water pouring and howling. . .

At breakfast Beethoven drank coffee, which he usually prepared himself in a percolator. Coffee seems to have been the nourishment with which he could least dispense and in his procedure with regard to its preparation he was as careful as the Orientals are known to be. Sixty beans to a cup was the allotment and the beans were often counted out exactly, expecially when guests were present. Among his favourite dishes was macaroni with Parmesan cheese. Furthermore, all fish dishes were his special predilection. Hence guests usually were invited for Friday when a full-weight *Schill* (a Danube fish resembling the haddock) with potatoes could be served. Supper was hardly taken into account. A bowl of soup and some remnants of the midday meal was all that he took. His favourite beverage was fresh spring water which, in summer, he drank in well-nigh inordinate quantities. Among wines he preferred the Hungarian *Ofen* variety. Unfortunately he liked best the adulterated wines which did great damage to his weak intestines. But warnings were of no avail in this case. Our Master also liked to drink a good glass of beer in the evening, with which he smoked a pipeful of tobacco, and kept the news-sheets company. . .

Beethoven's physique during this period has been sufficiently well documented to leave no room for fictionalisation or distortion. Schindler again is the source of this important primary description, and there is no reason to disbelieve him:

Beethoven could not have been much more than 5 feet 4 inches tall, Viennese measure. His body was thick-set, with large bones and a strong muscular system; his head was unusually large, covered with long, unkempt, almost completely grey hair, giving him a somewhat savage aspect, enhanced even more when his beard had grown to an immoderate length, which was quite often the case. His forehead was high and broad, his brown eyes small, almost retreating into his head when he laughed. They could, however, suddenly become unusually prominent and large, either rolling and flashing — the pupils almost always turned upwards — or not moving at all, staring fixedly ahead when one or another idea took hold of him. His mouth was well formed, the lips even (it is said that when he was young the lower lip was somewhat prominent), the nose rather broad. With his smile a most benevolent and amiable air spread over his whole face; this was of special benefit when he conversed with strangers, for it encouraged them. His laughter, on the other hand, often burst out immoderately, distorting the intelligent and strongly marked features; the huge head would swell, the face would become still broader, and the whole effect was not seldom that of a grimacing caricature. Fortunately, it always passed quickly.

Gerhard von Breuning, in his book *Aus dem Schwarzspanierhaus,* has given us one of the most lively pictures of Beethoven the man.

Mödling, the Square. Beethoven spent the summers of 1815, 1818, 1819 and 1820 here. Lithograph by Sandmann

Highly pointed, its imagery is marvellously projected, its atmosphere almost three-dimensional, its poignancy and loneliness vivid:

Beethoven's outward appearance, due to his quite peculiar nonchalance in the matter of dress, had something uncommonly conspicuous about it in the street. Usually lost in thought and humming to himself, he often gesticulated with his arms when walking by himself. When in company, he would speak quite animatedly and loudly, and, since his companion then had to write his rejoinder in the conversation book, an abrupt halt would have to be made; this was conspicuous in itself, and was still more so when the rejoinder was communicated in mime.

And so it happened that most of the passers-by would turn around to stare at him; the street urchins also made their gibes and shouted after him. . .

The crown of the felt hat he wore at that time had lost its shape and bulged towards the top where it had been stretched; this was the result of Beethoven's habit, on coming in, of clapping his hat over the topmost point of the hall-stand; should the hat be dripping with rain, he would simply shake it lightly first, which he also did at our house, without a thought for the furniture. The hat was rarely if ever brushed, before or after rain, and becoming increasingly dusty, it took on a permanent matted appearance. He wore it, when feasible, at the back of his head to have his forehead free, while his grey unkempt hair (in Rellstab's apt words, 'not frizzly, not straight, but a mixture of everything') flew out on both sides. . . The lapels of the coat (especially those of the blue frock-coat with brass buttons) were not fastened, and flapped back against his arms particularly when he walked into the wind; the two long points of the neckcloth, which was knotted about the wide shirt-collar, likewise flew outwards. The double lorgnette, which he wore for his nearsightedness, hung loose. The coat-tails were rather heavily laden: apart from a pocket handkerchief, which often showed, they contained a quite thick, folded, quarto music notebook and an octavo conversation book, with a thick carpenter's pencil. . . and at an earlier period, so long as it was of any use, an ear-trumpet. The weight of the music notebook lengthened the one coat-tail considerably, and the pocket was often turned inside out when notebook and conversation book were extracted from it. . . I often saw him thus from our windows, when I was not with him myself, coming at two o'clock — his dinner hour — from the Schottentor across the part of the Glacis where the Votivkirche now stands, sailing towards his lodgings in his customary posture, his body leant forward (but not bowed), his head erect.

* * *

By the end of 1826, Beethoven was a broken man, shabby, self-effacing, and racked with illness. For him 1815-27 were to be the years when his deafness became intolerable. He suffered, too, from rheumatism, catarrhal inflammation of the lungs, heart strain,

Sketches of Beethoven by Lyser

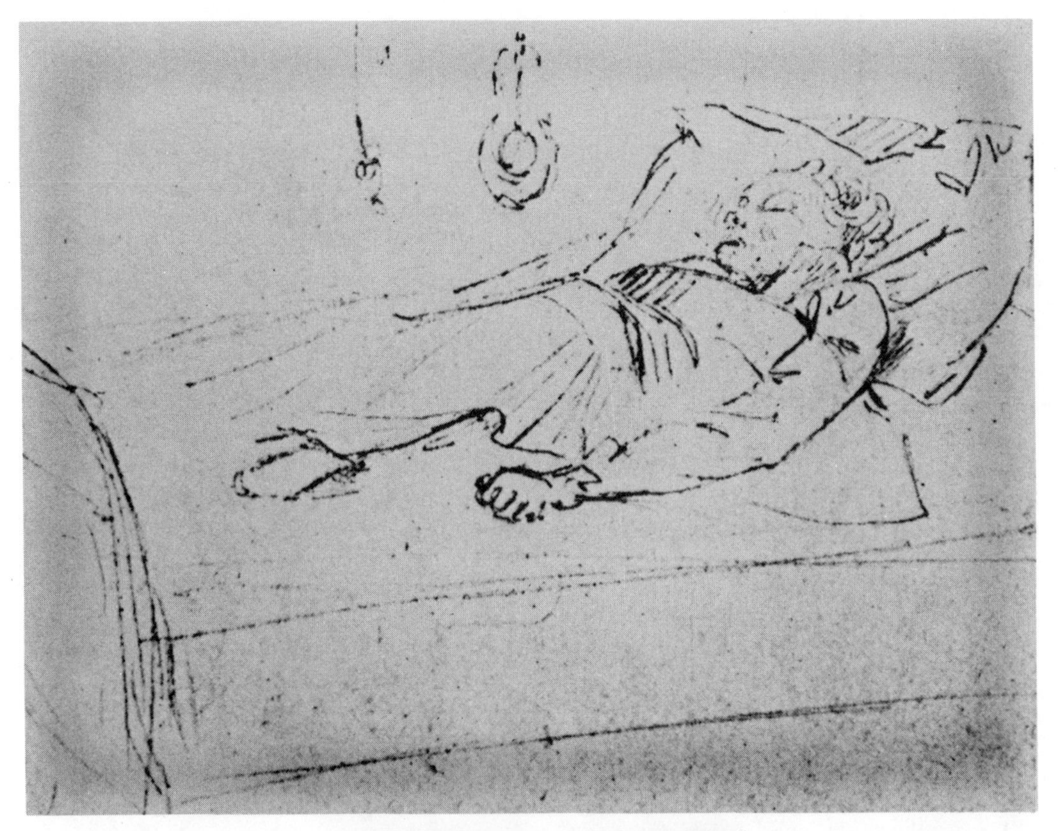

Sketch of Beethoven on his deathbed

Earlier picture of Beethoven in his study

jaundice (1821), a painful eye condition needing a darkened room and bandages (April 1823-January 1824), innumerable chills, nose-bleeding, appalling stomach disorders, ulcerative colitis, hepatitis and, in the end, dropsy, a terminal illness that took four months to run its course. It was four months of living death. In December 1826, Beethoven's doctor, Andreas Wawruch, reported:

I found him greatly disturbed and jaundiced all over his body. A frightful choleric attack had threatened his life in the preceding night. A violent rage, a great grief because of sustained ingratitude and undeserved humiliation, was the cause of this mighty explosion. Trembling and shivering he bent double because of the pains which raged in his liver and intestines, and his feet, hitherto moderately inflated, were tremendously swollen. From this time on dropsy developed, the segregation of urine became less, the liver showed plain indiciation of hard nodules, there was an increase of jaundice. Gentle entreaties from his friends quieted the threatening mental tempest, and the forgiving man forgot all the humiliation which had been put upon him. But the disease moved onward with gigantic strides. Already in the third week there came incidents of noctural suffocation; the enormous volume of collected water demanded speedy relief and I found myself compelled to advise tapping in order to guard against the danger of bursting.

Beethoven. A drawing by J.D. Böhm, *c.* 1819-20

At the end of February 1827, entries in the conversation book refer to bugs keeping Beethoven awake. Schindler says, 'The maid will put a wooden vessel under the bed so that the water cannot run over the room. No more straw in the house to fill the other mattress. The straw is all fouled.' Add to this the fact that medical science in the modern sense of the word did not exist in the 1820s and the scene of misery, degradation, helplessness and breakdown in the face of rampant, uncontrollable disease is complete.

The origins of Beethoven's deafness and the cause of his final illnesses have often been discussed. The former is usually dated to around 1799 (Beethoven's letter to Wegeler, 29 June 1801), though the Fischer manuscript speaks of a 'dangerous illness' in either 1796 or 1797 which was long assumed to be a contributory factor. The Heiligenstadt Testament, it will be recalled, also included a reference to a date as early as 1796. As for its main cause, and indeed as the primary cause of Beethoven's later ailments, it was George Grove in 1878 who first suggested that syphilis was the offending agent. This theory, however, is now generally discredited. As Edward Larkin has written, 'it is likely that Beethoven, like everybody else, caught gonorrhoea, but there is no evidence that either his lifelong illnesses or his deafness were syphilitic'.*

* In an Appendix to Martin Cooper's *Beethoven: The Last Decade* (1970)

Beethoven from behind. Water-coloured pencil drawing by J. Weidner (Bodmer Collection, Beethoven-Haus, Bonn). '. . . the impression of a man who has several heads, several hearts and several souls' — Haydn

Larkin later shows that 'the charge of alcoholism is likewise unsubstantiated'. He does, however, draw provocative attention to the state of Beethoven's mental health and, in the process, stresses his excessive, even pathologically emotional reactions, his general neurosis. One of his conclusions is that

> The picture . . . is of persistent ill-health, of a prevailing mood of depression, a highly strung, suspicious, 'persecuted' man, unstable, under stress, hypomanic at times, impulsive to the point of violence, perfectionist, deaf, irritable.

* * *

To add to Beethoven's problems, there was his family. His brother, Johann, for instance, who by 1822 had enough money to not only lend, but also buy a farm near Gneixendorf, the scene of Beethoven's last autumn sojourn in the country, and to live in Vienna during the winter months in the home of his brother-in-law, a baker. Gerhard von Breuning remembered that

> For several years after the death of the great 'brainowner', his brother the 'landowner', played a quite singularly naïve role. During Ludwig's lifetime, Johann was interested in his brother's works only for the profit that might be realized from them; now, however, he strove to feign the appreciative admirer of those same works. Splendidly bedizened (blue frock-coat, white waistcoat), he would be seated in the front row of the concert hall at performances of his late brother's works; following each one he would shout 'Bravo', his broad mouth wide open, while applauding mightily with his bony hands, clumsily gloved in white.

Johann's wife, who had been the cause of Beethoven's rage in Linz in 1812, cultivated the laxest morals, and repeatedly disgusted him. One climax out of many was in 1823. Johann had been ill and Beethoven wrote him a letter from Baden on 19 August (given here in the Thayer version):

> I received your letter of the 10th through the hands of the miserable scoundrel *Schindler*. You need only to give your letters directly to the post, from which I am certain to receive them, for I avoid this mean and contemptible fellow as much as possible — Karl cannot come to me before the 29th of this month when he will write to you. You cannot be wholly unadvised as to what the two *canailles*, Lout and Bastard, are doing to you, and you will have had letters on the subject from me and Karl, for, little as you deserve it I shall never forget that you are my brother, and a good angel will yet come to rid you of these two *canailles*, this former and present strumpet who slept with her fellow no less than three times while you were ill, and who, in addition to everything else, has your money wholly in her hands. O infamous disgrace, isn't there a spark of manhood in you?!!!

Beethoven a few days after the first performance of the Ninth Symphony. Julius Benedict likened him in his last years to King Lear or one of the Celtic bards, 'with his white hair that streamed down over his powerful shoulders, his knitting of the brows when anything specially moved him, and his prodigious laughter'. Chalk drawing by S. Decker, May 1824 (Historisches Museum, Vienna)

There was Beethoven's other brother, too, the consumptive Caspar Anton Carl, who lacked the business guile of Johann but whose choice in women was, for Beethoven at any rate, just as unsuitable. He married one heavily pregnant Johanna Reiss on 25 May 1806, and the issue of the marriage was a son, Karl, born little more than three months later on 4 September and destined to become the notorious nephew of Beethoven's last years. Caspar Carl died on 16 November 1815. His will of two days earlier appointed his wife and Beethoven as co-guardians of Karl. The phrase 'Along with my wife', however, was crossed through. A fragment in Beethoven's hand offers an explanation:

I knew nothing about the fact that a testament had been made; however, I came upon it by chance. If what I had seen was really to be the *original text*, then passages had to be stricken out. This I had my brother bring about since I did not wish to be bound up in this with such a bad woman in a matter of such importance as the education of the child.

An understandably worried Caspar Carl felt it suddenly necessary to add a codicil to the document:

Having learned that my brother, Hr. Ludwig van Beethoven, desires after my death to take wholly to himself my son Karl, and wholly to withdraw him from the supervision and training of his mother, and inasmuch as the best of harmony does not exist between my brother and my wife, I have found it necessary to add to my will that I by no means desire that my son be taken away from his mother, but that he shall always and so long as his future career permits remain with his mother, to which end the guardianship of him is to be exercised by her as well as my brother. Only by unity can the object which I had in view in appointing my brother guardian of my son, be attained, wherefore, for the welfare of my child, I recommend *compliance* to my wife, and more *moderation* to my brother.

Beethoven's youngest brother, Johann (1776-1848). He charged Beethoven rent for part of the time that he stayed in his house at Gneixendorf in the autumn of 1826. Oil painting by L. Gross (Historisches Museum, Vienna)

That codicil was the start of one of the longest, most tortured legal entanglements of Beethoven's life. He loved his nine-year-old nephew possessively, he enthusiastically saw himself becoming a father figure, he hated the boy's mother with a Shakespearean venom. He called her 'wicked and vicious', she was a person full of 'moral poison', she was for him the 'Queen of the Night', 'a raging Medea'. Others found her guilty of infidelity (she bore an illegitimate half-sister to Karl) and irresponsible. Breuning speaks of her as 'giddy. . . bottomlessly wanton, vulgar in her feelings and actions'. In February 1816, according to Beethoven, she was 'at the Artists' Ball until three a.m., exposing not only her mental, but also *her bodily nakedness* — it was whispered that she — was willing to hire herself — for 20 gulden! Oh Horrible! And to such hands are we to entrust our precious treasure [Karl] even for one moment? No, certainly not'. A conversation book for March 1820 contains the line that Johanna was 'born for intrigue, well-schooled in deceit, [and a] master of hypocrisy'.

Johanna nevertheless was Karl's mother, and had maternal feelings. The more Beethoven argued, the more she resented him. The outcome was a prolonged case dragged through the Vienna courts for nearly five years. Within weeks Johanna formally appealed against Beethoven's guardianship. By 20 February 1816 the court ruled in his favour. Beethoven was delighted: he arranged for Karl's schooling and education, he dreamt of the child fulfilling all kinds of lofty ambitions, of becoming a great musician, a classical scholar, he totally immersed himself in the problems of parenthood that he had always craved. His lifestyle, however, was singularly ill-adapted to the task, and it was not unknown for Karl to be restless and unhappy. Karl entered the Gymnasium in the autumn of 1818, following a lawsuit brought about by Johanna which claimed Beethoven was unsuitable as a guardian because of his deafness, that he was ill, that he had planned Karl's education badly, and that, finally, the child should be looked after by his mother. There was more than an element of truth in these arguments, but she again lost the case. At the end of the year, on 3 December, a crisis arose. Fanny del Rio wrote in her *Diary:*

> Never in my life shall I forget the moment when [Beethoven] came and told us that Karl was gone, had run away to his mother, and showed us his letter as an evidence of his vileness. To see this man suffering so, to see him *weeping* — it was touching! Oh! how dreadful it is that this man is compelled to suffer so on account of such outcasts... I would give half my life for the man! He always thinks of himself last. He lamented that he did not know what would become of his housekeeping when Karl was gone.

Beethoven turned to the police and got the boy back. Johanna, however, at once applied to the court again. The minutes of a hearing held on 11 December are revealing for what Karl apparently had to say:

Where would he rather live — at his mother's or his uncle's?
He would like to live at his uncle's if he but had a companion, as his uncle was hard of hearing and he could not talk with him.
Had he been prompted by his mother to leave his uncle?
No.
Had his mother commanded him to return to his uncle?
She had wanted to take him back to him herself, but he had resisted because he feared maltreatment.
Had his uncle maltreated him?
He had punished him often, but only when he deserved it; he had been maltreated only once, and that after his return, when his uncle threatened to throttle him.
Who had given him instruction in religion?
The same teacher who taught him other subjects, formerly the priest at Mödling who was not kindly disposed towards him because he did not behave himself in the street and babbled in school.
Had he indulged in disrespectful remarks about his mother?
Yes; and in the presence of his uncle, whom he thought he would please in that way and who had agreed with him.
Was he often alone?
When his uncle was not at home he was left wholly alone.
Had his uncle admonished him to pray?
Yes; he prayed with him every morning and evening.

Karl van Beethoven, the nephew (1806-58) in the uniform of a cadet. Anonymous miniature on ivory, *c.* 1827 (Historisches Museum, Vienna)

Some of Beethoven's stringed instruments (Fischer & Kock)

Pending the decision of the lower court, Beethoven toyed with the idea of giving up his guardianship. A letter written in July speaks of Karl's 'wicked pranks', 'his stubbornness, his ingratitude and his callousness': 'My patience is at an end, I have cast him out of my heart, I have shed many tears on his account, this worthless boy. . . My love for him is gone. *He needed my love*. I do not need him. . . I don't want to hear anything more about him'. But then later he cries out! 'You understand, of course that this is not what I *really* think. I still love him as I used to, but without weakness or undue partiality, nay more, I may say in truth that I often weep for him'. The court's verdict came through on 17 September 1819: Beethoven lost, he was no longer Karl's lawful guardian. Beethoven, however, was not by nature a loser and he was not going to give in now. With the formidable support of Johann Baptist Bach, Dean of the Faculty of Law at the University of Vienna, he took the case to the Court of Appeal. A lengthy Memorandum was drafted on 18 February 1820, beginning with yet another broadside against Johanna. On 8 April 1820, the Appeal Court found against the Magistrates Court and reversed the earlier decision. Beethoven was again Karl's legal guardian, this time with Carl Peters. Johanna continued to try and interfere. Karl ran away again, and life was scarcely easy for Beethoven. But the issue never went to court again.

In 1825 Beethoven persuaded Karl to enrol in the University. Karl, however, was no academic. He wanted to enter the army, or, failing that, a business school. In due course he was transferred to the Polytechnic Institute. In his free time he went to the theatre, he played billiards, he got into debt, he enjoyed the company of girls, he chose his own friends. Beethoven — distracted — watched and disapproved and admonished. Karl, though, had the measure of his uncle: 'I can do with him what I want, some flattery and friendly gestures make things all right straight away'. The tension between the two increased and reached another crisis point on 30 July 1826: Karl tried to shoot himself. He made a mess of it, however, and when found asked to be taken to his *mother's* house. Why Karl attempted suicide has been attributed to various reasons. Holz, who for a time replaced Schindler as Beethoven's amanuensis, reported that Karl 'said that he was tired of life because he saw in it something different from what [Beethoven] judiciously and righteously would approve'. To the police Karl said that he was 'tormented' by Beethoven: 'I grew worse because my uncle wanted me to be better'.

The incident left Beethoven, already weak, in a shocked state. He consented to Karl entering the army and from then on Karl went on his own road. He died eventually in 1858, and his son, Ludwig, something of a black sheep, ended up in New York. Ludwig's own son, Karl, born in 1870, died, incidentally, in Vienna in 1917. He was the last to carry the family name of Beethoven.

* * *

In April 1824, the *Allgemeine Musikalische Zeitung* printed a review of the last three piano sonatas, prefaced by a summary of Beethoven the musician, a summary of uncanny finality:

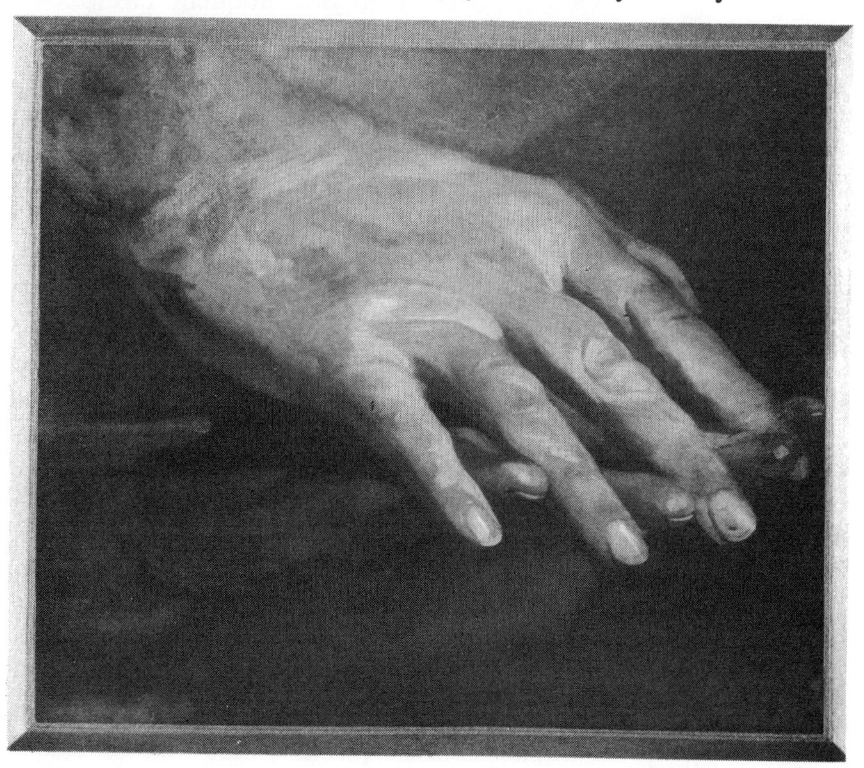

Beethoven's hands clasping a cross. Oil sketch by J. Danhauser, 28 March 1827 (Beethoven-Haus, Bonn)

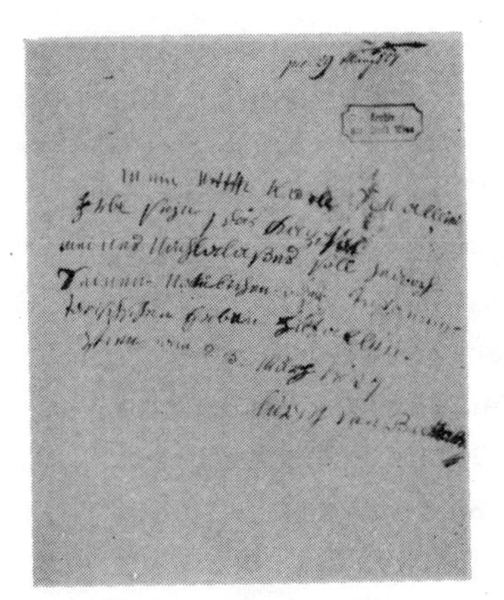

Beethoven's final Will, 23 March 1827. He left everything to Karl (Archiv der Stadt, Vienna)

It may be something over thirty years since the splendid manifestations of Beethoven's genius first enchanted receptive and understanding music lovers. This genius created a new epoch. All the conditions of a work of art: invention, spirit and feeling in the melodic, harmonic and rhythmic aspects of the music were fulfilled by Herr v. B. in a new way personal to him. The fact that opposition soon rose up against this originality is well known and indeed is usual in circumstances of this kind. Attempts to find fault, however, had only slight and short-lived success. The hero B. was completely triumphant. As soon as the first few of his works had appeared, his fame was established for ever. . . So rich an artistic life may, perhaps, best be compared to a splendidly landscaped garden with paths which wind to often wonderful effect among woodland, meadows, valleys and rocky gorges. As in gardens of that nature one comes, generally surprisingly, upon the most breathtaking views, which are often fully appreciated only by the experienced eye, so in a magnificent artistic garden such as that which Herr v. B. has created for us, certain enthralling features are particularly evident. Here, as there, the paths sometimes so suddenly change direction, and often just as one is at the most enchanting and restful spots, that one thinks, at least during the first moments, one is going back or that one has turned off from the route on which one had hoped for still more beautiful artistic pleasures, the loss of which one now regrets. However, both there and here, one should allow oneself willingly and submissively, to be guided by the creator of the work of art.

Three years later, in July 1827, the poet and historian Johann Sporschil published an obituary in the Dresden *Abendzeitung*. It was to be a no less eloquent farewell of Beethoven the 'Grand Mogul':

No longer will the citizens of friendly Vienna have the privilege of observing a man of compact build, carelessly dressed, a hat of indeterminate shape on his head, the head itself lifted up, the face with its grey shadows wearing an expression of deep abstraction. No longer will they see him hurrying through the street with his short yet firm steps barely touching the ground, until, fast as lightning, he vanishes around the corner. No longer will they be able to whisper with benevolent and indulgent pride to one another: 'Did you see? Beethoven!' Nor will the stranger, wandering through the romantically beautiful countryside of Baden or Mölding in the remotest part of the shady mountain woods again see the same man leaning against a tree trunk or sitting on a rock, a notebook in one hand, a pencil in the other, now fixing his gaze through the green and leafy cover to the blue sky, now hastily filling the page with strange hieroglyphs. No longer will the stranger be able to observe this curious but fascinating apparition without himself being observed. Nor will the stranger, once his presence has been noticed and the apparition has vanished towards yet more remote depths, continue on his way and, when he had returned to the company of his happy fellow men, describe what he has just seen and ask: 'Was not that, perhaps — ?' receive the answer — 'Yes, it was Beethoven!'

Take a hundred century-old oak tree, and write his name with them, in giant letters, on a plain. Or carve his likeness in colossal proportions like Saint Borromaeus on Lake Maggiore, that he may gaze above the mountains, as he did when living; and when the Rhine ships pass, and foreigners ask the name of that giant form, every child may answer — It is Beethoven, and they will think it is the name of a German Emperor —

Robert Schumann

Beethoven's deathmask by J. Danhauser (Historisches Musuem, Vienna) — 'To me the highest thing, after God, is my honour'

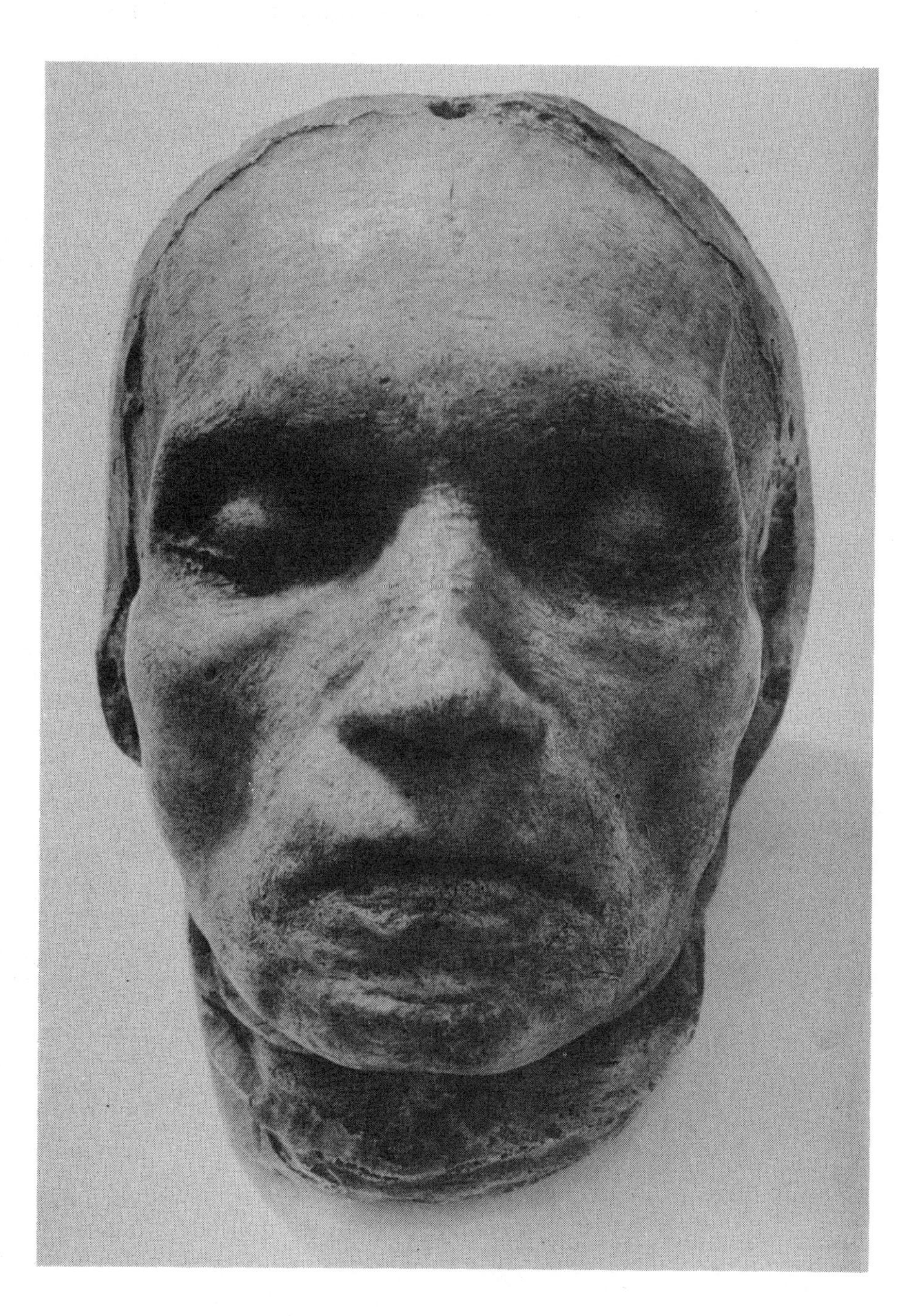

INDEX

Selective listing of references
Illustrations are indicated in bold type

Albrechtsberger, Johann Georg 47, 54

Bach, Johann Sebastian 10, 30, 48, 59, 75-76, 142
Beethoven, Caspar Anton Carl van (brother) 28, 49, 54, 78-81, 88, 108, 129, 132, 167-68
Beethoven, Johann Van (father) 21, 22, 23, 24, 28, 29, 31, 34, 36
Beethoven, Karl van (nephew) 108, 157, 166, 167-68, **169,** 170-71, 172
Beethoven, Ludwig van (grandfather), **22**-24, 26
Beethoven, Ludwig van *passim*
Heiligenstadt Testament 78-81, 104, 165
'Immortal Beloved' letter 103-05
Portraits **6, 8, 30, 73, 87, 88, 99, 117, 127, 133, 143, 159, 161, 166, 167, 171, 173**
Beethoven, Maria-Josepha van (grandmother) 22, 27
Beethoven, Maria Magdalena van (mother) 21, 22, 23, 27, 30, 34
Beethoven, Nikolaus Johann van (brother) 28, 54, 55, 78-81, 97, 120, 128-29, 158, 166, **167**
Berlioz, Hector 11, 12, 13, 15, 16, **18, 61,** 62, 89
Breitkopf and Härtel 18, 75, 112, 116, 118, 119, 123, 142
Brentano, Bettina 102, 125
Breuning, Eleonore von 32, 40, 47, 77
Breuning, Gerhard von 31, 32, 67, 163, 166
Breuning, Stephan von 31, 32, 78, 94, 147
Brunsvik, Countess Josephine 71, 96, 100-01, **102,** 103
Brunsvik, Countess Therese 71, 100, **101,** 102-04, 127
Bülow, Hans von 12, 18, 19, 20

Clement, Franz 82, 94, 109, 117, 123
Clementi, Muzio **110,** 111
Cramer, Johann Baptist 59, 111, 148
Czerny, Carl 8, 18, 19, 34, 51-53, 54, **61,** 72, 74, 106-07, 109, 116, 127, 140, 141, 145, 147

Diabelli, Anton 143, 151-52

Erdödy, Countess Anna Maria 101-02, **103,** 119, 124, 145
Ertmann, Dorothea von 103, **105,** 122, 123
Esterházy, Prince Nicholas 49, 111-12

Fischer family/manuscript 23, 24, 27, 28, 29, 30, 37
Franz I (II), Emperor 39, 43, 57, 68, 121, 122, 137

Galitzin, Prince Nikolas 147, 152-53, 159
Goethe, Johann Wolfgang von 60, 66, 67, 102, 124, 125, 126, 128
Grillparzer, Franz 8, 9, **10,** 11, 97, 141
Guicciardi, Countess Guilietta 100, **101,** 105

Handel, George Frederick 10, 16, 48, 49, 59, 138, 141-42
Haslinger, Tobias 9, 143
Haydn, Franz Joseph 10, **36,** 37, 39, 40, 41, 44, 45-46, 47, 53, 55, 61, 70, 82, 87, 108, 112, 114, 120, 166
Hoffmann, E.T.A. 114-15
Hoffmeister, F.A. 75
Holz, Karl 96
Hummel, Johann Nepomuk 8, 9, 112, 131, 151

Joseph II, Emperor 24, 30, 37, 50

Kinsky, Prince Ferdinand 119, 123, 129, 133, 162

Leopold II, Emperor 37, 122
Lichnowsky, Prince Karl 45, **47,** 48-49, 55, 57, 59, 71, 80, 82, 94, 106-07, 108, 127, 132-33, 135
Lichnowsky, Count Moritz 57, 124
Liszt, Franz 12, 13, **14,** 15-16, 18, 20, 57, 61, 147, 151, 153
Lobkowitz, Prince Franz Joseph von 49, **72,** 73, 77, 85, 93, 110, 112, 113, 114, 116, 117, 119, 123, 124, 129, 136, 162

Mahler, Gustav 15, 19, 66
Malfatti, Therese 102, 124
Mälzel, Johann Nepomuk 129-31, 133

Maria Theresa, Empress 24, 30, 42
Maximilian Franz, Elector **29,** 30, 33 35, 36-37, 38, 45-46, 55
Maximilian Friedrich, Elector 22, 24, **25,** 35
Mendelssohn, Felix 12, 13, 20
Moscheles, Ignaz 11, 16, **130,** 137, 151
Mozart, Wolfgang Amadeus 10, 20, 21, 27, 29, 30, 33, **34,** 36, 40, 47, 50, 53, 57, 59, 61, 70, 72, 82, 87, 95, 99, 112, 114, 144, 145, 153

Napoleon I (Bonaparte), Emperor 43, 57, **63, 69,** 84-85, 91, 94, 120, 122, 129
Neefe, Christian Gottlieb 26, **30,** 31, 33, 35, 37, 39, 44

Rasumowsky, Count (Prince) 49, **106,** 114, 116, 139, 140
Ries, Ferdinand 45, 49, 53, 54, 55, 74-75, 78, 82, 85, 86, 97, 115, **147,** 148, 149-50
Ries, Franz Anton 26, **32,** 33, 34, 36, 74
Rubinstein, Anton 12, 19
Rudolph, Archduke 113, 119, 120, **122,** 123, 124, 144, 151, **152,** 159

Salieri, Antonio 47, 54, 55, **57,** 56, 118, 131
Salomon, Johann Peter 24, 36, 148
Schikaneder, Emanuel 53, 82
Schiller, Johann Christoph von 60, 65, 67, 68, 125, 141, 151, 154, 156
Schindler, Anton 8, 15, 16, 19, 20, 57, 67, 69, 81, 100, 105, 111, 113, 115, 130, 134, 146, 147, 157-58, 159, 161, 162, **163,** 166
Schröder, Wilhelmine **145,** 147
Schubert, Franz 8, 57, 146-47, 151, 161
Schumann, Robert 13, 62, 108, 173
Schuppanzigh, Ignaz 8, 47, 56, 72, 82, 106, 107, 130, 134, 135, **144,** 145, 157-58
Sebald, Amalie 103, 128
Seyfried, Ignaz von 8, 57, 82-83, 89, 99, 117
Simrock, Nikolaus 26, 36, 142, 143
Smart, Sir George 14, 148, 149, 150
Sonnleithner, Joseph Ferdinand von **89,** 90, 139, 144, 157
Spohr, Ludwig 130, **131,** 135, 144
Steiner, Sigmund Anton 129, 142, 151
Swieten, Baron Gottfried van 46, 48, 49, 71, 142

Thayer, A-W. 18, 21, 24, 29, 44, 78, 87, 105, 113, 123, 131, 133, 139, 140
Thomson, George 13, 108, 122
Tomásek, Johann Wenzel 58-59, 139-40, 151
Treitschke, Georg Friedrich **93,** 94, 135-36

Umlauf, Michael 137, 139-40, 146, 157-58

Wagner, Richard **14,** 15, 16, 18, 19, 62, 89, 161
Waldstein, Count Ferdinand 34, **35,** 39, 40
Weber, Carl Maria von 62, 145, 147
Wegeler, Franz 21, 23, 30, 31, 32, 33, 34, 38, 48, **76,** 77, 96, 98, 165
Wölffl, Joseph 57-58

* * *

Beethoven: Selective listing of works

An die ferne Geliebte 73, 124, 143
Arias and songs 55, 72, 140
Bagatelles, Op 119 143

Battle Symphony **129,** 130-31, 133, 134, 135, 139, 143

Cantatas 37, 39
Cello Sonata, Op 69 122, 123, 145
Cello Sonatas, Op 5 55, 59
Cello Sonatas, Op 102 124
Chamber music with piano, general 71, 73, 75
Chamber music with strings, general 13
Choral Fantasia 12, 114, 154
Christus am Ölberg 82, 83-84, 123, 144, 147, 149
Concertos, general 12, 148
Consecration of the House Overture 142, 146, 150
Coriolan Overture 110, 113

Dances 53

Egmont 102, 124-26
Electoral Sonatas 30, 59
Equali for trombones 8

Fantasia, Op 77 114
Fidelio 11, 62, 85, 89-95, 96, 106, 110, 113, 115, 124, 125, 126, **135,** 136-37, 138, 142, 145-46, 147, 149, 154, 157

Glorreiche Augenblick, Die 139
Grosse Fuge, Op 133 145

King Stephen 127, 149

Leonore Overtures Nos. 1-3, 94

Mass in C 111-12, 114, 144, 145, 152
Missa Solemnis in D 11, 16, 62, 141, 142, 143, 147, 151, 152, **153,** 161

Namensfeier Overture 124, 149, 154

Overtures, general 12

Piano Concerto No '1' 58, 72
Piano Concerto No '2' 51, 53, 58, 72
Piano Concerto No '3' 11, 82-83 84, 86, 113
Piano Concerto No '4' 12, 96, 106, 110, 114
Piano Concerto No '5' 11, 12, 120, 122, 124, 127
Piano Sonata, Op 7 55-56

Piano Sonata, Op 13 (*Pathétique*) 59, 62, 68, 72
Piano Sonata, Op 26 8, 14
Piano Sonata, Op 27, No 2 (*Moonlight*) 14, 72, 100, 147
Piano Sonata, Op 53 (*Waldstein*) 12, 85
Piano Sonata, Op 57 (*Appassionata*) 14, 85-86, 88, 96, 106
Piano Sonata, Op 81 (*Das Lebewohl*) 122
Piano Sonata, Op 90 124, 143, 145
Piano Sonata, Op 101 103, 124, 143
Piano Sonata, Op 106 (*Hammerklavier*) 11, 13, 18, 124
Piano Sonata, Op 109 11
Piano Sonata, Op 111 11
Piano Sonatas, Op 2 47, 55, 58
Piano Sonatas, Op 31 81
Piano Sonatas, general 12, 14, 122, 141
Piano Trio, Op 97 (*Archduke*) 16, 124, 126-27, 135, 143, 145
Piano Trios, Op 1 **49,** 53, 144
Piano Trios, Op 70 119, 122
Polonaise in C 140
Projected Works 37, 45, 84, 85, 141, **142,** 155, 156
Prometheus 72-74, 86, 113, 136, 148

Quintet, Op 16 56, 57, 72, 82, 145

Ritterballet 37
Ruins of Athens 127, 133, 136, 149

Septet, Op 20 70, 89, 144, 145, 148
String Quartet, Op 74 122
String Quartet, Op 95 124, 143, 145
String Quartet, Op 127 11, 145, 147
String Quartet, Op 130 145, 147
String Quartet, Op 132 145, 147
String Quartets, Op 18 11, 70, 72, 73
String Quartets, Op 59 (*Rasumowsky*) 11, 106-07, 110-11, 144
String Quartets, general 11, 141
String Quintet, Op 29 72, 89
String Quintet, Op 104 144
Symphonies, general 12, 133
Symphony No 1 13, 70, 72, 82, 84, 89, 110, 144
Symphony No 2 11, 81, 82, 84, 86, 89, 108, 110, 113, 144, 156
Symphony No 3 (*Eroica*) 11, 14, 19, 20, 57, 62, 72, 84-85, 88-89, 91, 96, 110, 113, 116, 123, 144, 145, 148
Symphony No 4 96, 106, 108, 110, 113, 144
Symphony No 5 11, 12, 13, 19, 20, 72, 111, 114-16, 117, 122, 142, 144, 149
Symphony No 6 (*Pastoral*) 12, 13, 72, 114, 116-17, 122, 142, 144, 149
Symphony No 7 11, 12, 14, 124, 127, 128, 130-31, 133, 134, 139-40, 143, 144, 146, 149, 154
Symphony No 8 124, 127, 128, 130, 134, 143, 144, 154
Symphony No 9 (*Choral*) 11, 12, 14-15, **16,** 18, 62, 141, 142, 144, 147, 148, 150, 151, 153, 154, **155,** 156-58, 167

Triple Concerto 12, 85, 113

Variations (piano)
Op 34, in F 75
Diabelli 141, **151,** 152
Dressler 30, 151
Eroica, Op 35 12
God Save the King 84
Paisiello 53
Righini 37, 38
Rule Britannia 84
Viganò 53
Wranitzky 56

Violin Concerto 12, 96, 106, 109, 110, 111
Violin Sonata, Op 47 (*Kreutzer*) 84
Violin Sonata, Op 96 124, 127, 143
Violin Sonatas, Op 12 56
Violin Sonatas, Op 30 81

Statue of Beethoven

ILLUSTRATIONS ADDED FOR EXPANDED EDITION

In creating this expanded edition, more than forty illustrations have been added as unnumbered pages at various places within the text. Following is a key to those insertions.

facing page

Modern view of Beethoven's grave........ 10
Tributes to Beethoven........ 11
Engraving of Beethoven........ 14
Newspaper clipping about the Ninth Symphony........ 15
Hector Berlioz........ 18
Carl Czerny........ 18
Hans von Bulow........ 19
Arthur Nikisch........ 19
Beginning of Bach's *Well Tempered Clavier*........ 30
Title page for sonatas dedicated to Maximilian Friedrich........ 31
Stephan von Breuning........ 31
Painting of Beethoven........ 44
Engraving of Beethoven........ 45
Joseph Wolffl........ 58
Scene of Prague........ 58
Johann Wenzel Tomasek (Tomaschek)........ 59
Domenico Dragonetti........ 59
Manuscript for last movement of "Moonlight" Sonata........ 72
Title page of piano score for *Prometheus*........ 73
Manuscript for first movement of "Kreutzer" Sonata........ 84
Manuscript for beginning and end of "Waldstein" Sonata........ 85
Johann Wolfgang von Goethe in 1812........ 114
E. T. A. Hoffmann........ 114
Newspaper clipping about the Fifth Symphony........ 115
Beethoven letter to Archduke Rudolph........ 126
Title page for "Archduke" piano trio, English edition........ 127
George Frederick Handel........ 142
Johann Sebastian Bach........ 142
Beethoven letter to Steiner........ 143
Score for beginning of aria from *Der Freischutz*........ 146
Title page of Schubert work dedicated to Beethoven........ 147
Franz Liszt in 1824........ 147
Manuscript of the Kyrie from *Missa Solemnis*........ 152
Engraving of Schiller by J. P. Schweyer........ 153
Schiller's poem *An die Freude*........ 153
Drawing of Beethoven........ 160
Engraving of Beethoven........ 161
Sketches of Beethoven........ 164
Sketch of Beethoven on his deathbed........ 165
Picture of Beethoven in his study........ 165
Statue of Beethoven........ 176